Gardening

Through The Year

Gardening

Through The Year

John Dyer

ARCTURUS

Published by Arcturus Publishing Limited
For Bookmart Limited
Registered Number 2372865
Trading as Bookmart Limited
Desford Road
Enderby
Leicester
LE9 5AD

This edition published 1996

Printed and bound in Great Britain

ISBN1 900032 30 9

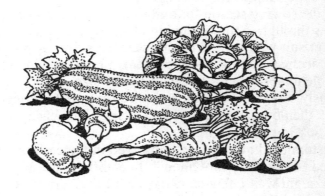

Onions And Leeks

A happy New Year to you - and with its coming it is time again to plan for new crops! The first job, if you have not managed to find time so far, is to settle down and finalise your seed order, so that the seed is ready to hand when needed.

The start of the year brings thoughts of leeks and onions, especially if you wish to try raising some of exhibition size. January provides opportunities for sowing both.

In fact the sowing season for onions extends from just before Christmas through to the beginning of April, and you can choose the time to suit your own circumstances. However, if you select a variety such as Robinson's Mammoth, a long growing season is desirable to allow bulbs to achieve large size.

Obviously, sowing at this time requires heat, but if none is available, then by tradition outdoor sowing commences on 12 March - St. Gregory the Great's Day.

The custom used to be so well observed in Lancashire that it was called "Gregory-great-Onion." If conditions are still bad, then you might wait a few extra days until St. Patrick's Day, 17 March, a time when the good Saint "turns the warm side of the stone uppermost," heralding the start of potato planting.

For the larger sized crop, sowing should be done before the end of the month. Use seed trays and seed compost and provide a temperature of 16C (60F) until germination, which should occur within three weeks.

After germination lower the temperature to 10C (50F) in the daytime with a night minimum of 7C (45F). To obviate the need for pricking-off, seed can be sown 3-4 to a pot with all but the strongest seedlings being removed.

Hardening-off can be carried out in March with a view to planting out in April.

If heated glass is not available, seed can be sown in frames or under cloches, but naturally germination will be slower. Outdoor sowing can commence from the last week in February through to mid-April, with early March favourite.

Seed should be sown thinly directly into the onion plot. Set them 12mm (1/2in) deep, in rows 30cm (1ft) apart. Following germination thin the seedlings to 5cm (2in), and subsequently to 15cm (6in) apart.

Thinning should be practised with care, minimising the amount of damage done and scent given off, and so lessening the chance of attracting onion fly.

You might do the job late in the evening when flies are less likely to be on the wing, and then water lightly over the rows to settle back the remaining seedlings and kill any scent. Throwing the thinnings onto the compost heap should be avoided, for they may still attract the fly from there.

Of the varieties, Ailsa Craig has been around for a long time and is well tried and tested. Many seedsmen offer their own selected strain. It is still a favourite variety, producing large, uniform bulbs with mild flavour.

While it has good appearance and sits pretty on the show bench, it does not keep for long periods.

Bedfordshire Champion is ideal for spring sowing, and produces good-sized globes which keep well. Strains of Rijnsburger yield well and also store well.

Anyone becoming hooked on onions will probably set aside a special bed where bulbs may grow for years to come. For most growers, however, they fit nicely into the normal crop rotation along with peas, beans, leeks, shallots, celery and radish. Organic matter can be dug in during autumn, and lime applied to bring the pH to between 6 and 6.3.

The aim is to produce a fine tilth, but following cultivation, the bed must be well firmed by treading. Where storage is intended, select an open situation with soil which is likely to be warm and dry. This should ensure sound, well-ripened onions.

That hasn't left any room to deal with leeks, so we'll have a look at those later.

Grey Mould

I'll start off the New Year with Botrytic cinerea - that grey mould of a disease that appears on chrysanthemum petals, causes core rot in gladiolus, ghost spot on tomatoes, neck rot on onions, blackleg in geraniums and so on and so on!

It is a common problem found on a very wide range of plants and crops. While in some cases the effect may be small, in others it can cause the wholesale decimation of a crop.

Only a slight variation to conditions which are ideal for normal plant growth, will create those in which spores of the fungus will germinate; giving rise to a mycelium which spreads into plant cells, produces more spores, and can lead to a very rapid spread of infection.

A range of plants are affected in bud and flower. While the symptoms may vary from host to host, grey mould will appear. Buds may rot, and flowers, their stems and petals may all sucumb.

In woody plants dieback is caused, and this can be a problem on gooseberries, currants and raspberries. First evidence appears when leaves wilt and then shrivel, changing to brown as they do so. Bark cracks, and in humid conditions the mould appears. In severe cases whole bushes may die out a branch at a time.

With fruit, botrytis is common on apples, grapes, strawberries, raspberries, blackberries and gooseberries, while in vegetables it is to be found on beans, brassicas, cucumbers, lettuce, tomatoes, peas, potatoes and also on celery and carrots in store.

Fortunately the fungus is not aggressive. In general, the door has to be left open a little to allow it to gain a toehole. Generally this occurs through a wound, when the host is in poor conditions or following frost damage.

Once an infection occurs, in susceptible tissue the fungus will establish and spread into living cells, causing them to die.

At the same time the mould, which is made up of a multitude

of spore-bearing growths called conidiophores, appears on the surface, and upon ripening releases the next generation of spores.

Needless to say, if conditions are not suited to the germination of the spores, perhaps because temperatures are too low or there is insufficient humidity, they lie dormant until the right conditions prevail.

Outdoor attacks are most likely to occur during rainy periods in summer, when both high temperatures and humidity are to be found. We all know how depressing it is to push aside strawberry leaves, only to be confronted with a soggy, useless mass of rapidly browning fruit covered by rampant grey mould.

At this time of year, attacks are most likely under glass, for this is the period when many plants reach the lowest point of their annual growth-cycle, and produce a wealth of susceptible decaying foliage.

This, together with high humidity due to overwatering and restricted ventilation to maintain temperatures, provides ideal conditions for the fungus.

So, it can be seem that providing the right cultural conditions is the most important way of preventing infection should lead to increasing heat, applying more ventilation, and reducing the amount of water given.

Good hygiene is critical, for the fungus can exist saprophytically on dead plant remains. Also avoid overcrowding, and seek to sustain buoyant plant growth wherever possible.

Damp and overcrowded conditions should also be avoided for outdoor crops, and of course, any crops stored should have been adequately dried before being placed in store, should have shown so signs of infection prior to storage, and should be inspected on a regular basis.

Both under glass and outdoors, any buds or flowers which have become moribund should be pinched off. Equally, when conditions sympathetic to the fungus prevail, it is a good idea to de-head any susceptible plants.

Your Gardening Week

✔ SEED LISTS Set to and list all the seeds you are likely to need over the next two or three months, and place your order without delay. This ensures that you will receive them in time for sowing, and makes it less likely that your chosen varieties will be sold out.

✔ FORCE SHRUBS Container-grown shrubs can be brought into the glasshouse for forcing. Maintain a minimum temperature of 13 C (55 F), and syringe with aired water each morning. Suitable subjects include rose, deutzia, lilac and viburnum.

✔ PROTECTIVE MOVE If there is a vacant sheltered spot in the vegetable plot, any exposed Brussels sprouts, savoys and late cabbage can be moved there if they are lifted with their roots intact.

✔ FORCE RHUBARB Continue to lift rhubarb roots, and leave them exposed to frost before bringing in and forcing.

✔ TURGID LILIES If lilies for potting arrive in a slightly shriveled state, place them in seed trays of moist peat for a few days, syringing them each morning.

✔ POT LEEKS Pot leeks can be sown now in a temperature of 15 C (60 F), using J.I. seed compost. Pot up when first true leaves have formed.

✔ FEED FEATHERED FRIENDS Don't forget to provide food and water for birds; they will bring extra colour and interest to the garden.

✔ GARDEN FURNITURE Bring in wooden garden furniture, and dry off prior to repainting or treating with preservative.

✔ SPARE STAKES Keep apple tree prunings and use the strong, whippy shoots to support bulbs.

✔ EARLY SALADS Stock up with seed of the salad onion White Lisbon, which can be sown in a glasshouse border or frame towards the end of the month.

6

Sowing Alpines

Winter's not a good time for the gardener. Days are too short and dark, and it's too cold (not for the gardener but for the soil to be workable).

It is, though, a period to take stock and to start planning ahead with catalogues, or giving thought to introducing new features to the garden.

When browsing through those lists of seeds, do not bypass the Alpines section, for there you will find an abundance of diminutive plants that can bring brilliant splashes of colour to the otherwise most uninteresting of sites.

In their native environments, they winter in the coldest of climates- and some seed which is naturally dispersed will not even germinate until it has experienced the bitterness of frosts. In our most cosseted conditions we need to take advantage of our winter, therefore, to simulate their natural conditions and get them off to a good start.

The seed planting is basically the same as in all other cases, with two exceptions.

Prepare the pots or shallow pans - first ensuring they are perfectly clean - by filling with John Innes potting compost. Then, turn the seeds out of their packet into the palm of your hand and, using a finger, brush them from the palm onto the top of the compost, as shown.

Now for the exception: First, sprinkle them over with a thin layer of fine sand, to keep them in place. For "fluffier" seeds, such as pulsatilla (see illustration) or clematis, use a heavier grit.

Secondly - and this is where you attempt to mimic nature - place them outside on a paved area, or raise them, so that slugs and worms cannot get at them. Choose a north-facing wall, so that they can experience the full rigours of frost and even snow. By March you can transfer the containers to a cold frame and, hey presto! by the end of that month the little plants should be pushing up through the compost.

A Hot-bed Of Production

While the term 'hot-bed' seems to have been absorbed into common usage to mean a place of activity - the practice of constructing real hot-beds to achieve early crops seems rarely to be encountered these days.

In years gone by, I suppose manure was more readily available than now; and that the other forms of energy on which we have come to rely, were either not available or prohibitively expensive for many people.

Perhaps the pendulum is swinging back a little as I find the cost of gas, together with coal and electricity, more than I would wish to pay.

I guess that we have also seen an increase in the population of horses, as more and more people have taken to riding for pleasure, so that the raw material required is commonly available.

Add to this a concern for the environment, an emphasis on recycling, and I think that hot-beds could usefully be revived. There is also the benefit that organic matter will be available at the end of the process which can be used to improve land.

The basic principle of a hot-bed, is that a heap of organic material is constructed which heats up as it decomposes. Soil is placed over the top, and early crops can be had, encouraged by the warmer conditions.

I can't give any hard and fast rules. If you want to give the idea to try, much will depend upon the materials readily available to you, the space in your garden, and the crops you wish to grow.

Hot-beds can be used under glass, where they will improve the output of a cold glasshouse, or contribute to some energy saving in a heated one.

For the purpose of this exercise, however, I'll deal with one that can be used outdoors as a heated frame.

Already the options start to pile up. At simplest, a rectangular bed of material can be built up to 1.2m (4ft) deep. A frame can be constructed on the top of this, but should be set back 30cm (1ft) from the sides and ends.

In other words, decide on the size of your frame, and make the bed 30cm larger all round.

This is because the sides of the bed have no additional insulation, and helps to ensure that heat will be provided evenly across the length and width of the frame.

If you are fairly confident that a hot-bed has a regular future with you, and some extra exercise has an appeal, then an alternative is to excavate a pit in which the bed can be contained, above and around which a frame can be constructed.

This has the advantage of being more accessible than a tall bed. A lot depends upon the state of the ground. If it does not drain well, then there is the danger that build-up of cold ground water at critical periods will prevent proper decomposition and leave a soggy, unproductive mess.

An alternative is to excavate a shallow pit, so that the heap is partly above and partly below ground level.

Siting the hot-bed is also important if maximum efficiency is to be achieved. Ideally, the bed should be set in a sheltered position which is not a frost-packet, and where the worst of cold winds are deflected.

Giving plants the benefits of bottom heat means that they are more advanced than would normally be the case in the growing year; and so taking full advantage of any light available is also important.

Thus the bed should face in a southerly direction.

The frame itself should be constructed well and of sound material, so that a minimum of heat is lost. It should be higher at the back than the front, so that maximum light penetration is achieved.

Painting it white will help reflect more light.

Later we will look at some of the materials that can be used in a hot-bed and deal with seed sowing for early crops.

Spring A Leak

So far we've covered onions - so now it's leeks. I don't really know why, but somehow it is fun to be involved in raising new stock at the same time as last year's sowings are still ready to harvest.

So many crops come and go within a twelve month period, and need a diary reminder that the time for action is approaching. With crops such as leeks, their diminishing numbers - as they disappear into pies, soups or as straight vegetables - seem to shout out that it is time to reach for the seed again.

Now, through to the end of the month, is the time to sow, in heat, for early crops and exhibition; with the resultant seedlings being planted out whenever the ground outside becomes workable, from early March to early May. The main season for sowing outdoors coincides with that time to be followed by planting out in June and the early part of July.

For the early sowings use boxes of seed compost and space-sow the seed 2cm (1in) apart each way. Keep under glass in a temperature of 55F (13C), and expect germination inside three weeks.

When the seedlings are 2cm high and large enough to handle they can be pricked off at double the spacing. All that is then needed is to make sure they are adequately hardened before going outside.

The later sowings take place outdoors on a seed bed. Ideally the seed bed should be fertile, and this can be achieved by cultivating the area, levelling and raking to produce a rough tilth, following which the area can be dressed with finely sifted, well-matured compost, before being trodden firm and raked again to produce the sowing tilth. Such a seed bed is also ideal for brassicas.

The earlier sowing can take place the better, with seed dribbled along 2cm (1in) drills. Provided seed is sown reasonably thinly,

no further action will be needed until planting time.

Leeks are less demanding than onions in their food requirements. They will perform in a wide range of soils, provided that
they are not waterlogged or heavily compacted. Nevertheless,
fertility will be reflected in results.

Ground that was manured for a previous crop is ideal, but if
not available a planting area can be prepared by digging in compost or well rotted manure and, as with onions, adding lime to
bring the pH to a range of 6 to 6.5.

At planting time the bed can be given a final light forking
before being raked level.

Use a garden line to mark the rows, which can be set 30cm
(1ft) apart. Using a dibber, make holes 15cm (6in) deep and
20cm (8in) apart.

Seedlings can be lifted from the nursery rows after being loos-
ened with a hand fork. Select the stronger specimens, and drop
one into each hole. Planting is completed by filling each hole
with water to settle in the roots. Do not fill the hole with soil.

There are several varieties to choose from. Musselburgh takes
some beating, having good flavour and winter hardiness. The
Lyon is good for exhibition, with good quality solid stems -
comments which also apply to Autumn Mammoth.

King Richard matures mid-season in late autumn and early
winter, producing long stems. Giant Winter is also very hardy,
and can be harvested in late autumn, but puts on a spurt of
growth in late winter and will stand until May.

During the course of the growing season, make frequent and
careful use of the hoe to keep down weeds.

The length of the usable white stem is increased by blanching,
which entails drawing dry soil around the stems when they are
well developed.

Successive earthing up can be carried on until the plants stop
growing around November. Soil can be kept from penetrating
between the leaves by wrapping the stems in paper while earthing.

Your Gardening Week

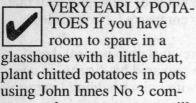 VERY EARLY POTATOES If you have room to spare in a glasshouse with a little heat, plant chitted potatoes in pots using John Innes No 3 compost, and young potatoes will be ready to harvest in April.

 BROAD BEANS Buy broad beans for sowing under cloches at the beginning of next month.

 EARLY TURNIPS If you like the tang that turnips bring, an early crop, from May onwards, can be had by sowing an early variety such as Jersey Navet, under cloches next month.

 WARM COMPOST If your seed and potting compost is kept in a cold place, remember to bring it into the glasshouse a day or two before use, so that is has chance to warm to the glasshouse temperature.

 SOW STREPTOCARPUS A sowing of Streptocarpus made now in a temperature of 18 C (65 F), followed by a second one in February, will provide flowering plants in autumn.

 SOW SWEET PEAS If not dealt with in September, sweet peas for exhibition can be sown now and germinated in a temperature of 13 C (55 F).

DELAY PLANTING Unless conditions are good, or you have prepared and protected the ground, heel-in any trees and shrubs which have not been planted and wait for better conditions in March.

SENSITIVE SOWING Why not buy some seed of Mimosa pudica, the 'Sensitive Plant' for sowing next month? Soak the seed in water for 20 minutes before sowing on top of seed compost. Do not cover, and germinate in a temperature of 21-24 C (70-75 F).

 FORCED FLOWER CARE Plants which are forced at relatively high temperatures, should slowly be acclimatised to lower temperatures before being set in cooler conditions when the flower has appeared.

Vines Inside And Out

Now is as good a time as any to give some thought to growing a vine—particularly if you have a greenhouse, which will allow you to take out a low panel, or to cut a hole in one through which you can train a plant to grow inside, when it is actually planted outside.

Dig out a hole about 2 1/2 ft deep and wide enough to take the teased out root system of the plant, put in a 6 inch layer of rubble and refill it around the plant with a loamy compost, to which should be added well rotted manure, some wood ash and bonemeal at the rate of 3 ozs to the square metre.

Having settled the plant into its bed, water well and immediately set about getting the plant poking inside greenhouse.

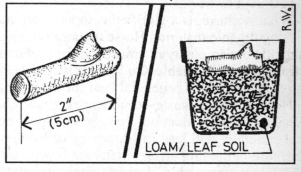

Let all the shoots make growth at first, and when they are about six inches long, pinch the tips of all but the strongest, which should attain about 6ft during its first year.

Another way to start a vine just now, is to prevail upon a friend, who may have heeled in some shoots from the winter pruning.

The idea is to cut a shoot into a number of 2 inch long pieces, each with a healthy bud, (see illustration).

Nick off some of the wood on the opposite side of the bud and plant the piece, by pressing it gently into a small pot of loamy soil.

Just leave the bud exposed (see illustration). Put the pots under glass with some bottom heat and, given a temperature of 15 to 20C, they should make nice vines.

Muck And Magic

We have already dealt with some of the general principles relating to hot-beds. Now I want to try and add a little more detail on preparation and growing techniques. But overall this is one of those "muck and magic" activities, where knowledge is only gained by experience, and weather conditions can have a great impact on success and failure. In reality you have to set the 'thermostat' at the time materials are chosen, and there is little scope to change it once Mother Nature has started to work.

What we have, is a glorified compost heap made from decomposing organic material. Horse manure is an ideal base, but should contain plenty of straw, and for preference be used straight from the stable. On its own it achieves high temperatures and provides beneficial heat for a couple of months.

Normal garden waste - dead leaves, straw, chaff; in fact any available organic material - can be incorporated in the mixture, but generally will lead to a lowering of temperature and an increase in the time over which heat is produced. So, given the muck that is available, deciding upon the mixture is where the magic comes in.

If you can forecast the weather and estimate the longevity of the bed, then the aim is to ensure that heat from the sun has built up to a sufficient level to compensate for a diminishing decomposition, so that the plants receive no check to growth.

Having settled on the ingredients, the mixture is made into a conical heap which should be moist. Within a week this is turned with a fork, so that the outside layers end up in the middle and vice versa.

A few days later the process is repeated. Following a further turning and a few days more, the mixture can be built into a flat-topped heap. As the layers are built up, they should be watered and beaten down firm with the back of a fork. Often the advice is to tread for firmness, but this can lead to excess compaction and result in too fierce heat if overdone.

The minimum depth of the bed to serve any useful purpose is 60cm (2ft), but increasing the depth to 90cm or 120cm will mean that heat production will continue for proportionately longer.

Over the top of the bed a 15cm (6in) layer of soil or compost is spread. Ideally this should be rich, light and dry, and should have been readied in advance and kept in a sheltered place.

At this point it is useful to have a soil thermometer which can be plunged into the centre of the bed to take successive readings. Initially it should indicate a build-up of heat in a fierce flush which slowly starts to abate. When the temperature has fallen to 24C (76F), sowing or planting can take place.

Although I say sowing, for crops which produce seedlings which can be transplanted, it is a good idea to start them off before the bed is made, so that full advantage can be taken of the heat produced. In these days, sufficient seedlings could be raised indoors, but in the past a practice was to build a small hot-bed in advance of the main one upon which the seedlings could be raised.

Seed raised in the hot-bed frame is best sown in a pot. This can be set into the soil of the frame and allowed to warm before sowing takes place.

Temperature can be controlled by sinking the pot deeper for greater heat or raising it for less, but regular inspection is required to ensure overheating does not occur.

Care is needed in ventilation, for at one extreme a build-up of steam could scorch seedlings or plants. Other than that, air can be given as conditions allow, and the lights closed in the after-noon to anticipate any drop in air temperature. If cold and frost is expected, additional protection can be given by using mats.

If the cold is such that the hot-bed itself may be affected, bracken or leaves may be piled round the sides to give added protection.

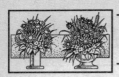

The Answer's a...

On this occasion the answer is not a lemon; but is at least an anagram of that fruit. The other clue is that while we tend to consider it a fruit it is really a vegetable. Yes, the answer's a melon.

Which ones to grow depend very much on the conditions you are able to offer: ranging from outdoor planting in the most favoured areas, to cold frame culture and, of course, under heated glass.

The sweet melon, Cucumis melo, belongs to the same family as the cucumber, is native to central Africa and is largely grown in warm regions. There are three types in common cultivation: cantaloupe, musk and winter.

Of these the musk and winter melons are best grown under heated glass, while cantaloupe varieties are suitable for cold frame or cloche, though they may be grown in the glasshouse with little or no heat.

Seed can be sown from mid-April using 75mm (3in) pots of seed compost. You may choose to set two seeds to a pot, removing the weaker seedling should both germinate. A temperature of 18-21C (65-70F) is needed for germination. This can be achieved in a propagating case, a heated glasshouse or by taking advantage of a sun-bathed windowsill. To maintain humidity, cover the pots with glass, or set in a clear plastic bag.

As soon as germination occurs, remove the covering and grow on the young seedlings in a temperature of 13-16C (55-60F). The aim is to plant out in late May or early June, so that if good growth is made, and the small pots fill with roots, it is advisable to pot the young plant on into 12.5cm (5in) containers of good compost.

Melons need a fertile, well-drained soil with a pH of 5.7 to 7.0. It should not be too rich, however, or excessive growth can occur to the detriment of crop producing.

If the frame or cloched area is not in use for any other crop, the ground can be dug three or four weeks before planting, at which time well-rooted manure or compost can be incorporated if required.

A couple of weeks before planting is intended, each individual planting site can be turned over again and have a dressing of compost or manure worked in. In frames, one plant can sit centrally beneath each framelight. In rows the plants can be set 90-120cm (3-4ft) apart.

Mound the soil at each planting station and if conditions are dry, give a thorough soaking. Put framelights or clothes in place to allow the soil to warm prior to planting.

Soft rot can be a problem, especially if water gathers at the base of the stem. To reduce the likelihood of this, make the planting hole a little less deep than the height of the rootball. So, after planting, the top of the rootball should stand 2.5cm (1in) above mound level.

Do not firm in, but rather settle in with water, taking care to keep water off the stem. After this, shut cloches or frames and keep closed for 7-10 days until the plants establish. Do shade if hot sun looks like being a problem.

Once the plants have established, shading can be removed and ventilation gradually increased. Once flowers appear, increase ventilation to allow a drier atmosphere, which helps pollination.

Unless you intend to rely on hand pollination, it is a good idea to remove the framelights of cloches entirely on warm days, to allow insects full access. The protection should be replaced, however, before the sun goes down.

After the appearance of the fifth leaf, the growing point should be pinched out. This will encourage the formation of sideshoots, which should be well in evidence after a couple of weeks. Select the four strongest and pinch out the rest.

In frames these shoots can be directed towards the corners, while for crops grown under cloches, two can be sent in either direction along the row.

Your Gardening Week

 WARM THE GROUND Where early crops are to be sown, cover the ground with cloches or spare frame lights, so that it is dry and comparatively warm before the seed goes in.

GARLIC AND SHALLOTS Unless you have well-drained land, start corms off in pots and grow on in a cold frame until March.

BOOST FRUIT Give a dressing of potash to red and white currants, strawberries and gooseberries.

KEEP CUTTING Cut back newly planted cane fruits, and complete pruning established fruit bushes at earliest opportunity.

MULCH ASPARAGUS Asparagus beds can be mulched with a generous layer of well-rotted manure, though application should be delayed if there is frost in the ground, or it will be sealed in.

KEEP OFF If you have managed to do any digging, keep off the cultivated land until conditions improve, or the soil structure will be impaired.

CYCLAMEN As cyclamen flowers go over, take care to remove the stems by grasping them and giving a sharp tug. This should remove the whole stem, which otherwise might rot and provide a breeding-ground for fungal infection.

SOW GERANIUMS If you aim to raise geraniums (zonal pelargoniums) from seed for summer bedding, then get them moving as soon as possible.

LONG-LIVED SEED When making out your order for vegetable seed, remember that beet, beans, carrots and lettuce should remain viable for three years, and cabbage, radish, swede and turnip for five.

 START DAHLIAS Dahlia tubers can be placed in boxes of moist peat, to encourage the production of shoots for cuttings. Ensure they have plenty of light, so that growth is not weak and leggy.

Shallots

One of the gardening adages that sprung to mind over the Christmas holiday, was that one should plant shallots on the shortest day of the year. Well, that's long past now; but in this case, as with many gardeners' sayings they provide a well remembered guideline. What is true is that you can plant them now, and that you should get them in as soon as possible, certainly by early March.

It's also often said that shallots are so easy, that all you need to do is 'Pop 'em in the ground'. True, they're easy. But pop 'em in and before long they'll pop up again to tempt the birds, who'll pull 'em out!

One good thing about shallots is that they are self-perpetuating producing off-sets which are plated the following year. Once you have  obtained the bulbs, you should henceforward be able to save enough off-set clusters to serve your needs.

Choose a previously cultivated strip of land, in a sunny spot, which has had time to firm down after manuring. Take out a drill just deep enough for the bulbs, and set them 4 inches apart. Turn back the soil, so that the tips just break the soil level. Another way is to trowel out separate growing holes for each bulb-again allowing the bulb point just to break the surface.

You can also start shallots from seed sown in January in boxes of seed compost. When sowing, place the seeds on a piece of paper on the seed bed, so that you can space them out using a pencil. Cover with glass and paper until germination. After hardening-off around mid-March, the seedlings will be ready for planting out in early April.

Invest In Seed

By now you should have a healthy collection of seed catalogues, and have given thought to ordering. I know that a trip to the garden centre is a pleasurable experience, but there is the danger of impulse buying. You may also spend your money on a few mature plants which would otherwise provide a multitude of seeds to sow.

It is important to calculate one's needs early and order in good time for sowing. It is therefore necessary to plan in advance, making sketches of the vegetable plot and annual border in particular. Even modest intentions can result in a fairly formidable list, but forethought will eliminate over-ordering and wastage of seed.

While I accept that variety is the spice of life, there is little point in ordering crops which will not be enjoyed by the family. A garden diary is also a useful aid, documenting the previous year's successes and failures and helping to fine-tune the list.

Work in the odd new variety and occasional novelty for interest, even though they may be a little dearer than standard varieties.

The next job is to check any seed that may have been left over from previous years, and which you are reasonably confident will still germinate. This can be deducted from your order.

It is also handy to build up notes over successive years about particular seeds. Catalogues can be notoriously difficult to interpret, with seed being offered variously by the packet, the pint, in grams or occasionally as a specific number.

In addition to listing plants, most catalogues contain valuable hints and tips. It is worth taking the time to read these before finalising an order. If the value of your order is significant - and it's amazing how the pounds mount up - it may be worth tracking down a horticultural or allotment association which can obtain discounts by ordering in bulk.

One vegetable you might like to include is scorzonera. Although it can be a little disconcerting to look at because of its dark skin, once scraped it has a distinctive and delicate flavour well worth growing for.

To produce good roots, a deeply cultivated light soil is best. Any stones should be removed to prevent the roots becoming distorted. Similarly, freshly manured ground is best avoided. The crop should follow one where the ground was well-manured in the previous season.

An April sowing is early enough. Seed can be sown thinly in 25mm (1in) deep drills with 30cm (1ft) between rows. For succession, a further sowing can be made in May.

When young plants are established, thin them to 20cm (8in) in the row and prevent competition from weeds. Some plants will be ready for lifting in September, but the main crop will mature in October and November.

Before any serious frost sets in the roots can be lifted and stored in sand. If you wish, however, some may be left in the ground and lifted as required throughout winter. Any remnants of the crop should be cleared by April, after which it will flower and run to seed.

There is only a little time to wait until I expect flowers to appear on Daphne mezereum, the native Mezereon. Growing to around 120cm (4ft), this interesting shrub has grey-green deciduous leaves. Rich, pinkish-purple flowers appear in February and March on second-year wood. They have the additional benefit of sweet scent, and are followed by clusters of bright red berries in May.

While seed from the berries may be used in propagation, care should be taken for they, like all parts of the plant, are poisonous.

There is a white variety 'alba' which produces yellow berries and makes a pleasing contrast.

The Mezereon is not always easy to grow, but does best in a moist, slightly shaded position. In hot, dry conditions it may fail.

Vegetables:
Where and When

Now is the time to sit down and work out your detailed requirements for the vegetable plot. You should have arrived at a plot with three basic areas to be planted.

Before going into detail there's a sin of omission to be dealt with, and that's the space for a nursery bed. It may be an open piece of ground or you may wish to utilise frames, or both. In either case, seedlings of some plants can be raised and grown on until they are large enough to be planted out in the row.

Now let's have a look at a cropping plan, bearing in mind that it can be altered in many ways to suit your own needs. The aim is to provide a basic range of crops which can be followed in succession by others, as soon as the first crop is cleared. Some, such as lettuce and radish, only occupy the ground for a short time, while others may be started in autumn to mature the following summer.

It is not possible to be precise about sowing and planting dates, for these depend on climate and locality, and will even vary from year to year with prevailing weather conditions.

It is important to secure succession so that a steady supply is achieved rather than a glut at any one time. Though obviously this does not apply to crops which are to be preserved or stored; the more the merrier in their case.

When planning rows, arrange that they run from north to south, so that during the day both sides are exposed to a share of the sun. If planted east to west, the north side of the row is in perpetual shadow.

In mentioning the crops I'll give general sowing dates, based on outdoor sowing in the south of England. In the north, times may be delayed by around three weeks, though this can be made up by using cloches, which bring the programme forward by

some two weeks.

I'll also indicate the expected time to maturity, but obviously this will vary from season to season.

In addition I will offer a guide to likely yields, but again this will vary with the season, soil fertility, the ravages of pests and diseases and the characteristics of the chosen variety. I have assumed rows 9m (30ft) long, but these can be extended or reduced as required.

Dealing firstly with the area which has been fed with animal manure or compost, we can look to include peas, beans, onions, leeks, lettuces, tomatoes, spinach, spinach beet and celery, with carrots and beetroot for succession.

Runner beans are sown 25cm (10in) apart in two rows 30cm (12in) apart, and so will need 60cm (2ft) of the plot. Sow half the row in mid-May and the remainder in mid-June, to extend the season. Expect maturity in four months. 125mls (pint) of seed is sufficient for a full row, and will yield 48kg (105lbs).

Catch crops of lettuce sown in half rows in mid and late March, and radishes sown in half rows in early and late March, can be had before the beans go in.

French beans can be sown a little earlier. Put half a row in at the beginning of May, and finish the row towards the end of the month. A yield of 12kg (24lbs) can be expected from 125ml (pint) of seed, with 25cm (10in) between the plants and allowing 45cm (18in) for the row.

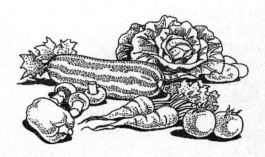

Your Gardening Week

FRENCH BEANS If heat is available, make a sowing of French beans, setting five or six in a 20cm pot. Cover with 25mm of compost and grow under glass at 15C (60F), expecting a crop in May.

LONG GLADIOLI To extend the flowering season, gladioli corms can be potted and plunged in a frame. In mid or late April, lift and plant out in their flowering positions.

FEED VEG Perennial vegetables such as asparagus, artichoke, rhubarb and seakale will benefit from a dressing of general fertiliser. This will have time to wash down to their roots, ready for the new growing season.

BIG BUD MITE Never mind big bud mite; in my case it has! Last season I spotted a limited amount of big bud on some blackcurrant bushes and endeavoured to prune it out. This year I see it has reappeared in force, so I will be lifting and burning those affected.

CUT PRIVET Where privet hedges have got out of hand, this is a good time to cut them hard back and encourage new strong basal growths.

POTATOES Buy seed potatoes as soon as possible. Set them off by chitting so they are ready for planting in late March or April.

SOW LUPINS If you can lay your hands on a few lupin seeds, sow them now for flower in late summer.

SWEET PEAS If not sown in autumn, sweet peas can be sown in a minimum temperature of 7C (45F), and will be ready for planting out in late April.

EARLY SALAD ONIONS For an early crop of salad onions, buy seed of the variety White Lisbon. This can be sown in a glasshouse border towards the end of the month, or outdoors under cloches in mid-February.

Making A Start With Dahlias

Despite the weather, now is the time when quite a number of things can be done that will, in fact, be preparation for displays during the coming year.

For instance, items that have been stored will need to be given attention. Check fruit to make sure that there is no sign of damage. Any suspect should be thrown away.

Check chrysanthemum stools and at the same time have a look at those left in the border. Waterlogging can prove something of a problem at this time and if that is the case, penetrate around each plant to their full depth with the tines of a hand fork. Remember too that new young shoots will make good cuttings to provide extra stock.

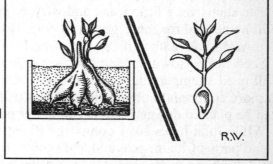

Much the same goes for dahlias. At this time in particular, the need is to check the health of the tubers. Damaged or rotting parts should be cut away and then dusted with flowers of sulphur.

If you find that the tubers have shrivelled, fear not; just steep them in a basin of tepid (not hot) water and leave them over night to regain their shape. They can then be returned to their boxes and covered once again with peat.

Later these can be started into growth by putting them in damp peat and, in February or March, they will throw shoots (pic left) which can be taken, with a piece of the original tuber, (pic right) to make excellent cuttings.

The cuttings can be started quite easily by planting in a three inch pot filled with sand above a layer of loam or peat. Kept in a greenhouse and given some bottom heat, they will soon form roots and can later be transplanted into 5 inch pots.

Into Hot Water!

A little tender loving care can be rewarded by a pleasing display of flowers if you should choose to grow Achimenes. This, the Hot Water plant, takes its name from the Greek "cheimaino", which translates as "to suffer from cold" - and gives an indication that temperature is important.

Modern hybrid varieties carry masses of large tubular flowers in colours of white, blue, purple, pink and yellow. While each bloom is short-lived, a succession are produced from June until October.

The stems are a little weak and wiry, so the support of twigs will be needed for those grown in pots. However, this limitation is turned to advantage if they are used for basket work.

Seed can be sown in March to flower in the second year and will need a temperature of 21-27C (70-80F) for germination. It is more common to obtain small tubers called tubercles. These can be planted during February in either pots, pans or boxes.

While John Innes No 1 compost will suffice, a mixture of equal parts of loam, peat and leaf mould, together with a dose of sand might be more appropriate. Set the tubercles 25mm (1in) apart and cover with 50mm (2in) of the compost. Water in well - preferably with tepid water - and keep in a temperature of 16C (60F) in shade, until shoots appear. When this happens the temperature can be dropped to 13C (55F) but should not fall below that level during the growing season.

Increase the amount of tepid water given as growth progresses, taking care to achieve the balance of keeping the compost moist at all times without overwatering. Feed can be given at 10-day intervals.

When large enough, box-grown plants can be set in pots or baskets. Those expected to remain upright should have branched twigs pushed in to give support before they become too large.

Humidity around the plant can be increased during drier periods by misting with tepid water, but try to avoid wetting the foliage. Although bright light is appreciated, direct sunlight should be avoided after mid-April.

During autumn, flowering will diminish and water can be reduced until they are completely rested. Once dry, cut off the stems and store the tubercles in dry peat or sand in a frost-free place.

Stock is easily increased by dividing the tubercles at planting time, or by taking stem cuttings in April or May.

If you had a Winter Cherry over the festive season and would like more of the same next time, then it is easy enough to achieve. In the first instance your existing plant can be grown on for many years. Prune the stems back by half in February, and keep almost dry until March. Repot before encouraging back into active growth. The prunings can be used to provide stem cuttings.

An alternative is to raise fresh stock from seed. As existing berries start to shrivel, select a few of the best and as they ripen, remove them and open with a knife to expose the seed. This can be sown from late February through to early April.

Space-sow in a pan or box of seed compost and cover lightly with fine compost. After watering, cover with a sheet of glass which can remain until germination starts.

Pot into 75mm (3in) pots using No1 Compost, and pot on as growth demands.

When the young plants reach 10cm (4in), pinch out the tips to encourage the formation of sideshoots and repeat this operation twice more before the summer.

From June to September, plunge the plants in a sunny frame or in a border so that insects have ready access to the flowers. This will encourage a high rate of pollination and ensure plenty of cheery berries for next winter's display.

Keep the compost moist and mist the leaves regularly. During winter the highest excesses of central heating should be avoided. Aim for something around 10-15C (50-60F).

Start Early Vegetables

Although I dealt with melons, we barely touched on different varieties. As mentioned, the cantaloupe are more suited to cold frame or cloche. Look for Ogen, which has small round fruits, good flavour and is suited to cooler areas. Charantais, again has small fruit, but with flavour best described as excellent. The same comment applies to Sweetheart, which gives larger fruit and is also suitable for cooler conditions.

Glass with enough heat to keep an average temperature of 10-12C (50-55F) at this time provides an opportunity to consider raising early seedlings of some vegetables for planting out later. Onions and leeks have already been mentioned but several more can be brought on over the next week or so. Beans, Brussels sprouts, summer cabbage, early summer cauliflower, parsley and peas are all suitable.

It is important, however, not to get carried away and allow the temperature to rise too high. If it does, the rate of growth will outstrip the light available and result in drawn, leggy seedlings which are likely to suffer shock if an attempt is made to transplant them.

Cabbage varieties such as Primo and Hispi, sown in mid-February, should be ready for cutting in June. If space-sown around 25mm (1in) apart they should not need transplanting until set outdoors in early April. Where heat is not available, they can be sown outdoors in April and transplanted in May or early June for an August crop.

The earliest cauliflowers come from sowings made in frames during September, but are quickly followed by crops raised from sowings made now. Polaris and Snowball are both fast maturing varieties and some extension of cropping can be achieved by using All The Year Round, which matures more slowly.

While seed should again be space-sown, the young seedlings are best moved into 75mm (3in) pots before planting out in

April. Further sowing can be made outdoors in late March or early April to transplant in June for cropping in August and September. These may be followed by autumn varieties sown in late April or early May to transplant in late June.

Autumn sowing of broad beans outdoors is only a prospect in mild areas on a sheltered site with free-draining soil. Seed sown now, individually in pots, for planting out in April, will bring an early summer crop and can be followed by sowing outdoors in late February or March. The Sutton, which is a dwarf variety, can be sown in succession from March through to July to give a long cropping season. If you wish to carry a crop through winter, it can be sown from November onwards provided that cloche protection can be given.

Even under glass, dwarf French beans are not started until the end of March or early in April. Set them five or six to a 20cm (4in) pot, covering with 25mm (1in) of compost and growing on in a temperature of 15C (60F). Successional sowings outdoors commence at the end of April and continue until the beginning of July. Two to try for flavour are The Prince and Nassau but both should be harvested young to be at their best.

Peas can be started from now on and are best sown singly in pots. Early varieties to try include Early Onward and Kelvedon Wonder, but for flavour you might choose the second early variety, Hurst Green Shaft. Outdoor sowings can commence in late March, continuing though to the beginning of June.

If a little more heat is available why not try some early aubergines? They can be sown in pots from now until March, but need a temperature of around 16C (60F). Germination should take a couple of weeks, and as growth is made the plants can be moved on into 12.5cm (5in) pots of John Innes No 1 compost, and later into 20cm (8in) pots using No 3 compost.

When the plants reach 15cm (6in) pinch out the growing tip. Subsequently, after four fruits have set, remove any remaining flowers and pinch out sideshoots. Water well and apply liquid feed in summer.

Your Gardening Week

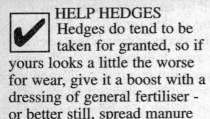

HELP HEDGES Hedges do tend to be taken for granted, so if yours looks a little the worse for wear, give it a boost with a dressing of general fertiliser - or better still, spread manure over the area of root run.

SOW VEG Sowings of cabbage, lettuce, peas and cauliflower can be made in a temperature of 13C (55F).

APPLY LIME This is a good time to apply lime to any ground that needs it, particularly the vegetable plot. Lime and manure are never worked at the same time, so that soil dug and enriched in autumn can now be treated.

PLANT RHUBARB Rhubarb crowns can be planted now some 75-90cms apart, just below the soil surface.

CHECK CLOCHES Check that cloches have not moved out of alignment, or unwanted cold air may find its way to your crops.

USE STRAW If the weather is wet and warmish then don't worry, but if a cold spell threatens, crops such as spring cabbage can be protected by spreading straw about them.

BUY CELERY SEED Purchase celery seed for sowing under glass in March or early April, to produce plants to be set out in late May or early June.

TOP DRESS Pot plants which are not to be repotted, will benefit if a little soil is removed from the top of the pot and replaced with fresh compost.

SOW PARSNIPS While clearing the last of the current crop, it is time to think of sowing fresh parsnips. Get on with it as soon as the ground will allow.

USE CLOCHES Sowings of early carrots, lettuce and salad onion can be made under cloches. Peas may be sown in between the rows, and left to grow on as the others are harvested.

Raspberries

One good thing about gardening is that even in the depths of a snow-bound winter, you can think ahead of the good times to come - summer's sun and the fruits it will bring. Providing that you get down to some hard work as soon as the climate allows.

One such thought is of raspberries and cream. Raspberries are an excellent fruit for the beginner to tackle for they are fairly trouble-free.

They grow well in most soils, providing it is moist and free-draining. Even those with clay or chalky soil should not be disappointed by results, provided a little more attention is given, particularly by ensuring the plot is well manured and mulched.

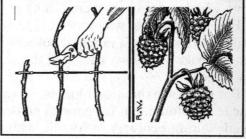

Plant your raspberry canes now, about 2 1/2 ft. apart, digging out a wedge of soil about five inches deep. Tread the soil around the roots, after planting. At each end of the row place a stake to reach about 5 1/5 ft. above the ground. Then stretch galvanised wires across at 3 ft. and 5 ft. heights. As the canes grow, just tie them in to the wire.

If you already have plants, then they will require some attention. Autumn fruiters should be cut back to about nine inches above the ground, whilst those fruiting in summer will be showing growth above the top wires and should be tip-trimmed. Cut back to a bud just above the top wire (as shown above).

In March, give a feed of sulphate of ammonia (about a dessertspoon to the square yard) and a good mulching.

Then all you'll need to do is to arrange a good supply of thick cream!

Super Sweet Peas

If you take up your catalogue and turn to the section devoted to Sweet Peas, the number of entries will serve to confirm the popularity of this beautiful flowering plant. Its popularity is justified by pleasing blooms, a wide range of colours, a long flowering-season and an exquisite scent.

Sadly, all these benefits cannot be had without some effort. Sweet Peas require preparation and care if you are to have the best of them. Part of the problem is in providing support, for many varieties will grow several feet tall. But others are available which only reach 45cm (18in) or 90cm (3ft).

Probably the best way to start is to select a mixture of varieties which will provide a range of colours. Then in future years you might make your own choice of the self-colours that have greatest appeal.

For the best exhibition blooms, sowings should have been made in autumn, but for general garden use sowings can be made during February or March, with the benefit of frame protection during cold spells. Alternatively, seed may be sown outdoors in late March or early April, when germination will be encouraged by cloche protection.

Some varieties have very hard seed coats, and will benefit from being filed or chipped with the point of a knife to allow moisture to penetrate more readily. Take care that this is done on the opposite side to the eye, and don't go so deep as to damage the inner white tissue. Otherwise they may be soaked in water for 24 hours prior to sowing. This will cause most of them to swell - any not having done so and remaining hard can be chipped so they will germinate at around the same time.

When sowing under glass, use pots or deep boxes and John Innes compost. Space-sow the seed at 5cm (2in) centres and set them 25mm (1in) deep. Water in and cover with sheets of glass. These should be turned daily to allow condensed moisture to drain off. During periods of strong sunshine, give shade.

As soon as the seedlings push through the soil with their stems bent over, all coverings should be removed. When they reach 75-100mm (3-4in) with one or two pairs of leaves, the growing point is pinched out to encourage busy growth.

So far thing are quite straightforward. However, sweet peas are possessed of a deep and extensive root system if given the chance. They make rapid growth when the days are warm, producing a long succession of flower and so need easy access to plentiful supplies of food and water.

If you want to go the whole hog then ground may be cultivated three spits deep and well supplied with manure. If that doesn't appeal, try two spits. Where even this may be too much, settle for digging the top spits and working in well-rotted manure. During the growing season this resource can be augmented with water as required, and the occasional dose of liquid feed.

When the ground has been prepared, supports should be erected before planting or outdoor sowing takes place. Here you are faced with a number of choices.

If tall varieties are grown in rows, 240-300cm (8-10ft) canes can be set in a double row 30cm (1ft) apart with 20cm (8in) between. The plants are then trained as cordons. Alternatively netting or trellis can be set up for more informal training.

If the plants are to be accommodated in a mixed border, it is a good idea to use large pea-sticks which can be formed into a wigwam by tying the tops together.

Sweet Pea seedlings are fairly hardy and should withstand normal spring frosts; but if cold east winds threaten it is advisable to provide a windbreak. The protection of short pea-sticks or even netting may be needed to prevent young shoots being damaged by pigeons or other birds.

Most important when planting is to make great efforts to avoid damage to the long roots. Take out a large enough planting hole and carefully spread the roots in this, leaving the lowest sideshoot joint at ground level.

Plan For Sprouts

One of the vegetables mentioned already, but not expanded upon, is the good old Brussels sprout. By choice of variety and successional sowings, crops can be had in season right through from the end of September into March next year. This means that care of the crop spans the full 12 months with normal sowing starting in the middle of March just as the last buttons are being picked.

Fortunately Brussels sprout seed remains viable for around four years and so, provided vast quantities of each are not required, it is possible to keep several varieties on the go while only purchasing one or two fresh packets of seed each year.

When choosing varieties there are two basic types to select from: the long-serving old favourites and the newer F1 forms. The F1 varieties have been bred with commercial production in mind and should be judged in that light. They tend to be compact and produce regular sized buttons which mature at the same time. This is fine if you expect to need a lot at a time or have a freezer to keep them in.

Alternatively you could go to the trouble of growing very small numbers of a particular variety, or making regular successional sowings to extend the season a little.

Among the best known of these varieties is Peer Gynt which produces medium-sized, good quality sprouts from October to December; and Citadel, with firm, tight sprouts from December to March.

On balance I still tend to the older varieties which can produce the tallest plants with the heaviest yields, the largest sprouts, and have the advantage of producing these in sequence over a long harvesting period.

Of these, Bedford Fillbasket produces large, solid sprouts from autumn into the New Year; Roodnerf produces medium buttons around Christmas which also keep well; and Winter Harvest

makes strong and hardy plants cropping from October to February.

One other advantage of the non-F1's is that they are less than a third the price of their newer relatives.

To grow sprouts to the best advantage a deeply worked, firm and well-manured soil is needed. Ideally sprouts should follow a crop for which the ground was heavily manured, but which has had time to rot down and consolidate. Prior to planting, work in a dressing of superphosphate and sulphate of potash. Late cultivation, fresh manure or loose soil may well produce lush growth and lead to blown sprouts.

Sowings can be made under glass, in frames or in a sheltered seed bed. When the seedlings are around 15cm (6in) high - having been hardened off if necessary - they can be planted out, generally in late May or early June. For most varieties a spacing of 75cm (2ft 6in) each way is adequate, but for the more vigorous varieties increase this to 90cm (3ft).

Conceivably the ground may dry out between now and planting time. But planting is best carried out following rain, and it does no harm to fill the holes with water just prior to planting.

Both cabbage rootfly and club root are hazards to beware of. As a preventative measure it is a good idea to wash the roots and then dip them in a thick paste of four per cent calomel dust and water. When planting, set the seedlings so that the lowest pair of leaves are just at soil level, then firm in well using either a dibber or your heel.

Keep the hoe going throughout the growing season and apply water during dry spells. Liquid or foliar feeds can be given in early summer to boost growth. Varieties expected to stand during late autumn and winter can be staked as a precaution against wind damage. Drawing a little soil up around the stems will also increase stability.

Harvest the buttons by working upwards from the base of the stems, picking evenly across the plants rather than stripping individuals to excess.

Your Gardening Week

 CHECK SUPPORTS If you have any wall-trained fruit trees or bushes, check that the supports are in good order before the new season's growth makes fresh demands on them.

 EXTRA HELLE-BORES Although prefering to be left, helleborus niger, the Christmas Rose, should re-establish if propagated by division immediately after flowering.

 LAWN CARE Any turfing should be completed as conditions allow. By the end of the month it will be time to think about preparing ground for sowing new areas.

 SUMMER BEDDING If not yet dealt with, summer bedding schemes should be planned at the earliest opportunity so that seed orders can be sent in as soon as possible.

START FUCHSIAS Fuchsia stock plants can be started into growth to encourage the production of shoots which will serve as cuttings in March.

 FORCING As temperatures improve there is less need to bring seakale and rhubarb inside for forcing. They can be covered where they are planted.

 CAMELLIAS When pot grown camellias pass out of flower they can be top-dressed or repotted to sustain them through the growing season.

 BULBS As early potted bulbs cease flowering, the pots or bowls can be laid on their sides and the bulbs allowed to die back naturally. This allows food in the foliage to be drawn into the bulbs, building them up for next season. As an alternative they can be heeled-in in a nursery plot, provided they are first hardened-off.

 SEED SOWING The busy season for seed sowing approaches, and it is always worth sowing thinly. This way seedlings have room to develop, and will not become overcrowded if pricking off is delayed.

A Right Royal One For The Pot

There is something very regal about gloxinias; a regality characterised by their velvety flowers in rich tones of red, through blue to the deepest of purples, which makes them superb plants for indoor decoration from May right on in to July.

As such they are well worth trying for the average gardener; either from seed planted this month, or by starting tubers in March.

By far the easiest way of course, is the latter method, but since February is still with us let us deal with the cheaper method with seeds first.

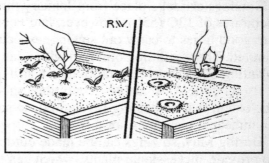

Fill a seed tray with damp John Innes seed compost and gently knock the seed from the packet or from a piece of paper on which they have been emptied. The seeds are very fine and will need to be sown as thinly as possible. Then just lightly press the seeds on to the top of the soil. Cover the tray with a sheet of glass, keep in good light and maintain a temperature of around 20c (70 F).

Once germination has taken place, the temperature can be allowed to drop to 15c (60 F). When they are big enough to handle transfer them, spaced at 1 1/2 inch intervals to trays of John Innes No 1, laid over a bed of peat (see left). As the plants develop they can be moved on into separate pots, first of 3 inch size, later 5 inch.

To grow the easier way, obtain healthy tubers with good centres. Plunge them into trays of peat (see right) and, once they have formed roots transfer them to 5 inch pots which should be filled with John Innes No 2 over a good layer of peat.

When they are brought into the house, find them a windowsill which will allow good light, without them being in direct sunlight.

Half-hardy Annuals

This is the time to start sowing half-hardy annuals to add to the summer display in your garden. If large numbers are intended, a glasshouse or frame will be needed; but much can be achieved using the airing cupboard and a windowsill.

What are half-hardy annuals? Basically they are annuals and some perennials which tend to be grown as annuals, which will not stand frost. Thus, they need to be raised in a protected environment until the danger of frost has passed.

Sowings can take place from January through to May in temperatures of 13C (55F). However, late February and early March are good times to carry out sowing, especially where space is limited. There is little point in having plants ready too early for planting out if outside conditions are still too cold.

By the time April arrives, conditions should have improved to the extent that no heating is required, so sowings can be made in an unheated glasshouse or a frame.

During May, sowings can be made outdoors. These are useful to provide successional plants, which can be set out to replace plants from earlier sowings that have passed their best in summer.

Inside, make sowings in boxes or pans using a seed compost. Generally, and especially with very fine seed, it is good practice to water from the bottom so that the seed is not washed too deeply into the compost. As ever, sow thinly so the seedlings have room to develop and do not become overcrowded if pricking-off has to be delayed for a day or two. Cover the containers with glass and paper until germination takes place, turning the glass at least once a day to prevent condensation droplets building up.

Once the first seedlings appear, remove the paper. The glass can be left in place for a few extra days, though it should be tilted slightly to allow some air circulation.

When large enough, the seedlings can be pricked-off into potting compost, but should be shaded from strong sunlight for a day or two until they re-establish in their new environment.

Planting out can take place around the end of May or early in June when the danger of frost has passed. Prior to this, the plants should be gradually hardened-off so that there is no sudden change in the general temperature.

A temperature shock can cause growth to stop, and it takes a while for them to recover, so they never seem to reach their full potential.

Hardening can be achieved by transferring the plants to a cold frame. Gradually increase the ventilation until the framelights are left off altogether unless frost is likely. If no frame is available, gradually increase ventilation in the glasshouse until both doors and vents can be left open day and night.

The advantages of raising the various plants treated as annuals from seed, are that for a comparatively small sum it is possible to raise many plants and - perhaps more importantly - the opportunity is there to make changes in the types and varieties chosen. So each year the garden has something new to offer and you might achieve a substantial variation in atmosphere by, for example, selecting a range of varieties with a similar colour. But whatever the colour, I find flowers cheering.

There is not the space to mention many, but here are a few half-hardies to consider.

The blue flowers of Ageratum, the 'Floss Flower', are in season throughout the summer, and mix well with many other informal plantings as well as making a good edging to formal bedding schemes. They will thrive in any ordinary soil, but prefer sun.

Making a fine pot-plant, Amaranthus caudatus, 'Love-lies bleeding', is also useful in sub-tropical bedding schemes. It grows to 60-90cm with long, red, drooping flowers like a fox's brush. Similarly, various forms of Celosia, the 'Cockscomb', are ideal for both bedding and pot work.

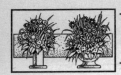

Your Gardening Week

Delightful Daphnes

I know of those who question the point of growing sweetly scented flowers which come into season early in the year, at a time when they are unlikely to sit out in the garden. Another factor to be recognised is that the weather tends to be more turbulent and the scent scattered on the wind. I think they miss a point, for how much more precious is the pleasure when it is more scarce?

I have already recommended Daphne mezereum as one of the shrubs that gives me pleasure from the appearance of its fine scented flowers in February and March. But as I mentioned, there are many other deserving specimens in this genus.

In fact the flowering season for Daphnes starts in December or January, as the reddish-mauve buds of D. bholua open to reveal white flowers with a reddish-mauve reverse.

These are carried in terminal ambles each made up of twenty or more flowers. The shrub is deciduous or semi-evergreen with stout, erect branches which can reach to over two metres (6 ft).

If planted in an exposed position, hard weather may damage the flowers, but it should do well given shelter.

Flowering at around the same time as the mezereon, but with similar form to D. bholua, is Daphne odora. It is very fragrant and makes a small bush from 1.2 to 2m high (4-6 ft). It will withstand quite severe frosts, but a sheltered position, ideally against a west wall, is again to be recommended. Where there is some doubt as to its performance, it may be pot-grown to give the benefit of additional protection.

Although it will make acceptable growth in a shady position, a sunny position improves the ripening of new wood and also seems to encourage flower-bud initiation. The flowers themselves are rosy-purple, particularly on the reverse of the petals, and there are also forms in pure white. The flowers are held in dense heads of ten or a dozen blooms.

Another form is D. odora 'Aureo-marginata' which sports white margins to its apple-green, evergreen leaves. It is hardier and may be a better bet to grow, but nevertheless is best protected from north and east winds.

To continue the succession of scent, the pink flowers of Daphne mantensiana appear in March or April. Compared to some, it grows reasonably quickly to form a rounded evergreen bush and may produced a second flush of flower in late summer.

By now the season is advancing and a wider range of these plants come to flower. First to spring to mind is Daphne burkwoodii 'Somerset'. Again reasonably fast-growing, this semi-evergreen shrub grows to make a dense dome of around one metre (2 ft).

The well-scented flowers are a soft mauve-pink and are carried in clusters on short, leafy shoots spread along the branches. They appear in May and June with a second flush, again in late summer.

It looks well set among heathers, bringing an extra flush of flower to the area they occupy.

As a rule Daphnes will thrive in any reasonable garden soil, though a rich loam is to be preferred. Soil on the sandy side should be well bolstered with organic material. The usual rule of free-drainage with adequate retention of water applies.

The biggest threat to their existance comes from hot, dry conditions. Where these occur the effects can be mitigated by the application of a mulch and the giving of water as required.

Other than at the extremes, pH does not seem to be a problem. In the wild, many of the species grow on limestone soils, but in the garden they appear tolerant of some degree of acidity.
Having said that, some, such a D. odora 'Aureo-marginata', may exhibit signs of chlorosis on chalky soils and can be treated with a sequestered product.

It is doubtful whether I have scratched the surface in dealing with the genus Daphne. There are many more to choose from, and I can only suggest that you give some of them a try.

Your Gardening Week

WORK FOR THE WEEK

✔ SOW ONIONS For a crop of onions in August or September, seed should be sown as soon as the land is workable. Shallots can be planted, but onions should be held back until March or April when the ground is warmer.

✔ START PARSNIPS Long-rooted varieties of parsnip need a lengthy growing season and should be sown as soon as possible. Shorter rooted varieties can be left to March or April.

✔ BROAD BEANS Sow an early variety of broad beans for an early summer crop. If the ground is too wet, raise in pots and plant out in April.

✔ MUSTARD AND CRESS I know that mustard and cress is readily available in the shops, but it is easy to grow your own. Sow in shallow boxes and start the cress four days before the mustard so that they are ready together.

✔ SPROUT GLADIOLI Early blooms can be had from gladioli if a number of corns are chitted by spreading them out in a box and exposing to maximum light. Turn occasionally and plant out during mid-March.

✔ HARDEN CAULI-FLOWERS Autumn sown cauliflowers being overwintered in frames, should be hardened-off as conditions allow to be ready for planting out in March.

✔ STORED POTATOES Regularly check late potatoes you have in store. As sprouts appear rub them out.

✔ REGULAR TURNIPS A favoured piece of ground could allow a small sowing of turnips. Follow up with successional sowings every three weeks.

✔ FORCE LILIES A batch of pot-grown lilies can be forced into early flower if brought into a temperature of 13C (55F). For succession, start another batch in about four weeks.

Gladioli

I would anticipate that by now, Australian ambassador extraordinaire, Dame Edna Everage, would have ensured she had ordered the Gladdie corms to brighten her London or Home Counties patch. If not she, and you, should get down to it pretty quickly.

Gladioli come in three main categories: Firstly, large-flowered which grow up to 5 ft; then primulinus which are smaller, in both height and florets and, finally, the smallest-butterflies which are delightful as cut flowers.

In the most clement parts the corms can be started into growth from mid-February. Although, mid-or even late March may be more advisable.

However, to get good blooms over a long period, say from part through July to November, plant corms on an interval basis of every two weeks.

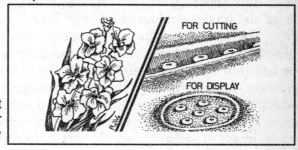

Ideally you want a light soil and the corms should be planted about 3 ins (7.5cm) deep. If your soil is on the heavy side, then 2 ins (5cm) should be all right. Plant in groups, about 5 ins (12.5cm) apart if they are for decoration in a mixed border. Growing in rows is best if specifically required for cutting. Planted in rows, the bigger blooms will need to be planted about 4 ins (10cm) deep and about 8 ins (20cm) apart. You will need a gap of a foot between rows.

Use a trowel for planting in groups, but take out a drill for rows. The large-flowered varieties will need separate staking about five feet in height, whilst those planted in groups may have a number of stakes around the area, joined with criss-crossing twine.

Something Odd In The Garden!

As a rule we tend to look for the graceful, the colourful and imposing when choosing plants for the garden. There are, however, a number of plants falling outside these categories which can make a useful contribution and certainly provide a talking point.

The idea of growing plants with green flowers may at first have little appeal. Certainly catalogues tend to concentrate on large and brightly-coloured flowers. However, too many colours close together can compete with one another and have the effect of reducing their impact. 'Greens' can act as a foil and will also be found to have more subtle attractions of their own.

First to come to mind is Euphorbia wulfenii (syn. E. veneta), which grows to over a metre (4ft) with a spread of around 90cm (3ft). It is a handsome perennial, with grey-green foliage which backs heads of yellow-green flowers from spring to summer.

Thriving in any reasonable garden soil, this euphorbia prefers a slightly sheltered position. While other species are easily propagated by division, seed is more appropriate here and can be sown in spring. Alternatively, softwood cuttings taken in spring can be inserted outdoors under a cloche.

We usually select roses on the basis of their large and attractive blooms. In the case of Rosa chinensis 'Viridiflora', by some accident of nature a seedling rose appeared which has become known as the green rose. While not the most beautiful it has a certain curiosity value. Growing to form a small shrub, its flowers are double and consist of tightly packed, petal-like scales.

'Fasciation' is an abnormal form of plant growth which can be described as a lateral fusion of stems. Instead of stems being round and branching out, a number of them remain joined together to form a broad, flat shoot. This condition can be found occasionally in a range of plants but is more prevalent in some.

I suppose the purist would seek to rogue them out. However, the Japanese have a yen for this type of feature and have perpetuated some species of willow which exhibit regular fasciation together with other contortions. Salix sachalinensis 'Sekka' (syn 'Setsuka'), is one of these. The condition may be encouraged by hard pruning, and the resultant branches are useful for floral decorations. The display of catkins is less satisfactory than in other forms, for they only open at the same time as the first flush of leaves appear, rather than in advance.

Salix matsudana - the Pekin Willow - has given us two interesting and contrasting forms. 'Pendula' makes a graceful tree, and can be regarded as one of the best forms to grow if a traditional weeping form is needed. In complete contrast, S. m. 'Tortuosa' takes amazing twists and turns as it quickly grows to make a sizeable tree. It will thrive in drier conditions than those required by many willows. Both are easily propagated by making cuttings, but even branches pushed deeply into the ground when dormant are likely to root.

Our brethren over the water cannot claim a monopoly in this field. Corylus avallana contorta is, I think, a gem. Discovered in a hedgerow in Gloucestershire in the mid-nineteenth century, its branches snake and twist and have earned it the names of the Corkscrew Hazel or Harry Lauder's Walking Stick.

Propagation can be achieved by layering and new plants grow quite slowly, taking many years to reach their ultimate height of around 3m (10ft). The impact is enhanced by a pleasing display of catkins in the early months of the year.

Not distorted in the branches, but in the leaves, Ilex aquifolium 'Ferox' is reputed to be the oldest identifiable cultivar of holly still in cultivation. It has been known since the early 17th century, and its small leaves, puckered covered with short, sharp spines, have led to its name of the Hedgehog Holly. It is a slowish growing male form and can be attractive as a specimen, although its prickly nature makes it ideal for a barrier hedge.

A Handful Of Herbs!

A lthough a winter with few real frosts is fine for plants of doubtful hardiness, it can also mean that many pests which would have succumbed to cold will survive. Fortunately the same will be true for ladybirds which, in the more common species, should emerge from hibernation to lay eggs in spring. The larvae which hatch from these will welcome a plentiful supply of aphids on which to feed. A shortage of such food may mean that they resort to cannibalism in order that the fittest survive.

When fully fed they attach themselves to a leaf and turn into a chrysalis, from which the adult emerges soon afterwards.

But from the world of the ladybird to the varied world of herbs There is a real pleasure in growing your own herbs. Not only can they enhance a meal, but in the majority of cases are attractive within the garden.

Things do tend to go in cycles. At the beginning of the 19th century a wide range of herbs were in regular use. A hundred years later the number in regular and extensive use had declined to mint, parsley, sage and thyme. Now a look at the proliferation of boxes and jars on supermarket shelves serves to confirm that herbs are in wide use again.

One of the attractions of herbs is that anyone can grow them. In large gardens a distinct herb garden can be created to hold a wide range of plants.

On a smaller scale a border may be set aside to accommodate a few or they can be integrated within mixed borders or the vegetable plot.

In extreme cases where gardens are small or non-existent, they can be grown in pots on a window sill or balcony.

Many of the herbs we grow are native to warmer areas and will need shelter from prevailing winds, but with an open, sunny aspect. Where no shelter exists some of the hardier, shrubier

types can be used to provide better conditions for lower-growing companions. Artemesia, lavender, sage and rosemary can all be used in this way.

Some herbs are annuals, so fresh stocks need to be raised from seed each year. Basil, borage, caraway, chervil, corn salad, parsley, purslane and summer savory all fall into this category. For initial stocks seed or plants must be purchased, but once you have made a start, seed can be saved from your own plants each summer. Make sowings outdoors in a seed bed during April or, if you wish to start a little early, sow in seed pans in gentle heat next month, thinning and hardening off before planting out in May.

Several herbs such as angelica, clary, evening primrose, sage and verbascum are biennials and need to be sown during summer to flower in the following year. Some of these, grown for their foliage, can be encouraged into longer life so that they grow as perennials. This can be achieved if flowering stems are pinched out as they appear. Nevertheless, it is better to raise fresh stock each year.

Many perennial forms are readily available in pots from garden centres, although if you want some of the less common types it will be necessary to seek out a specialist grower. Most, such as chicory, comfrey and lemon balm can be raised from seed initially. Once these plants have reached a reasonable size they can be propagated by cuttings, division or offsets. The more woody types such as lavender, rosemary and santolina can be increased by cuttings taken with a heel in July, or struck in a frame in spring.

Overall, herbs will grow in a wide range of soils, although the usual improvements will lead to better growth. Thus, sandy soils will need humus to improve water retention, while heavier soils can be lightened using compost. Needless to say, requirements do vary from plant to plant. The likes of rosemary, marjoram and thyme thrive in baked soils, while angelica and mint prefer a moist soil in a lightly shaded position.

Your Gardening Week

 RANUNCULUS AND ANEMONES Ranunculus and anemones can be set out this month, but on heavy and wet soils anemones will benefit from a raised bed.

 SOW HELIOTROPE To provide a filler and background among other bedding plants, heliotrope can be useful. Sow now in seed compost and germinate in a temperature of 20C (68F).

 TRAIN BLACKBERRIES Keep an eye on blackberries, and take care to tie in new growth as it occurs. This is much easier than wrestling with strong shoots later in the season!

TRIM HEATHERS Once winter-flowering heathers pass out of flower they can be lightly trimmed with shears. This helps keep them tight and bushy. Take care not to cut back into older wood.

 SOW TOMATOES Make a sowing of maincrop tomatoes for planting in the glasshouse during May.

 SUMMER SPINACH Summer spinach can be sown now and will be ready to harvest in May. Maintain successional sowings every three weeks until July, to give crops in season through to September.

 PRUNE HYDRANGEAS The old flowering heads of hydrangeas, left on through the winter to give some protection against frost, can now be pruned out.

 BREAK WIND Strong winds can be a problem. So check over stakes and ties. Any newly planted stock, particularly evergreens, can be susceptible to the drying effect of such winds. They will benefit from the erection of temporary windbreaks until roots are established. Do make sure the breaks themselves are secure.

 MORE FRENCH BEANS Make further sowings of French beans in pots and under glass.

A Touch Of Flavour For The Roast Beef

There's nothing quite like the flavour from home grown parsnips to give that final touch to a traditional English Sunday lunch of roast beef and Yorkshire pudding.

To get them, however, you have to plan early; planting seeds certainly by the early part of March, though later sowings will produce acceptable specimens for the pot.

As soon as possible, set about providing the best conditions for growing. A fine tilth will be necessary.

You will need to cultivate fairly deeply too, because parsnips are very deep rooted.

The area, ideally, should have been manured in the autumn so fresh manure should not be added now.

When preparations are complete allow the area to settle.

Just before sowing dress the ground with Growmore at the rate of about 3ozs to the square metre and hoe it in.

In general sowing can be done by taking out a drill into which the seed can be placed, just deep enough to be covered by soil. To allow for somewhat erratic germination you can sow fairly thickly, thinning out afterwards.

For really big, prize specimens the best way is make room for them first; use a dibber to its full length and wiggle it to make a V shaped hole (see pic left).

Fill the hole to the top with good soil or potting compost and put 4 or 5 seeds on top, finally sprinkling more soil on the top (see right). After germination just leave the best specimen to grow into your prize parsnip.

Green, Purple And White!

February through to May is the season when sprouting broccoli is at its best. It is also the time to be thinking about preparations for next year's crop. Although March and April are peak harvesting periods, crops can be had from July to November in the form of calabrese.

There is little doubt that calabrese or green sprouting broccoli is popular. It's readily available from shops in fresh and frozen form.

However, it is easily raised in the vegetable plot so that regular fresh supplies should be available in summer and autumn, augumented by heads that have been frozen.

This is because the plant is not winter-hardy, although it will continue to produce throughout winter if no prolonged periods of frost occur.

After the turn of the year, both white and purple sprouting varieties come into their own. The purple forms are a mite hardier and are ready for harvesting during January in mild winters, but will be delayed if conditions are hard. White sprouting is less hardy, and so should benefit from a more sheltered position to bring it on.

I suspect that less broccoli is grown than could be, for not only is it pleasant to eat, but also simple to grow. There is no need to check your diary for sowing dates, and no need to plan for succession. All sowing can be achieved in April and the job completed at one go.

Following preparation of a seedbed, seed can be sown thinly in 1cm (1/2in) drills set 22.5cm (9in) apart. Sufficient thinning should be carried out to ensure that the seedlings do not become drawn and spindly. Calabrese can be transplanted in late May when 8cm (3in) high, at 50cm (20in) apart in the row with 60cm (24in) between rows. Broccoli are moved when a little taller at 10cm (4in), and need a little more space at 60cm in the row with

75cm (30in) between rows.

Ideally, as with other brassicas, soil should be rich in organic matter. While good drainage is needed, a soil on the heavy side allows adequate firming. Set the young plants a little deeper than they were in the seedbed, firm in well and give a thorough soaking.

It may be necessary to give protection against pigeons and sparrows; but other than that, all that is necessary is to keep weeds down and provide water during dry spells. Broccoli will benefit from mulching, and in autumn can have soil drawn up around the stems. In exposed positions use canes for additional support.

Crops should be harvested when the flower shoots or 'spears' are well formed, but before the flowers have had chance to open. The most well-developed will be the central spear, and this should be cut first. Its removal will stimulate fresh growth from the leaf joints. If flowering occurs, the production of fresh spears will cease.

Of the calabrese varieties, Mercedes and Express Corona are in season during August and September, and can be followed by Green Duke and, for a late crop, Autumn Spear.

In broccoli, Improved White Sprouting and Purple Sprouting are the ones to go for. If you fancy missing out the sowing each year, try Nine Star Perennial. This will mature in late March and early April, showing a central head surrounded by smaller ones. Provided that each of these are picked, the plant will crop for several years.

Perhaps not so appreciated, but nevertheless valuable - especially in hard seasons - curly kale can be dealt with in a similar manner.

However, besides manure it needs lime and should have a ph of 6.5 to 6.8. Plant out in July at 45cm (18in) centres.

Plain-leaved kales are sown in July, in the plot where they are to mature. Set the rows 45cm apart, and gradually thin plants to a similar distance within the row.

Health Indicators

The genus Nicotiana was named in honour of Jean Nicot, a French Consul to Portugal who introduced tobacco into France and Portugal during the sixteenth century. Whether it would be regarded as an honour or a condemnation, is debatable these days.

Fortunately the genus has more to offer in colour than nicotine stains, and provides a number of useful ornamental tobacco plants for the garden.

Notable among these is the F1 hybrid Lime Green, which produces striking flowers in pale green which are held upwards and so display well. They are also ideal in flower arrangements. Suited to a partially shaded spot, the plants sit well in a mixed border and also have a pleasant scent. If scent is an objective, then mixtures such as Evening Fragrance can be had with flowers of white, pink, rose, red, lilac and purple.

The F1 formula mixture Nicki produces even plants to around 40cm (16in), in colours of red, rose, lime and white which are useful for bedding. 'Roulette' is an F2 mixture and 'Domini' an F1 mix, both of which reach around 30cm (1ft) and display their flowers well.

These plants should thrive in any reasonable garden soil. Seed can be sown from now through to April, in a temperature of 13-16C (55-60F), using John Innes seed compost. After hardening they will be ready for planting out in June.

If heat is not available, sowing can be carried out outdoors towards the end of May, in the position where the plants are to flower. In favoured areas the plants may set their own seed. This will germinate in the following spring, but will not be true to type in the case of hybrid varieties.

When to prune roses is always a matter of judgement. Do it early and they spring into growth with the promise of early flower. But there is the risk of frost damage, in which case noth-

ing is gained. The safest and latest time for pruning is the beginning of April, though the job can be carried out during March.

When a shoot is pruned back - perhaps by a half or more, depending on circumstances - the rising sap which was flowing to the top of branches and feeding buds there, is forced into lower, dormant buds which stimulates them into growth.

We do experience late frosts and occasionally severe ones too, although generally roses suffer little damage. If they are caught, the tender leaves opening in the bud will brown at the tip. They will grow away again, but the bush may be given a check.

Where the check is apparent, it seems to have the effect of encouraging suckers on budded varieties. These should be pulled out at the earliest opportunity. During April apply a dressing of rose fertiliser, and lightly prick into the soil surface.

While rose foliage might become brown and crinkled at the edges as a result of frost damage, the foliage is also a good indicator of the general health of the plant.

If stems are stunted and weak, and the leaves small and pale, the likely cause is a shortage of nitrogen. Red spots may also be found and early leaf fall will occur.

Similar poor growth with early leaf fall, but with the young leaves small and dark green and showing purplish tints on the underside, is an indication of a shortage of phosphate.

Where potash is deficient (a common problem on light, sandy soils), the young leaves take on a reddish hue. As they mature the edges become brown and brittle and flowers will be small.

Two contrasting effects are achieved by waterlogging and manganese deficiency. With the former, the leaves exhibit large, yellow areas, spreading out from the midrib and veins. Shortage of managanese works the other way round, with yellow areas appearing between the veins, the oldest leaves affected first.

A shortage of magnesium produces pale areas, but these start in the centre around the midrib. As the effect continues, dead patches appear in the middle of the leaf. Again, older leaves are affected first and premature leaves fall may be expected.

Your Gardening Week

✓ **THIN RADISH** If you have started to sow short rows of radish for succession, don't forget to thin the seedlings before they become overcrowded. Left too long they will produce all leaf.

✓ **ONIONS FROM SETS** Depending upon the state of the ground and the weather, onion sets may be planted from now through to the end of April, though mid-March to mid-April is probably best for most areas. Try Stuttgarter, which has a mild flavour, stores well and is unlikely to bolt; Sturon, which is also bolt resistant and produces large bulbs; or old favourites like Ailsa Craig or Dutch Yellow.

✓ **SOW PEAS** If not already started, round seeded varieties of pea such as Feltham First or Meteor can be sown now under cloches.

✓ **GLASSHOUSE CARE** This can be a difficult time in the glasshouse, with sun in the middle of the day causing temperatures to rise quickly - only to fall just as quickly when it disappears. Open ventilators when possible, but risk the heat rather than the cold if you can't be sure of getting back to them.

✓ **LETTUCE** Early lettuce sown under glass can be set out under cloches during March.

✓ **LEEKS** You may already have sown leeks under glass. If not, it's time to acquire seed for sowing outdoors in late March or early April.

✓ **HARDENING OFF** As weather conditions improve, frames containing seedlings and cuttings from autumn should be ventilated to harden them off.

✓ **CLOCHE STRAW-BERRIES** If you have cloches, partly cover the strawberry patch to bring forward the fruiting season.

✓ **PREPARE FOR ANNUALS** If an annual border is part of your scheme, cultivate the ground soon so that no time is lost when conditions allow sowing.

Dahlias

Plant a bed of mixed dahlias, and you can be certain of a variety of forms and colours for nigh on a third of the year, from July to October, or when the frosts cut them down. If that is not recommendation enough, bear in mind their cut-ability for the house; the more you cut the blooms, the more you get.

To ensure the longest possible flowering period, it's best to get them into bed as early as possible.

They do well in any soil provided it is neither too acid, nor too alkaline. But they do like a rich bed, full sun and plenty of water when the conditions are dry.

So choose a sunny spot and prepare well for them. Dig in plenty

of well-rotted manure and give a dressing of bonemeal at the rate of, say, 8 ozs. to the square yard.

Start now if you are introducing dahlias for the first time. Make your selections from the catalogues and order so that they arrive in time for planting mid to end of May.

If you have plants which you have overwintered, then now is the time to start them into growth again, particularly with a view to increasing stock.

Take the old tubers from their storage place and spray them with tepid water, daily if possible. This should prompt them to produce new shoots which can be removed (as shown) for rooting on a frame or greenhouse.

Take shoots which are about 7.5cm (3in) long and remove the with a sharp knife as near to the base as you can.

Remove the lowest pair of leaves and cut straight along beneath the joint of the removed leaves. Dip them in hormone rooting powder and insert into small pots of about an inch in depth of John Innes potting compost.

Put the pots into a glass covered frame, or cover each pot with a polythene bad and they should root easily.

At the end of March you should be able to start raising dahlias from seed as well.

Prune Clematis

If you pause for a moment and let your mind wander to a sunny day last summer, the chances are that you can recall seeing a mass of clematis blooms looking resplendent in the light. If such a mental picture is based in your own garden that is fine, but if not there is the opportunity to plant one now.

Such action should provide the basis for a long and happy association; for to obtain the best from your plant there is a need to appreciate its needs, particularly for pruning.

The time and method of pruning is affected by the form of growth and time of flowering, though it may be refined to influence size and also to alter the natural flowering period. Thus you may vary things over successive years, particularly if you have several specimens, until you settle on the system that is best for you, your plant and your garden.

There are over a hundred varieties available, descended from a range of species. For most practical purposes they can be classified into three groups, based on their natural flowering time.

The first group includes such species as C. alpina, C. armandii, C. chrysocoma, C. cirrhosa, C macriopetal, C montana and C. spooneri, together with their varieties and cultivars such as Columbine, Elizabeth, Maidwell Hall, Markhams Pink, Pamela Jackman, Tetrarose and White Moth. They flower in spring before mid-May, carrying flower on the ripened stems of last year's growth.

Pruning is not essential, but may be practised to keep them in bounds or to encourage sturdy growth in early years. The job is carried out when flowering is over, removing flowering trails and dead or weak stems. Any later activity may damage new stems which will carry the following year's flower.

The remaining two groups both require attention at this time of year, though care must be taken to classify them correctly for their treatment is completely different.

Group 2 consists of large-flowered cultivars, both single and double, which bloom in early summer before mid-June. The list is formidable, but includes such as Barbara Dibley, Bees Jubilee, Bracebridge Star, Countess of Lovelace, Dawn, Duchess of Edinburgh, Henryi, Horn of Plenty and Kathleen Wheeler.

These carry their first flush of flower on last year's wood. In their first couple of seasons they can be cut back to 30cm (12in) and then 90cm (3ft) to encourage more stems from the base. In subsequent years the key thing is to wait until the buds appear, plump and green at around this time. This will allow differentiation between living and dead wood. Cut out all the dead, then shorten back the young vines to the topmost buds for the tidiest effect.

Alternatively, pruning can be left until after flowering when poor growths are removed to make way for better ones. Don't, however, be tempted to remove stems which have just carried flower, for new wood will arise from these to carry a second flush of flower later in the season.

In contrast to the limited pruning required for Group 2, the treatment for Group 3 is more severe. This group is made up of plants which flower from late June onwards, carrying bloom on the current season's growth. Therefore pruning is aimed at preventing a proliferation of unnecessary old non-flowering wood and encouraging the production of vigorous new shoots.

Again the list is long and includes cultivars such as Abundance, alba luxurians, Comptess de Bouchard, Etoile Voilette, Gypsy Queen, Hagley Hybrid and Huldine.

It may be that in dealing with this group you will have to harden your heart, for at the time of pruning there may well be a number of healthy green shoots making valiant efforts to grow. Don't hesitate, cut all growths back to 60-90cm (2-3ft), selecting a strong auxiliary bud just above which the cut should be made.

Although March is the best time for this cut, in milder areas or a sheltered spot it may be done in November, so that untidy growth is removed from sight.

Green Leaves For Summer

D id we all go through a phase of not wanting to eat our vegetables? I know that I used to hate spinach, and even Popeye's instant, bulging muscles could not tempt me to clear the plate. Now, of course, things are different and I regard spinach as a key crop in the vegetable plot.

If conditions are right it can be regarded as an easy crop to grow; but the soil must be fertile, with an ample supply of organic matter to retain moisture and a pH between 6.5 and 6.8. The other important factor is the sun. Spinach is a relatively short-lived annual, and too much sun or dry conditions can cause bolting, which means you lose the benefit of a full crop.

This has its plus side, for it allows summer spinach to be grown between rows of taller-growing vegetables where it will have the benefit of dappled shade. It is also a reasonably fast-growing crop taking 8-11 weeks to reach maturity, and so can be treated as a catch crop.

Sowing can start from the end of February with successional sowings, about every three weeks, through until July. These should provide leaves to harvest from May into autumn.

Prepare the seedbed and rake in a dressing of general fertiliser before sowing at a rate of 4oz to the square yard - or 140g to the square metre if you have a new set of scales. Take out drills 30cm (12in) apart and 1cm (1/2in) deep. Water along the bottom of the drills and then sow thinly, subsequently covering the seed and firming down the soil.

Once the seedlings appear, they can be thinned; initially to 75mm (3in) and again a week or two later by removing alternate plants. Then all that is needed is to keep weeds in check and supply plenty of water during dry periods.

If all this isn't enough, winter varieties can provide a follow-on. Make a sowing in August and a further one in September to provide leaves for picking from October through until spring. In

all but the most favoured areas it will be necessary to give protection, either by using cloches or straw.

Of the varieties, Long Standing Round is a summer variety with good flavour. Sigmaleaf is hardier and can be used for both summer and winter crops.

By now we will hopefully have experienced something of a dry spell, allowing heavy ground to became workable. If so the new bouyancy in the air introduces a sense of urgency, particularly if jobs like digging and planting have been delayed.

In the fruit garden, any new planting should be finished as soon as possible, preferably by the middle of the month. If a mixed batch is being dealt with, try to sort out the early starters first. The order should be peaches, cherries, gooseberries, plums, pears and finally apples.

Well prepared sites are essential, having been deeply dug and poorer light soils enriched with manure and compost. Some coarse bonemeal worked into the second spit will provide a yield of phosphatic food over a few years and benefit root growth.

The right depth is also important, for tree roots breathe, and to pack them tight too low down will impair their performance causing distress and suffocation. The safest guide is to ensure that the uppermost tier of roots is not more than 75mm (3in) below the soil surface after firming in.

Make any planting hole large enough to accommodate the full spread of roots and loosen the bottom with a fork. Work good topsoil in and around the roots in stages. Firm one layer around the lower roots, tread carefully and build up in stages until the top is reached.

Peaches and nectarines grown in the open are more susceptible to peach leaf curl than those grown under cover. The problem is also more prevalent following cold, wet springs which are not entirely alien to Britain.

Take preventative measures by applying a temporary covering of polythene or sacking held close to the bushes, and spray with three per cent lime sulphur as the buds begin to swell.

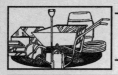

Your Gardening Week

✔ **STOP SLUGS** The appearance of new shoots on the likes of herbaceous perennials will prove attractive to slugs. Bait tubs with milk or beer and sink them into the ground for the slugs to drown in. Not a pleasant prospect for the slug, but I suspect it is preferable to a chemically induced demise!

✔ **STOP STRANGLING** As the sap begins to flow and the stems and trunks of trees and shrubs begin another season's growth, check around any ties. If they are tight, slacken them a little to allow room for expansion.

✔ **SOW ZINNIAS** Zinnias can be sown now in a sheltered frame. Once started, they should be growing without check up to flowering in July.

✔ **POLLINATE STRAWBERRIES** As forced strawberries come into flower, give them a brush over with a rabbit's tail or a feather to ensure adequate pollination. This is important at a time when insects are scarce and it prevents the appearance of misshapen fruit.

✔ **SOW CELERY** Celery for planting out in early June can be sown now under heated glass.

✔ **READY WITH POTATOES** Make sure that you have stocks of second early and maincrop potatoes ready for planting out in April or early May.

✔ **KILL MOSS** If moss is a problem in your lawn, then now is the time to take remedial action.

✔ **GARLIC AND SHALLOTS** Check the bulb of garlic and shallots, and if they seem loose firm them down.

✔ **START GLOXINIAS** Start Gloxinias into growth by setting them in boxes of light, moist soil. When shoots have formed, the tubers can be potted singly.

✔ **ANNUALS** Annuals sown now in a temperature of 15C (60F) can be used for bedding out or for pot work. They should come to flower by the end of May.

Sowing For Summer

The nice thing about spring is that with brighter sunnier days the ground warms up allowing one to make a start sowing seeds, to provide the colour for summer's garden.

Cold soil is no good for sowing hardy perennials. Now, as the soil warms up, you can start thinking about putting in some of the seeds of hardier plants such as Alyssum, Clarkia, Godetia, Lavatera and, of course, Iberis, the ever-popular and very colourful candytuft.

Turn the soil over first and break it down to a fine tilth. This is one of those jobs which is made so much easier if you have an electrically operated power weeder, otherwise treading and hoeing is the best answer.

Then mix in a general fertiliser and rake level.

When taking out drills for the seeds, mark out first with a line and then draw the drill with the corner of a hoe blade (see left). Shake seeds out from the packet and allow as much space as possible between them.

This is as good a method as any for distribution. When they have germinated you can take out the weakest of any that are growing too close together.

Having prepared the bed and planted the seed, it is of vital importance to ensure the safety of the young seedlings. A polythene tunnel, open at both ends, will protect them from the possibility of late frost; but where the climate is kind you will only need to protect them from birds. A hoop of wire at each end of the row, with cotton lines stretched from one to the other (see right), will do the job.

Companionable Cactii

C acti and succulents can make good specimen house plants, with a wide range of shapes in their habit of growth, a goodly range of sizes to choose from and - in many cases - spectacular flowers in vivid colours. By and large they require little attention, but last for many years and instil themselves as part of the household.

If raised from seed, some species will flower in the year after sowing. Others will take a couple of years. There are some that will never or only rarely flower in this country, for there is insufficient sunlight to induce flowering.

We tend to imagine that in nature the cactus is a plant of the desert, but that is not the whole story. Some are found in prairie country intermingled with shrubs and trees, others on rocky mountainsides, and the epiphytic types are found in the forests of Brazil, where they grow on trees.

If you have existing plants whose natural resting period is from October to March, then these will have been kept very dry through the winter. Now it is time to think about increasing the amount of water given and perhaps give them fresh compost to sustain them through the growing season. At first only a little water is needed, but as growth increases during April and May they might need watering once a week, and more frequently still through the summer.

As a rule cacti are so uncomplaining, going from year to year without showing obvious signs of distress, that it is easy to overlook them. However, one day you may realise that they have become pale or are showing signs of browning.

This does not mean they have to be pampered. Repotting every two or three years will be adequate for most, and is a job to be carried out in the spring with the first signs of new growth.

Compost must be open in texture, allowing free drainage. If you like to make up your own, one containing two parts of good medium loam, one part of leaf-mould (or if you have none, peat) and one part of sharp sand will be fine for the majority of species. To this you can add a few pieces of charcoal to keep the compost sweet, together with three-quarters of an ounce of ground chalk, three-quarters of an ounce of sulphate of potash, one and a half ounces of superphosate and one and a half ounces of hoof and horn to each bushel. Here I must apologise if you are metricated; but I still use a bushel box and an old pair of scales with weights!

If such ingredients do not come easily to hand, or if you prefer compost of the pre-packed variety, then good old John Innes will do the job provided, that additional sharp sand is added in a ratio of one part of sand to five parts of compost.

For most types use J.I. No1, but for epiphytes, which are used to a richer soil in nature, use J.I. No2. which is also suitable for Cerei, Crassulas, Opuntias, Sedums and the like.

While underfeeding will lead to a gradual reduction in vigour, overfeeding must also be avoided, especially for the more spiny types. If given too much nutrient they are likely to become lush and soft in growth, which increases the chance of their rotting off during winter.

If you don't already have cacti, then have a go on the lucky dip. Many seedsmen offer a mixed selection of seed, and this can be sown in pots or pans using J.I. seed compost. Besides the thrill of expectation as you await germination and growth, the choice of mixed seed can lead you into the thrill of the chase as you try to identify your new plants.

After sowing water from the bottom and, for preference, place them in a propagating case at 21C (70F), covering with a sheet of glass and then paper. If you cannot manage the temperature don't be deterred. You will just need a little more patience, for the seed will still germinate though it will take longer.

Young plants should be kept away from direct sunlight during their first year, but make sure they receive plenty of indirect light or they will become drawn.

Fine Foliage

M any of the plants that we use as annuals are not true
annuals at all, but may be tender perennials, trees or
shrubs. What they do possess in common is an ability
to grow quickly from seed and provide interest in the first year
of their life.

Of course most subjects are chosen for their flower, but there
are a number interesting for their foliage.

These may be used as contrasting dot plants in bedding
schemes, as a foil in mixed borders or even as a focus of attention in their own right.

First to spring to mind is the castor oil plant, Ricinus commu-
nis. This is the only species in the genus and while treated as
half-hardy here, is a perennial in the tropics where it makes a
small tree.

Nevertheless, given the right conditions, plants can make 1.8m
(6ft) or even more by late summer. This size is matched by presence, and the plant has a fine spread of large palmate leaves
which are deeply cut with 5-12 lobes. They may be in grey-
green, brown or deep red and held on strong stems which themselves have good colour.

Fuzzy heads of flower in red or yellow may appear in summer
and these in turn are followed by prickly seed heads in late summer. The seeds are quite large and are the source of castor oil.
Now it may be that you regard this as 'sort of' poisonous; however, the seeds are extremely poisonous, producing an alkaloid
called ricinin.

There are a number of cultivars to be had. 'Gibsonii' is the one
I have been used to growing, which is more compact with dark
red stems and leaves. 'Mizuma' has deep bronze-coloured leaves
which contrast with its red stems and veins; while 'Impala' has
maroon leaves.

Seed can be sown in 75mm (3in) pots any time in March or

early April, but in a temperature of 13-16C (55-60F). In higher temperatures, germination and growth will be more rapid. Grow on under glass until early June, then harden off before planting out around the middle of that month.

This plant resents any damage to the roots, so if you think that potting on will be needed, it is best done into 125mm (5in) pots before they become pot-bound.

They can be used in a variety of ways; ideal as dot plants in large and bold bedding schemes, making a striking statement if planted in a large group or, if grown in 125-150mm (5-6in) pots, providing a decorative specimen for the cool glasshouse, conservatory or living room.

I'm never quite sure about Ruby Chard in the flower garden. This form of Swiss chard or seakale beet is undoubtedly bright and ornamental, but somehow it still has the look of a vegetable. That doesn't mean it should not be tried, and seed can either be sown in pots under cool glass in April or sown directly into the ground during May. The beetroot-like foliage is a fine deep green with red veination, carried on stout stalks of deep shiny scarlet.

Seakale beet itself can be grown as a contrast, having paler green foliage and striking broad stems in shining white. While ruby chard is edible, it is not as palatable as the other form. Both may be set in sun or partial shade.

Basil is well known as a herb, but there are a number of ornamental cultivars grown for their foliage. One such is Ocimum basillicum 'Purple Ruffles' that grows to around 45cm (18in) and has large, crinkly purple leaves. 'Green Ruffles' has green leaves while 'Dark Opal', in deep purple is smaller and less crinkly.

Seed can be sown under glass in April in a temperature of 16C (6OF), and the seedlings pricked out and grown on for planting out in June. A sunny, shelterd spot and light soil are needed. In this position the leaves should give off their clove-like scent in warm, still conditions.

Your Gardening Week

 PLANT RANUNCULUS If you have ranunculus which were lifted for storage last autumn, they can be planted as soon as ground conditions will allow. They should be set about 5cm (2in) deep.

 SOW CHRYSANTHS Cascade and Charm chrysanthemums can be sown now in gentle heat. Cascades need careful training to obtain the best results, but Charms are an easy way to a riot of flowers.

 SOW SPINACH BEET From now to mid-April is a good time to sow a row of spinach beet for a summer crop. This is a cut-and-come-again crop which should be ready in July.

 SOW CELERIAC Ideal for celery soup or as a boiled vegetable, celeriac sown in heat can be grown on for planting out in May.

 FIRST CUT? On a fine dry day, any debris can be removed from lawns and the turf tidied by giving the first gentle cut of the season - with the height of cut set well up.

 FINISH PLANTING Plan to finish all permanent planting at the earliest opportunity. Herbaceous perennials can be lifted and divided during the course of the month, and may provide a chance to colonise any bare areas of ground.

 DIVIDE CROCUS Where crocus have become well established and overcrowded, they can be lifted and divided prior to replanting. If you would rather wait until foliage has died down, be sure to mark where they are.

 FEED BEANS Encourage autumn-sown broad beans with a dressing of superphosphate stirred into the soil along the rows.

 FEED FIGS Figs growing in the open or under glass will benefit from a dressing of bonemeal together with a mulch of compost over the root run.

Shrubs

For many, the answer to gardening - and certainly to easy gardening - is to fill the borders with shrubs.

In many ways, of course, they are right. There is certainly not the constant need to be planting, digging and watering.

But to think that just to plant shrubs is the answer to everything is to be sadly mistaken. For, like all other plants, they do need care and attention if they are to give of their best, particularly if they are bloomers.

Now is the time to give attention to a number of the more popular shrubs. There are two main kinds of shrubs; firstly those that produce flowers on the new season's growth and secondly, those that give flower on last year's growth.

The former should be pruned in the spring, whilst the latter will benefit from attention immediately after flowering.

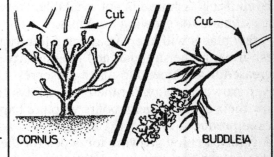

It is the first, then, that currently concern us. Start with the ever-popular Hydrangea. Remove any dead heads which have been left on over the winter and cut out any really old wood. Then cut back the remaining shoots by about a third, to a bud.

Cornus, perhaps best known for those bright red stems, should be cut back hard to within just a few inches of the groun. (see left).

Just a light cutting back, to take out damaged or weak shoots, is the requirement for cistus, hebe and potentilla, whilst it's back as far as possible to new wood for hardy fuchsias and the profuse bloomer Lavatera olbia rosea, the tree mallow.

Though, strictly speaking, buddleia - the beloved of butterflies - should be pruned of its flowering panacles immediately after blooming, the quality of the blooms may be increased by now tip cutting the new wood (see right).

Remember, too, that you can now take cuttings of Rhus (sumach).

There's Pleasure In Tomatoes

I always use a bushel box for measuring compost mixtures. While scales and tape measures are readily available with both imperial and metric calibration, the chances are that a bushel box will have to be of the DIY variety.

A bushel is a dry measure of volume, not of weight, and a box measuring 22x10x10 inches approximates to that size.

You can grow them in a border, in raised beds, use ring-culture or even growing bags, but if you have an unheated glasshouse don't fail to grow some tomatoes.

Even if a glasshouse is not available, there are plenty of varieties suitable for growing outdoors.

A few plants will keep an average family well supplied with fresh fruits in the summer, and the quantity grown can be increased if you intend to make preserves. Usually you could never grow too many, for there are always friends who do not grow their own and neighbours who are happy to buy fresh-picked produce.

Anyway, I enjoy growing tomatoes for themselves. At the end of the season they can look a little scraggly, brown and shrivelled. But while growing and producing fruit, their development is a joy only marginally sullied by the hard scrubbing that is needed to remove stained fingers following a session of removing sideshoots!

Really the sowing period for raising crops to grow under unheated glass is coming to a close, having started in mid-February.

It can easily be extended, but you may have to reduce the number of trusses allowed to develop on each plant. As one door closes another one opens, and from now to mid-April is the time to sow for outdoor crops.

Perhaps the first thing to do is make a selection of seed. As usual, I would recommend that you try more than one variety, in subsequent years varying the one that does least well or has least appeal, so that over time you discover the varieties that best suit you and your conditions.

Ailsa Craig, Moneymaker and Alicante are all suited to both indoor and outdoor culture. Ailsa Craig is a well tried and reliable variety producing heavy crops of even, medium-sized tomatoes with good flavour. Moneymaker is more reliable still, giving large trusses of medium-sized fruits with an adequate flavour. Alicante is popular and produces medium to large fruits with good flavour.

If crops will be raised only under glass, try Eurocross. That has the advantage of setting fruit freely even in poor summers, and produces good crops of fairly large fruit. If something really large is required then Big Boy is worth a try. Not for the faint-hearted, it can give fruits weighing up to a pound and a half if the plants are stopped at the third or fourth truss; however, I would limit the number of plants until you are sure it meets your needs.

Outdoors it is a good idea to use some of the bush varieties such as Gardener's Delight, French Cross and Amateur. Gardeners Delight is ideal for growing in a container on the patio, where its long trusses of small, sweet fruit can develop to their best.

French Cross is a high-yielding variety, giving many trusses of fairly large fruit, while Amateur produces medium-sized fruits and remains popular. You may also find a mixture of small varieties offered and these are a bit of fun!

Make sowings in seed boxes or pots, using a seed compost and providing a temperature of 16C (60F) to encourage germination. Indoor crops will be planted at the end of April, while those for outdoors will need to be given protection until mid-May or early June depending upon the season.

When the seedlings have formed a pair of true leaves, prick them off into 75mm (3in) pots using potting compost, allowing plenty of light and a minimum temperature of 13C (55F).

Pieris Presence

From being a most popular plant - following its introduction well over a hundred years ago - Pieris japonica suffered a decline, as other species were introduced. The ministrations of plant breeders encouraged people towards new species and away from the Pieris japonica. Yet over the last thirty years or so, a range of new cultivars have appeared to put fresh life into the genus and it has experienced something of a revival.

The name is derived from Pieria, the abode of the Muses in Greek mythology. The genus contains some ten species of hardy evergreen shrubs or small trees which produce stimulating displays when at their best. They belong to the family Ericaceae and, as with their relatives, require a lime-free soil with a pH of 6.5 or less. The soil should be well supplied with organic material and hold moisture, but still be free-draining.

Why mention them now? The reasons are that most are in season from late February through to the end of March or early April, so there is the chance to see them with bright new foliage or following display and make a choice. Then April or early May provides an opportunity for planting, during mild periods, giving the plants time to establish before next winter. Even so, it is a good idea to cover the roots with a deep mulch of leaves and erect a windbreak against the colder winds from the north and east, together with light overhead shade for the first two or three winters. This is particularly true for P. formosa and P. formosa forestii 'Wakehurst' which may suffer from frost damage during colder winters.

The varieties of P. japonica will grow away quite happily in full sun, but will have a tendency to smaller flowers and less attractive foliage. The best situation is within the dappled shade provided by other shrubs and trees, which has the additional advantage of giving some shelter.

While the basic evergreen shrubs have their attraction, refine-

ments are to be found in flower displays and coloured foliage, each of which can have their place in the garden.

Probably the most well known is 'Forest Flame', a hybrid resulting from a cross between P. japonica and P. foresstii 'Wakehurst'. It makes a superb large shrub which may reach 3 metres (10 ft) with dense habit and brilliant red young growths in spring. These pass through pink and white before turning to green. The white, lily-of-the-valley-like flowers are held in large terminal, drooping panicles and appear in March.

'Forest Flame' combines the brilliant foliage of 'Wakehurst' with the hardiness of P. japonica. Look also for 'Mountain Fire'.

P. japonica 'variegata' is a naturally occuring form found in the wild. Slow growing, it makes but a medium-sized shrub although the foliage is coloured in green and creamy-white to make it one of the most attractive variegated shrubs. Look also for 'Flaming Silver' and 'White Rim'.

For flower there is a wider range to choose from, though you may need to search out stockists. Look for forms of P. japonica such as 'Dorothy Wyckoff', 'Purity', 'Valentine' and 'Delight' and if you have a mild, sheltered spot try P. formosa which produces large scented flowers and has large, finely toothed, leathery green leaves.

Little is needed but to enjoy these plants. Pruning is minimal, unless they have become straggly or outgrown their space. In either case prune immediately after flowering. During dry spells it is desirable to water freely and the ground can be kept in good condition by regular mulching if suitable material is available.

Propagation can be effected in a variety of ways. Seed is sown either in November or March in a cold frame and using a peat/sand mixture. If suckers appear they can be harvested, or shoots can be layered in early autumn. Cuttings are taken with a heel in August/September and can be set in pots of peat/sand mixture and rooted in a cold frame. Try a little of each on a successional basis through the year, to see which method is most successful for you.

Your Gardening Week

 SOW CHILI Seed of Capsicum annuum, the Cayenne Pepper, can be sown now to give some home-grown heat. Plants may be set in a glasshouse border at 45cm (18in) spacings, or a small-fruited variety can be sown in mid-april and grown on in a frame.

 MORE CAMELLIAS As Camellias pass out of flower, between now and early May, they can be propagated by taking leaf-bud cuttings.

 DAHLIA CUTTINGS Dahlia tubers prompted into action last month should have made sufficient growth for cuttings to be taken. Sever or break off stems around 5cm (2in) long, and insert in a sandy compost. If placed directly into pots, no further disturbance will be needed prior to planting out.

SUSPENDED SPUDS While it is possible to plant potatoes using a large dibber, there is a danger that the tubers will become suspended in the hole, and so not have full contact with surrounding earth. Although taking a little longer, it is better to use a trowel.

 SHADING Many young sensitive plants could be damaged by strong bursts of sun. It makes sense to have some form of temporary shading that can be put in place when needed, but also removed to make the best use of indirect light.

 BOOST BEANS Seedling broad beans will benefit from a dressing of superphosphate hoed in along the rows, to encourage root action and firm growth.

 TRANSPLANT ONIONS Transplant autumn-sown onions to their final quarters, spacing them alternately at 30cm (12in).

 NATURALISED BULBS Check over naturalised plantings of bulbs. Where overcrowded, mark them for lifting and replanting either after flowering or in the autumn.

Sweet Peas... A Fragrant Feature

Of all the flowers that one can grow in the garden at home, there surely can't be one to beat sweet peas.

They are superb both in the garden and in the home for their form and excellent colour range, but most of all, undoubtedly for their exquisite fragrance.

For best results, of course, work should start in the autumn, when the bed should be prepared, enriching it with well rotted manure.

Growing from seed is the way the expert does it to ensure that he has the best plants to produce the best possible colours and scent.

But we can't all do that, so now is the time for the rest of us to buy our pots of seedlings and put them in to soil which has been enriched, as previously explained.

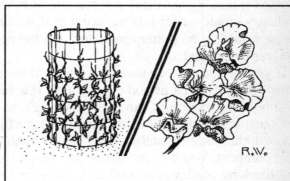

It is important before planting to decide how you wish to display the plants in the garden.

All too often they are planted at the bottom of a fence or wall where they will be teased up strings or canes as they grow.

But far nicer is to make a feature of them in the middle of a bed, at the end of a pathway or perhaps set into a corner of the lawn. Where the latter is concerned, an area of grass will need to be lifted so that the plants have their own space. Insert 3 or 4 tall canes around which netting can be swathed, tube-like (see pic above).

Then using a dibber to make holes big enough to take the young plants with their roots spread out they can be planted at the base of the climbing tube.

Immediately after planting, put slug pellets around the plants to ensure their safety.

Cyclamen Persicum

O ften, plants of cyclamen persicum which have given pleasure around Christmas and in the early weeks of the following year are discarded as useless. Sad, for a little care through the summer will see them in even better fettle next season. With similar treatment in future years, they will last for decades.

The cyclamen is one of our most popular flowering house plants, and countless thousands are sold each year. I suppose it is a good job many are thrown away, for without this the nursery industry would suffer just the same as if we did not crack cups there would be no pottery industry; and the old one about ladderless stockings!

If you decide to keep them, then after flowering has ceased they can be given a period of rest. This is achieved by gradually withholding water and hardening them off, so that they can be set outside in a dry frame or plunge-bed for the summer.

In August they are started back into growth by soaking the pot and compost. You will recognise that when I say "soak the pot" I am thinking of clay pots, and certainly I find these most satisfactory for any plant that is to be kept for an extended period.

Shortly, tiny leaves will begin to sprout, and at this point the compost can be refreshed. If the plants are only in their second season, it will suffice to carefully remove the top 25mm (1in) of compost from around the tuber and replace it. With older specimens, complete repotting is advised. While John Innes compost will be perfectly satisfactory, your own made from two parts loam and one part leaf mould and sand should serve them better, though the loam should be of a gritty, open nature.

Care must be taken not to cover the tuber, and the compost should be brought up to the circumference.

Following this, the plants are best kept in a close frame for a few days until they re-establish. Subsequently, shade and a moist atmosphere, together with a temperature around 13-16C (55-60F) are the conditions to aim at. Water moderately and bolster with weekly liquid feeds through the flowering period which, with successive batches of plants, can extend from November through to March.

New stock can be had from seed. While it is possible to have plants in flower at Christmas from sowings made from January to March, I still favour mid-August to mid-November sowings intended to produce good flowering plants in the winter of the following year.

Such plants need a period of growth of about 16 months from seed sowing. Space sowing can take place in deep boxes, in drills one centimetre (half-inch) deep and 25x25mm (1x1in) apart. After sowing, soak thoroughly and keep close and shaded in a temperature around 10-16C (50-60F). Germination can be expected in four to six weeks; and the following two or three months require a degree of patience as the first true leaves can be slow to show, particularly if temperatures fall below 13C (55F).

February or March should be a time when the young seedlings can be handled. They are pricked off into thumb pots or set in fresh boxes at twice the spacing. Another couple of months and they should be blessed with three or four leaves and be ready for 75mm (3in) pots or larger depending upon the amount of root.

When the roots are well established, it is time for another move. Generally 125mm (5in) pots or thereabouts will do, but if vigour demands go up to 175mm (7in).

Allow plenty of space while growth takes place and ensure ample light and air, but avoid full sunlight and draughts. Keep the atmosphere moist, spraying overhead several times a day if required in summer. Better control of conditions can probably be achieved if they are grown on in a cold frame during summer. A glasshouse is more prone to larger fluctuations in conditions.

There are many good varieties to choose for sowing, and I like to include at least one which is well scented.

See The Lady in the Bath!

S o many of the plants that we can grow have only a short flowering season. Perversely, that can be an attraction as their scarcity value makes them all the more appreciated when in flower.

If sufficient space is available to provide for a wide variety of planting - which enables a constant succession of delight as one species passing out of flower is replaced by another's bursting buds - then all is well.

Where space is limited, or to provide some continuity of colour, plants with longer flowering seasons come into play.

As an aside, I was talking to a chap the other day and he was telling me how he had been tidying up a part of his garden; chivvying out the odd weed and spreading a little compost about. In a rough and ready fashion he had levelled the compost with his spade and afterwards wondered what had happened to his only clump of snowdrops.

These had disappeared beneath the compost and we can all imagine the skipped heartbeat as he realised that he had sliced the stems with his spade. However, in the circumstances he did the right thing, apologising profusely and hoping that the snow-drops would recover well enough to come up again next year.

On with the plot! Of perennials with long flowering seasons, one of the first to come into my mind is Nepeta mussini 'Six Hills Giant'. This is a plant I grew up with, for it was used as edging around rose beds in front of the house where I used to live. Coming to flower in June, its spikes of deep violet-blue are held over pleasant mounds of restful grey-green foliage. After the first flush of flower fades, the spikes can be cut hard back to stimulate further flowering which should continue until frost occurs.

Even without the flower this plant makes a pleasing edging to roses, being sufficiently tall to hide the stems, but allowing the

flowers of HTs and floribundas to show above. When in flower, the blue-hued flowers contrast well with the reds, yellows, oranges and whites of any rose.

Another spikey subject that flowers well is Polygonum affine 'Donald Lowndes'. We have a good patch mid-way between the door and garden gate. So from July, often into November, our daily wanderings are enlivened by its cheerful pink blooms, held in short, thick spikes.

Making good ground cover, but also prepared to colonise rocks and drystone walls, the carpet of foliage turns a bright reddish-brown in autumn and can remain a feature all winter.

Of course there are some plants which come to flower earlier and persist into late summer.

Dicentra, a member of the poppy family, is one of these. I have an affection of Dicentra spectabilis from having spent time in manipulating the flowers to achieve the effect that has lead to its common name of 'Lady in the Bath'. If you don't know what I am talking about, then here is an added incentive to go out and buy the plant. When it comes to flower, and provided that nobody is watching, take hold of the heart-shaped flower, turn it upside down and pull at the edges of the petals. You will see the lady in the bath!

Here is a plant with fern-like foliage and stems which carry drooping flowers in pink and white. Dry conditions are not helpful and may shorten the flowering season, but in a cool, moist position with plenty of leaf mould in the soil, these plants will thrive. A number of forms are available; 'Bacchanal' with wine-red blooms and bright green foliage, 'Pearl Drops' in pale pink with blue-grey foliage, and 'Luxuriant', again in red, to name but a few.

Also best in a soil that does not dry out is Viola cornuta 'Alba', This, the 'horned violet', will grow in sun or partial shade to form ground-covering clumps of small, neat light-green leaves. These are topped by tall-stemmed, violet-shaped flowers, backed by a long spur appearing from mid-spring onwards.

Your Gardening Week

 TREES AND SHRUBS It may not be necessary to say this if wet conditions prevail, but if we have any dry periods, take care to ensure that newly planted trees and shrubs are given sufficient water. In extreme conditions it may also be necessary to syringe or spray over the foliage.

THIN LETTUCE Early sowings of lettuce should be ready for thinning. At this time the thinnings can be transplanted if needed - a practice which should not be carried out later in the year because of the danger of bolting.

FEED ROSES By now the roses should have been pruned, and will benefit from a top dressing of rose fertiliser.

SOW CAMPANULAS A nice trailing, free-flowering pot plant which can be sown now is Campanula isophylla. It can be had in both white and blue flowered forms, but must be grown under glass.

TIDY IVY Ivy growing on walls can be clipped now, using shears. If the job is left, growth may become excessive and untidy during the summer.

 CLEAR CROPS Where just a few plants of crops such as leeks and celery remain, they can be lifted so that the ground can be prepared for new crops.

SOW SUNFLOWERS For your own pleasure or for something to interest children, why not sow a few giant sunflowers? Many seedsmen offer varieties which will grow to 6-8 ft and will carry enormous flowers. Sow now under glass or outdoors when ground conditions allow. Remember that they make big plants and will need a rich soil.

TOO BIG? House plants such as the ' Rubber Plant' can outgrow their station. Make new, smaller versions of the rubber plant by aerial layering; and prune back the cheese plant, propagating new plants from sections of stem.

Waterlilies

On balmy summer days there are two most welcome sounds in the garden. First, the rustling of leaves caught in a gentle breeze; secondly, the sight or sound of water.

The average garden can play host to both through trees and a pool, — but not too close together, if the pool water is to be kept sweet!

The end of April is a good time to start planting a pool, so you really need to get down to some hard graft now, by choosing a site and cutting out the ground for a pool liner, if you are going to introduce one this year.

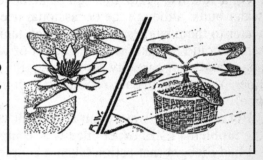

On ledges or base areas where you want plants to be set, give a good 6 inches cover of soil. If you don't plan to plant on the base itself, then cover that area with about 5cm (2in) of soil, which will be sufficient to provide a bed for important oxygenating plants.

Waterlilies are a 'must' for the decorative pool and these will be best planted in deep plastic containers, which can be lowered to the base — best just off-centre.

You can also, of course, use pierced containers to house marginal plants for the edge or ledges.

When planting waterlilies in containers, use a good quality soil and make sure that it is well soaked. Plant them at an angle of about 20 degrees and so that the crown is just below the soil's surface.

When it comes to filling the pool, a worthwhile tip to stop any unnecessary disturbance of plants and soil: put a bucket on the base of the pool, lying on its side. Then lay the hose on the bottom, with the nozzle directed into the bucket.

Your Gardening Week

Feed Lawns

Water companies in various parts of the country can often seek emergency powers; not necessarily to restrict the use of water immediately, but at least to be in a position to do so should the need arise during the course of the year.

While this is not a problem every year, and will depend on the average rainfall, it does remind me of the desirability of making arrangements to have some water storing capacity in the garden.

On a smallish scale, this can be achieved through the use of water butts, although the occassional need to pipe used bathwater to them suggests that a sunken tank is best. An alternative which could retain a greater amount of water, depending on space and your capacity for digging, might be the use of a pool liner. You might even go so far as to construct an ornamental pool.

But a supply of water won't solve all your problems. One of the problems I still experience is a resurgence of moss in lawns.

I had thought that action taken a couple of years ago to kill the moss and improve the soil by adding sand, would have ensured that this was a matter of history. However, relatively mild winters and often waterlogged ground conditions mean it will return with a vengeance.

Nevertheless, lawn turf is growing more quickly and needs to be mown more frequently over the next week or two, so that the sward is kept in good condition. This helps ensure that coarser types of grasses are not allowed to expand to the detriment of finer species which add so much to appearance.

Obviously this enhanced rate of growth consumes more food. To replace this, fertiliser can still be given. Ideally this should contain all the major elements of phosphate, potash and nitrogen. You might think this a little silly, and wonder what is the point of encouraging more growth when this will only lead to still more frequent mowing.

The answer is that if you want to keep your lawn in good condition it must be allowed to grow strongly, so that it makes a thick sward, resistant to invasion by both weeds and moss. Don't forget that so long as you practice good husbandry, the mowings will be recycled either as mulches or through the compost heap, so the nutrients will go round again!

Dry feeds can be spread by hand or by using a spreader, and if you want to sustain a regular colour, care must be taken to spread it evenly. With a spreader, work in parallel runs across the lawn. With luck you will be able to see the wheel marks, and these should just overlap.

If broadcasting by hand, there are two good practices to follow. Firstly the fertiliser can be bulked-up, using sand. This ensures a better spread and makes it less likely that you will deposit too much fertiliser in one place, which could lead to scorching. Secondly, split the material into two parts, and apply one portion in one direction and the other at right-angles to it.

In any event the soil should be moist and the grass dry when application is made. If by any chance rain does not fall within a couple of days of application, the lawn should be watered to prevent scorch, but do check that there is no likelihood of a hosepipe ban.

An alternative is to apply liquid feed, a job I would not recommend unless you have a dilutor which can be attached to the end of a hosepipe. Trying to do the job with a watering can is slow and heavy work.

Colour And Charm From Polyanthus

Let's hope for another good spring for polyanthus, whether set in a formal bed as harbinger of spring, and then background colour to tulips - or used informally in border or natural area. If you draw back the curtain in the morning or reach out the door for the milk only to find that none are in prospect, then it is time to put this right for next year.

There should not be a garden in the country without its share of polyanthus, for these beautiful spring-flowering plants are consistant each year. I never cease to be amazed at the number and quality of blooms which can appear on a single plant, and their brightness and simplicity make them a pleasure to behold.

Also, they are versatile, looking equally at home in a border outdoors or as an attractive pot plant.

If you already have stock plants then it will soon be time to start thinking about increasing numbers of the most attractive ones by vegetative propagation. If there are no stock plants then the best and cheapest way of starting a collection is from seed, and now is as good a time as any to get them on the move.

If you happen across a particular plant that takes your fancy in a florist's shop or nursery, it could be propagated from and give rise to many new plants during the course of the year.

Polyanthus are, in fact, primulas which are believed to have originated as a hybrid, from a cross between the primrose (Primula acaulis) and the cowslip (Primula veris). Since then plant breeders have produced many strains in a variety of sizes and colours, so most seed catalogues have a number to choose from.

Probably the best way forward is to choose a couple of mixed strains and then, in future years, propagate those with most appeal by vegetative means.

Seed can be sown in early autumn, from January to March in gentle heat, or from March to the end of May in a cold frame, unheated glasshouse, or in the open. If sown in containers cover with glass and brown paper until germination. Outdoors, choose a plot with dappled shade so seedlings are not shrivelled by sun.

Germination should be complete in 10-15 days, and the seedlings can be pricked off or thinned. By August, the young plants will be sufficiently developed to stand on their own and can be set in their planting positions. They perform best in a soil enriched with well-rotted manure or leafmould. In addition they prefer a little light shade.

Plants may also be potted in August using John Innes No 1 compost to which well-rotted and riddled leafmould can be added. Alternatively, make your own compost by blending leafmould, sharp sand and loam in a ratio of 1:1:2.

Potted plants can be stood in a shady frame with a northerly aspect until October. Then, as the sun becomes weaker, they may be moved to a frame facing south. During autumn and through until March, just give enough water to keep the compost moist. Then water more freely for the rest of the year, incorporating weak liquid feeds from March until flowering is over.

I have already mentioned vegetative propagation a number of times. At its simplest, this consists of lifting the plants when flowering is over and dividing the multiple crowns. Although the roots will be entangled, having eased them apart they can be replanted straight away.

Even if you do not require more plants, the vigour of modern hybrids is such that they will soon become overcrowded unless dealt with like this at least every couple of years. In any event, spare plants are useful for swapping or could find their way to a charity stall, rather than being dumped.

Where larger increases are required, root cuttings are the answer. After lifting wash off the roots, select the thickest and cut them into 25mm (1in) lengths. Lay the pieces on top of boxes of seed compost, cover lightly, keep moist and wait.

Your Gardening Week

 SOW SWEET CORN Sweet corn can be started under glass. Either sow singly in pits, or space sow at 50-75mm (2-3in) centres in deep boxes.

 EARLY SPUDS First early potatoes can go in now, on the basis that there should be little danger of frost damage by the time shoots appear.

 START RUNNERS Runner beans can be started now, though frame protection should be given until there is no danger of frost.

 LAYER SHRUBS Many shrubs can be propagated by layering. Select a suitable branch or stem which can be encouraged to bend down to the ground, and make a slicing cut part way through a joint. If needed keep the wound open with a small stone. Bury the cut part just below the soil surface, keeping it in place with a wooden peg or a stone until rooting takes place.

 BUY CHICORY Chicory seed can be bought now for sowing at the end of the month. When forced, it makes a useful salad for autumn and winter.

 STAKE EARLY As fresh shoots appear on herbaceous plants, give them support with twigs and small branches to lessen the chance of damage. Placed with care, they will eventually disappear as the foliage grows through and around them.

 SOW ANNUALS Once the atmosphere becomes a little bouyant seed of annuals can be sown outdoors in the place where it will flower - an easy and colourful way of filling gaps in the border.

 ONIONS OUTDOORS If not already raised under glass onions can now be sown outdoors. Draw drills a foot apart and sow the seed thinly along them. Young plants raised under glass can be set out at the end of the month or in early May.

The Time Is Ripe For Tomatoes

The beginning of April is just about the right time to start planning for a good crop of tomatoes. Given a sunny windowsill, and some of those long plastic seed boxes, which come complete with their own mini-greenhouse tops, you can now start sowing to raise your own plants.

Fill the seed boxes with seed compost and try and space the seeds about 2.5cm (1in) apart. Finish off by scattering compost over them before laying a piece of folded newspaper on top.

Germination should take just under a fortnight at which point the paper and plastic cover can be removed. Just keep the seedlings in as good a light as possible.

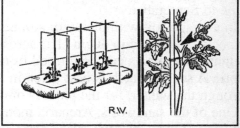

When the plants have developed two leaves you should be able to prick them off and plant them separately in 7.5cm (3in) pots filled with John Innes No 1.

They will still need cover so the pots will need to be kept on a window ledge or, better still, in a greenhouse. Make sure that they are always kept moist.

By mid May, given reasonable climatic conditions, you should be able to start hardening them off ready for planting out in June.

When that time comes one of the best methods of growing on is to plant them in growing bags, which are filled with the perfect growing medium and which will allow you more room for other crops either in the greenhouse or in beds.

Choose a warm and sunny spot for the growing bag site, and if possible install it in one of the special frames, which are designed to give adequate support for the plants (see left).

You can expect to get about 3 plants in each bag.

Pollination should take place quite naturally, but nip outside shoots growing in the leaf axils and once you have four trusses of fruit set take off the top of the growing plant as illustrated in pic above.

Alpines In April

The change in the seasons felt around this time, denotes a period when thought can be devoted to increasing stocks of alpines. Several useful plants can be propagated during April and early May, either from seed or by making cuttings.

While antirrhinum majus has experienced extensive attention from plant breeders to give us the highly ornamental bedding plants we enjoy, the same cannot be said of A. glutinosum from Spain. In contrast it is not erect, grows to form a prostate plant with grey-green leaves and flowers in yellow or cream from June to September.

In average soil with plenty of sun and good drainage, it may be expected to spread to 30cm (1ft) across and reach 15cm (6in) in height. New plants can be formed from cuttings taken during April. A second batch is best taken in August and protected through the winter, for the plant is of doubtful hardiness.

One of the sandworts, Arenaria montana, can be propagated by division However, stock raised from seed seems to fare better. This plant is happiest in sandy soil and when it is exposed to plenty of sun. Once established, it will grow to some 45cm (18in) across, and its loose habit is ideal for trailing over rocks. Large white flowers are present in May and June, and the foliage is evergreen.

There are two astilbes that can be increased by division about now. Both require moist, shady places with an acid soil augmented with leaf mould. A. crispa has curly, feathery leaves, bright red on the back and surmounted by typical short spikes of flower in white, pink or rose during July and August. It will spread to 15cm (1ft) and reach half that in height. Somewhat smaller, but no less attractive, is A. simplicifolia which produces spikes of pink flower in June and July.

Campanulas provide some of the most attractive plants we have. Two which are a bit of a mouthful but well worth remembering are C. portenschlagiana and C. pascharskyana. Ideal for the rock garden or alpine collection, both can be propagated in April.

C. portenschlagiana trails to cover an area around 30cm (1ft) across. It has smooth shining green leaves that are held in a tight mat and is covered with sprays of violet/purple flower. C. poscharskyana is somewhat larger with flowers of powder blue.

I must mention Campanula glomerata even though it is more suited to a wild garden area and has a tendency to spread if left unchecked. This is a native plant growing to around 45cm (18in) with round heads of close-packed flowers of a strong deep purple evident from June to August.

I have found Campanula glomerata though difficult to establish is well-established in my mother's garden. Each year I lift a little and bring it home. And each year it disappears! I think a combination of slugs and heavy land are to blame, but this year I have raised an area of ground and will try again.

Another native is Anagallis tenella, the Bog Pimpernel. This is very hardy and when established, provides a useful background carpet against which to grow bulbs. As its name suggests, a moist spot is required where it will grow to just 25mm (1in). While the carpet of foliage is maintained throughout the year, it is enhanced by a carpet of attractive pale-pink flowers in June. Stock is readily increased by division of the roots in May.

Finally, another plant for a dry position is Antyllis montana rubra. Again readily increased by cuttings taken with a heel in May, this plant produces a carpet of silver foliage against which flowering heads of rich crimson are borne.

While seed will produce plenty of new stock, a single plant purchased and increased by cuttings or division should meet most needs. There is also less chance of the variability which might be introduced by seed.

Having said that, there is still a place for seed and still the thrill of seeing young plants break through the soil surface for the first time.

Bay Watch

Polygonum bilderdyckia baldshuanicum is a name near as long and rampant as the plant it belongs to! More often it is called by the shortened synonym of P. baldshuanicum or by its common name of Russian Vine.

Here is a plant with a purpose if ever there was one. If there is an eyesore that needs disguise, then plant a Russian Vine alongside. Growing with rapidity, its slender whippy stems will scramble and climb to reach the best part of 12 metres (40ft), obscuring fence, tree-stump or even rubble as they spread. The rate of growth has led to its other common name of 'mile-a-minute plant' which seems but a slight exaggeration.

The leaves are ovate or heart-shaped and a delicate pale green in colour. The flowers are white with a slight tinge of pink. Although individually small, they are borne profusely on dense panicles to give a decorative and long-lasting display that persists through summer and into autumn.

Although I always tend to think first of P. baldshuanicum because it was the first of its kind that I came to know, it is quite similar to P. aubertii, which is probably the more commonly planted of the pair.

Similar in size and habit, it is differentiated by the fact that its flowers are carried on short, lateral branchlets. They are also white but may take on a greenish tinge, only being touched by pink after pollination.

While not really specimens for small gardens, both forms have their attractions. Stock can be increased - should you ever need more than one - by rooting cuttings in sandy soil under a cold frame during August.

Laurus nobilis, the sweet bay or sweet laurel can make an attractive, dense evergreen pyramidal shrub or be set in a container where it responds well to clipping. In colder areas the container becomes a near necessity for there is a need to provide

protection from frost.

Besides its ornamental attractions it is the source of the aromatic leaves used in cookery. Unfortunately these very leaves are also attractive to a number of pests.

There are many different species of scale insects attacking a wide range of plants, some of which live on the underside of leaves next to the leaf vein. This is because the vein is a ready source of the sap on which they feed. They emerge from their eggs as tiny, oval, six-legged creatures and as they grow, finally come out from the protection of their dead mother's scale. They move over the plant until a suitable feeding place is found, insert stylets to absorb sap and settle down for the rest of their lives.

One such insect is soft scale (Coccus hesperidium) which attacks the sweet bay. As it matures, it turns into a flat oval scale, yellowish brown in colour and grows to about 3mm in length. Besides depleting the plant's food, the pest excretes a sticky honeydew which falls onto the surface of leaves below. This honeydew provides an ideal habitat on which a black superficial fungus known as sooty mould may develop.

While mainly a pest of the summer months, scale may continue to breed through the year on plants under glass.

Tortrix moths are small, night-flying creatures with fringed wings. Problems are caused by the caterpillars, which make a shelter for themselves by joining leaves together with silken webbing, wherein they feed on the leaf cells.

Attacks on bay can start in March and with pupation taking place on the host plant, will continue through successive generations until autumn. Infestations are normally light and can be contained by hand-picking.

Another sap feeding pest is the bay sucker. It overwinters as an adult in a sheltered spot, either on the host plant or nearby. Emerging in spring, they feed from soft growth at the margins of new leaves, causing them to thicken and curl. Eggs are laid at the affected points, a new generation appearing in May or June. Light infestations can be controlled by hand-picking.

Your Gardening Week

WORK FOR THE WEEK

✔ ANNUAL BORDER
While annuals can be sown in among other plants, there is some value in having an area devoted entirely to them. Sowings for such an annual border can be made now, in situ. Remember to hoard twigs and prunings for supporting taller types.

✔ SOW PANSIES
Pansies flower well in mild conditions. To have a supply for next year, sow now in boxes of light soil. Transfer the seedlings to grow on in a frame prior to planting out in October.

✔ SOW ARTICHOKES
There's just time to make a sowing of globe artichokes, which can be planted out on light or loamy soil in a sunny position. If your ground is heavy, either spot-treat the planting area or grow something else.

✔ BROAD BEANS
Successional sowing of broad beans can continue through to the end of May, to give cropping through to the end of September or early October.

✔ POT TOMATOES
Tomato plants started in January should be ready to move into their final pots or be planted direct into a glasshouse border.

✔ FRENCH BEANS
While early crops of French beans might have been started under glass, sowings can now be made outdoors but with the benefit of cloche protection. By starting now and continuing in succession until mid-July, you should have crops from the end of June through to October.

✔ LEAF BEET Spinach beet or the varieties of chard can be sown now, 10cm (4in) apart, in rows 37.5cm (15in) apart. Thin to 30cm (1ft) in the rows and harvest from late July right through to next June. There's value for money!

✔ WINTER GREENS
The early sowing of winter greens made under glass can now be followed by sowing outdoors or in a frame.

Hanging Baskets

There are certainly few more welcoming sights in summer than a hanging basket massed with flowers in bloom at the entrance to your house. Certainly they can be used to superb effect placed at strategic points — such as patios — around the outside of the house.

Given a cold greenhouse, or any other glass-covered area, you can make a start planting them now, so as to get them hardened off and settled in to start blooming as early as possible.

Many people seem to struggle unnecessarily with the basic filling procedure. They balance the half glove wire basket with one hand, trying to position the liner, and then fill it with growing mix and, in the process, spill everything.

Yet the solution is so simple. Just take a bucket and use it to cradle the basket in the top (as in the illustration). It's as simple as that! "Ah, but what about those half-circle shapes?", you might ask. Just as simple. Place two back-to-back and temporarily join them together at the top with a twist of wire before placing on the bucket top.

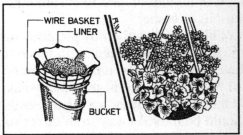

The choice of linings is vast today, but remember that the aim is to allow drainage (so that the plants do not become waterlogged), yet to retain the moisture necessary during hot summer periods.

Pre-shaped liners, sheets of plastic with holes punched in, or even plastic foam are excellent; though there is still nothing really to beat sphagnum moss or thin turves (grass side out, of course) particularly for 'finish'.

When choosing plants to fill the basket, bear in mind the colours of the blooms and particularly the forms of the plants. Aim to have some trailing, such as lobelia and campanula, begonias, or carnations. Then you will need height. To achieve this there are, of course, geraniums, fuchsias and petunias — just to give an idea of range for a nice long flowering period.

Finally, a word of warning. Once the good weather arrives keep an eye on the baskets that will need watering well at least once a day.

Plan For Christmas Cheer

There must be countless thousands of them spread throughout the land. Some will go on from year to year, just clinging to life by a thread. Others will thrive and grow to bring pleasure for a lifetime. To some botanists they will appear as a hybrid in the genus Schlumbergera. However, to many of us they remain Zygocactus truncatus, the Christmas Cactus.

What a joy they can be, hosting a succession of red flowers from December through to the end of March, and then needing but a minimum of care to ensure repeat performances for many seasons to come.

While many cacti enjoy plentiful sun, this one hails from eastern Brazil and is content with much lower levels of light. During their flowering season they do fine on a south-facing window sill because the sun is generally weak.

Once out of flower, and as the sun's intensity increases, they should be moved away from direct sunlight. Within the house, a room which has medium light is ideal, but in a glasshouse shading will be needed.

In addition, warmth and humidity, augmented by repotting and feeding when required, will produce large plants with many tens of flowers and which may last for 50 years or more. Needless to say, many do not survive for this length of time, despite their tenacity, eventually succumbing to starvation or an excess or shortage of water.

As a rule of thumb, repotting should be undertaken every second year or when the plant becomes too large for its existing pot. The period immediately following flowering is the right time, and while John Innes No 2 compost can be used, it will benefit if leaf mould and coarse sand is added.

Propagation is easily effected in early summer by taking sections of stem made up of three segments and carefully breaking them from the parent plant at a joint. These cuttings can either be set in a propagating case or dibbled directly into a pot containing a mixture of leaf mould and sand. Because each plant does not have a crown, a single specimen can be one-sided. This is overcome by setting three to a pot.

Once established with good roots, the cuttings can be moved into 125mm (5in) pots without being separated. If your new plants have a different habit to their parent, this will probably be due to the parent having been grafted onto Pereskia stock to make it taller.

In June, plants may be set outdoors in a semi-shaded position, the traditional and ideal place being in the fork of an apple tree where dappled shade is found. This also has the advantage that worms are less likely to enter the compost and slugs to reach up, though aphids may be a problem.

Growth is made following flowering, and may extend through to July or August. Established plants will benefit from regular weak liquid feeds at three-weekly intervals. Use such as tomato fertiliser, which is high in potash.

During dry periods in summer, syringe the plants with water, but by and large allow them a rest period. In September bring them inside and place in a position where they will not suffer from drafts or excessive changes in the atmosphere or buds may drop. When these new buds appear, commence a programme of feeding again and water normally.

While a temperature of 10C (50F) will have been adequate, once the buds appear it should be increased to 16C (60F). If the normal winter position is a window sill, move away with care if frost should threaten. Give water when compost has almost dried, probably at least once a week, and improve humidity by standing the pot on moist gravel.

The other common names of Crab Plant and Lobster Plant give some indication of habit, but hardly do justice to what can be a glorious specimen. Varieties include 'altensteinii' with brick-red flowers, 'crenatus' with smaller flowers in blue-violet, and 'delicatus' which is more upright in habit with pale-pink flowers.

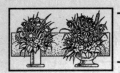

Sweet Peppers

There is no doubt that sweet peppers have become a regular visitor to the kitchen; their colour and taste both playing a part in that popularity.

They are related to the potato and tomato and their cultivation follows similar lines to the latter; though I would never aim to grow anywhere near the quantity of those two. Nevertheless, they can have their place, and a few plants add a little interest.

They perform at their best when given protection, and a cool glasshouse is ideal; but if space is limited a frame or cloches will help them along. In favoured areas they can be grown outdoors without protection, given the benefit of a south-facing border, backed by a wall or fence.

Most commonly grown are forms of Capsicum annuum, varying from the large sweet green peppers to the long, tapered pimentos, with a variety of shapes and sizes in between. The colours generally relate to maturity, for most are green when young, turning to yellow and red as they ripen.

For crops under glass, sowing can commence in February. However, middle to late March is early enough for plants to be grown outdoors. Early to mid-April should still be time enough (so get your stakes on), but glasshouse protection and even a little heat at the end of the season may be needed to bring the crop to maturity.

Seed, which is slightly larger than that of tomatoes, can be sown individually in soil blocks or pots, or may be space-sown in boxes.

Germinate in a temperature of 18-21C (65-70F).

When box-sown seedlings are large enough to handle they can be potted up, initially into 65mm (2.5in) pots and then subsequently into 10cm (4ins). During this period aim for a day temperature of 20C (68F) and 16C (60F) at night, ventilating at 23C (74F) on sunny days.

Space out and turn as growth is made, and take care not to over-water while the plants are small.

If the crop is to be grown under glass, pot on progressively into 20cm (8in) pots using John Innes No 3 compost. Those to be planted outdoors can be hardened off with a view to setting them out in late May or early June.

Should planting be delayed for any reason, don't let them become pot-bound, but rather move them on again into 15cm (6in) pots.

Outside, set the plants 45cm (18in) apart and cover with barn cloches. If the plants are placed in a slight depression, the cloches can be kept on longer.

Eventually though, the cloches will have to be removed, but their effect can be prolonged if they are placed on end around the plants. Place the cloches in position a couple of weeks before planting, to warm the soil. If it is comparatively cold, a slight check to growth may occur.

Best results seem to be produced when planting takes place just before the first flower buds open, though if growth is a little on the soft side a delay until the first flowers open is sensible.

Many of the problems of pest and disease found in tomatoes are also to be found in sweet peppers. That can be important when choosing varieties, for a number are resistant to tobacco mosaic virus.

Three fast growing or early F1 varieties which fall into this category are Gypsy, Luteus and Midnight Beauty.

Gypsy should give a good crop of slightly tapering fruits, which turn to yellowish green and then deep red when ripe, though a little heat may be needed. Luteus is fast growing and gives fruits which turn to yellow. Midnight Beauty is very early, with large fruits which turn to purple and then deep red.

If you would prefer smaller plants to grow in containers, which can be moved in and out as conditions allow, then try Redskin. This variety grows to around 37cm (15in) and produces medium-sized fruits which turn from green to deep red.

Your Gardening Week

 TRIM LOBELIA Blue lobelia which is growing well can be trimmed back a little to make it thicken out.

 SOW PEAS Ensure succession by making a sowing of second early peas.

 LEEKS A late crop of leeks to be harvested between January and the end of March, can be had from sowings made now. The seedlings can be planted out in June.

 LAST SPROUTS This is about the last chance to sow a late variety of Brussels sprouts which can be planted out in June.

BETTER CARROTS Heavy soil can be restricting to long-rooted carrots, so if you want some large ones try making holes with a crowbar and filling them with good compost before sowing a pinch of seed on top.

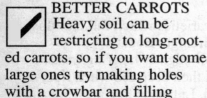 **PLANT SWEET PEAS** Provided they have been well hardened off, sweet peas sown in January should be about ready for planting. Take out a large hole with a trowel, and spread the roots before covering.

 STOP STRAWBER-RIES If you have a new plantation of summer fruiting strawberries, then there is merit in pinching out the flowers in the first year, to give the crowns a chance to establish and bulk up before producing fruit.

THIN ANNUALS Hardy annuals sown during March, should be making growth and must be thinned before they become overcrowded. Pull out the weakest, leaving the remainder 5cm apart. Further thinnings may be required as more growth is made.

 BETTER BLOOMS If you want bigger and better blooms in the perennial border, then try thinning the number of shoots down to half a dozen per plant. Plants which will benefit include delphiniums, heleniums, lupins and phlox.

Two For The Price Of One

You often hear it said that you can either grow plants in the house or you can't. Some people certainly seem to have no problem. One relative just cannot even get "babies" from her spider plants yet another, given the same conditions in the very same house, has them running wild.

Those who do do well with plants, particularly the larger ones, are very often faced with another problem - that of them taking over the house. When they outgrow their welcome, you can of course ensure you have a replacement from the very same plant.

The rubber plant is a case in point. This can be propagated by air layering, which usual-ly involves taking the top portion of the old plant and getting it to grow roots whilst it is still attached in its entirety.

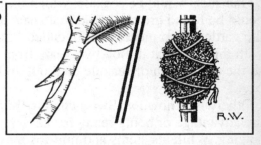

You will deal with that portion of the main stem which is new - using a sharp knife to make a cut upwards into the stem, just below a leaf joint so that there is a tongue of new wood protruding (see illustration left). Alternatively you can cut a ring of the bark away below a joint, removing a 1/2 inch width ring of the bark.

In either case, dust with hormone rooting powder and, in the case of the "tongue-cut", push a little sphagnum moss to keep it open before binding the wound with more damp sphagnum moss which can be tied to keep it firmly in position (right). Add a piece of stake to help support the cut portion of stem.

Finally, bind some polythene around the sphagnum moss, tying securely around the top and bottom of the moss to ensure that moisture is retained.

Before long you should see roots making their way towards the polythene cover, at which point the top will be a new plant ready for cutting away and potting by itself.

But don't throw away the old plant. Cut it back and you should see new growth - there you have it, two for the price of one!

Swiss Chard And Lobelia In Pots

If you grow vegetables for their economic value, it can be difficult to decide which ones to concentrate on for the best results. If you grow for pleasure, then the choice is less critical and there should be scope to try different types and varieties just for the fun of it – particularly if they are unlikely to be available in shops.

One such would be seakale, which used to be widely grown. It could be found growing wild in coastal areas, and was raised in the garden from pieces of root called 'thongs'. The drawback with this was that it took two years from planting to harvest, and so the cultivation of seakale died out, to be replaced by seakale beet.

Otherwise known as Swiss chard or silver beet, this crop has the advantage of being ready for harvest about four months after sowing. While its stems and midribs may be used to substitute seakale, the leaves may also be used as a substitute for spinach. It has the further advantage of being more tolerant of hot summers and cold winters.

Seakale beet will also perform in a variety of soils and in positions of partial shade or attracting full sun. It will grow in light, sandy ground in which true spinach would struggle and also in heavy clay although - as with the other beets which are grown for their roots – it needs lime, and a pH of 6.5 to 6.8 should be the aim.

Try to follow a crop for which the ground was manured the previous year, and encourage leaf production with a dressing of general fertiliser in early summers.

General practice is to sow in April and again in July. Space rows 45cm (18in) apart and set three seeds to a station 38cm (15in) apart in the rows. After germination, thin the seedlings to leave the strongest. For the spring sowing, cloches can be used to advantage, being removed about six weeks after germination. The July sowing should be in a protected position and cloches will be needed throughout the winter.

Of the varieties, Silver Beet is white and green, while Ruby Chard has red stems but is less palatable. Both make plants of attractive appearance, so that if space in the vegetable plot is limited in summer, odd plants will not look out of place in ornamental borders.

To harvest, pull stems from the outside of the plants, allowing the remaining central ones to develop. Do not be tempted to cut the stems or the remaining stump will bleed.

Spring-sown plants should be ready from July and remain productive until autumn. Crops which have been overwintered can be pulled from in both spring and the following autumn.

Beside providing an attractive edging in contrast to many bedding plants throughout the summer, the pleasant blues of lobelia can also prove decorative under glass during winter. Save some seed from your sowings for bedding and make a note to bring the packet out again in June. Then, during the first fortnight, sow sufficient seed to provide for a few plants in pots.

As soon as the seedlings are large enough to handle, pick them off, subsequently potting on into progressively larger pots until by September they are well established in 12.5-15cm (5-6in) pots.

Use John Innes No 1 potting compost, but if the plants are slow in growth give a boost with liquid feed. During the growing period try to take the trouble to pinch out any flower buds which appear.

Toward the end of September place the pots in a cold frame to give protection against frost. Then in mid-October they can be taken into the glasshouse.

The reward for this activity will be a splash of background blue right through to February. A nice change in the winter when blue flowers are in short supply.

Pepper Cultivation

Having dealt with sowing and planting peppers I now want to go a little further into their cultivation. For crops grown outdoors the selection of a suitable plot is important, with the quality of the soil being the most essential consideration.

It is crucial that there is a reasonable supply of organic matter - too little and the roots will struggle leading to poor growth; too much and the growth will tend to be over-vigorous. This may lead to the production of masses of foliage at the expense of fruit production.

The same effects are true of fertilisers and so, unless the ground is in poor shape I'd advise that you don't apply any. All you need is a well-drained soil in a sunny position with an average level of fertility.

The aim with sweet peppers is to form strong, bushy plants before allowing them to fruit. This is achieved by pinching out the growing tips when plants are around 37.5cm (15in) tall. If, when the first flowers appear, plants are still on the spindly side, then pinch out that first flush of flowers to give more time for them to make up before fruit is set.

Given strong growth and a sheltered position staking should not be necessary. But to be on the safe side, they can be secured by tying-in to a single cane or by running strings down either side of the row.

During the season keep them well supplied with water to ensure that growth is not checked and, ideally, cover the root run with a light mulch. Moisture is also important in helping to ensure a good set of fruit.

To this end it is useful to spray over the plants with a fine mist once or twice a day. Once the fruit has set a better supply of food is demanded. This can be given in the form of soluble or liquid feed given at two-week intervals.

Plants being brought to maturity in a cool glasshouse can be potted on until they reside in 20cm (8in) pots or set in a border. They should be spaced in double rows, some 45cm (18in) apart, with 37.5cm (15in) between the plants. Support can be given exactly as for tomatoes, using canes or string. As the amount of growth in these protected conditions should well exceed outdoor plants, it is worth giving feed once a week.

The outdoor crop should be ready to harvest in late August or early September. Indoors, fruit should be ready at the end of July or early in August and - subject to frost - cropping can extend into November, just showing how useful even a cool glasshouse can be!

In anticipation of frost, the plants can be pulled, complete with roots, and hung in a frost-free shed where fruit will continue to mature.

Naturally you will wish to allow some fruits to turn red to enhance the presentation of meals, though sometimes our summers are not good enough to allow this. In any event, start to pick when the first fruits are still green, but have become swollen and glossy. This leaves the way clear for the plant's energy to be devoted to those remaining.

Besides tempting our palates, peppers also seem to attract a wide range of pests such as aphids, red-spider mites and caterpillars.

However, provided that you follow good cultural practice, using sterilised compost for propagation and potting, the removal of decaying flowers and foliage and avoidance of injury to plant tissues, then disease should not be a problem.

Nevertheless, where tomato problems have been experienced in the past, infections are more likely. Look out for white rot, botrytis, verticillium wilt, various virus complaints and blossom-end rot.

If, by any chance, we have a long, hot summer, then soft light coloured areas can develop on the fruits which dry out and bleach. This 'sun scald' can be avoided by light shading.

Your Gardening Week

WORK FOR THE WEEK

✔ **RE-USE DAFFS**
Daffodils which have been forced can be knocked out of their pots or boxes and planted among trees and shrubs to establish themselves for flowering in the open next year. Where bulbs are naturalised in grass, mowing should be delayed until the foliage dies down. It is a good idea to give a light dressing of fertiliser to plump up the bulbs and corms.

✔ **FERTILISER FEEDS**
Dressings of fertiliser are appropriate at this time for vegetables, fruit, roses and really any plant that is making rapid growth. In dry weather use dry feeds, hoeing them into the surface where they will be washed in by watering or rain. If liquid fertiliser is used, never apply to dry plants, or the concentration taken up may be detrimental. Always give a soaking with plain water first.

✔ **THIN RASPBERRIES**
Young raspberry canes are appearing in profusion, and any which will not be required should be removed.

✔ **SOW MARROWS**
Marrows can be sown outdoors from now to the end of May when conditions allow. Prepare pockets of enriched soil spaced from 60-120cm apart depending upon whether bush or trailing varieties are grown. Sow three seeds per station, thinning in due course to leave the best. If it remains cool, sow singly in pots under glass.

✔ **TOMATOES**
Glasshouse tomatoes are growing away well and should have unwanted sideshoots pinched out regularly. Any growing in bags should be given feeds from about four weeks after planting, while those grown in rings or in a glasshouse border will not need a boost until the first fruits have set and are about the size of marbles.

✔ **SOW CINERARIAS**
Start sowing now for flower at Christmas, and follow on with successional sowings in May and June.

Tidying Climbers

With better weather here and frosts less of a threat, wall shrubs and climbing plants should be making good growth.

Until they really get going though, they tend to look twiggy and rather untidy; yet those most prone to this — such as that favourite, the clematis - do not need pruning at this time.

It is best to tie-in the stray, twiggy bits to ensure that as little as possible is taken out, so that the plant to bloom abundantly. A point worth remembering about tying-in is that you are adding to the strength of the plant, which will better withstand any stormy times ahead.

If the plant has become so 'matted' that it is felt necessary to open it up, then cutting back should be done as sparingly as possible — just enough really to keep the plant tidy looking. Using secateurs, cut back to immediately above a shoot (as in the illustration).

Another occasion for clematis pruning, and even then only lightly, is after the free-flowering varieties, such as Nellie Moser (a popular pink) and Barbara Jackman (a reddish-purple) have given their first blooms. They can grow as high as 20ft, so may need a light cutting-back, even if only to ensure the qualify of future flowers.

Hard pruning is only necessary for the large flowered hybrids, such as Jackmanii and Ville de Lyons. These bloom after June and may be cut back to within a foot of the ground around February (but not later), to encourage the new growth on which they flower.

For the rest, just keep your clematis well watered and give it a good mulch. It will do you proud.

Odds And Ends In The Garden

Once daffodils start to fade, there is merit in pinching off the spent flowers; not only because they become unsightly, but also to prevent unnecessary development of seed heads. These will only absorb energy that is best conserved in the bulb itself, to contribute to next year's display.

The same is true for tulips, especially the smaller varieties such as greigii and Kaufmanii. Although the seed heads are not so prominent and therefore less likely to be considered unsightly, they still absorb energy. These varieties are normally planted in permanent positions rather than being treated as bedding subjects.

Water in the form of a pond or stream adds an extra dimension to the garden. Not only is it visually rewarding in its own right, reflecting the various moods of nature with either a mirror sheen or bounding ripples, but being important to life it seems to create a special affinity. Of course it also provides an additional habitat for aquatic plants. The best time for planting is April through to mid-June, a time when they have not made too much growth, but when the weather, and also the water, is warming up.

Water lilies are the queens of such a situation, and there are many available in a wide range of colours. They inhabit a depth of water ranging from over a metre (3ft) down to barely 15cm (6in), though the widest choice is from plants which will flourish in 30-45cm (12-18in) of water.

Reliable, free-flowering forms include the deep red 'Escarboucle', 'Sunrise', which is bright yellow and the white 'Virginale'.

Late May or early June is the time to make sowings of perennials and biennials. Perennials, of course, have the advantage that once established they will go on for many years. The majority of biennials that can be sown this year to flower next, will either die out after flowering or should be replaced by fresh stock. They are best discarded, as if grown on, they tend to become woody and straggly in appearance.

Both types can be sown in nursery rows, and should be thinned as growth is made and then planted out in autumn in their flowering positions.

For the border, Shasta Daisy, Gypsophila and Delphinium are all attractive. If you intend to have spring bedding, try Forget-me-Not, Bellis (the double form) and Wallflower, all of which can be interplanted with bulbs. If flower arranging is your forte then Eryngium, the Sea Holly, Echinops, the Globe Thistle and Dipsacus (the Teasel) all have something to offer.

While you are sowing, why not pop in a few annuals such as Schizanthus, Kalanchoe, Celosia and Calceolaria. These should be grown under glass to give plenty of colour during late winter and early spring.

In the glasshouse, more care will have to be taken in shading a range of plants as the sun gains in strength. Many foliage plants, particularly ferns, will suffer if exposed to intense light and heat for too long. Both gloxinias and tuberous rooted begonias will benefit from light shading.

A more bouyant atmosphere will naturally increase the demand for water. Particular attention should be paid to crops such as tomato and cucumber to ensure they never dry out. Plants take time to recover from stunted growth caused by lack of water and this can have an adverse effect on crops at a later date.

Ventilators should be used more frequently during the day and may even be left open a little at night unless real cold threatens. One of the drawbacks of closing them fully is that there can often be a sudden and significant rise in temperature shortly after sunrise if the morning is clear. Unless you have some automated form of ventilator control, that really means your first job on such mornings should be to dash out and open the vents - even before you clean your teeth!

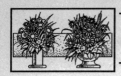

Kiwi Fruit

Traditionally described as the Chinese Gooseberry but now perhaps more widely recognised as Kiwi fruit, Actinidia chinensis is an interesting plant to try in the garden. With a seemingly plentiful supply of the fruits available all year round you may feel there is little point, but this plant does have other virtues.

Despite the superimposition of its new name, the plant is native to China and was introduced here around the turn of the century.

It makes a vigorous climber which may reach to 9m (30ft) or more. Certainly in the wild it twines its way through trees or spreads across rocks and embankments.

Such method of growth may be encouraged in the garden, although if that sounds a little on the wild side, it can be grown on wires as you would blackberries or be kept in bounds in a container.

The ideal is for a warm, sheltered position either in full sun or with partial shade. While not too fussy as to soil, a good loam is preferred. As a general rule, ensure that drainage is good. Soil should also be enriched with organic material prior to planting, working in a dressing of general fertiliser at the same time.

So, what do you get? If home-grown fruit is your aim, it is advisable to obtain two plants to allow for cross-pollination.

This is because the flowers are normally unisexual. Other than that, you will be blessed with reddish, hairy shoots holding heart-shaped leaves up to 25x20cm (10x8in) in an attractive shade of deep green.

These provide a background to the creamy-white fragrant flowers, which are about 4cm across and can be in season from June through to August. These mature to an attractive buff-yellow as they prepare to turn to fruit.

If the plants are to be left to their own devices, set them about

3m (10ft) apart. Where the root is restricted by growing in containers, top-growth will be less. Use John Innes No3 compost augmented by liquid feeds in the growing season.

By and large the plants can be trained to fill the space available. Any excess growths can be cut back to 15-20cm (6-8in) towards the end of July or early in August. Any winter pruning should be completed before the end of January to limit the possibility of bleeding.

While fruits should ripen from green to the well-known brown in late September or early October, in less favoured areas this may fail to occur. In such areas cultivation in containers is the answer, allowing the plants to be given some protection at the end of summer.

I don't know why, but I always feel pleasure when confronted by campanulas. There is just some indefinable effect created by the way the flowers are formed that appeals and ensures I always have a number on the go in garden or glasshouse.

One worth growing if you have not tried it before is Campanula pyramidalis, the Chimney Bellflower. Quite how it was given the name I don't know, but it can be used indoors or outside.

The normal method is to treat it as a biennial, sowing seed now to flower next year. The seed may be sown in pans in a cold frame, the resultant seedlings being potted singly and gradually potted on until they are in 12.5cm (5in) pots, which should be sufficient to see them through the winter. Take care when potting not to bury the crown.

By next February or March they can be moved on into 20cm (8in) pots, in which they will flower.

While pot-grown plants can be plunged into a border, the alternative is to grow them on in a cold frame bed, lifting and planting in March.

With luck you will be rewarded with three or four stems on each plant, making a pyramid of blue flower around 120cm (4ft) or more high during June and July next year.

Your Gardening Week

✔ SET SUPPORTS Herbaceous perennials are putting on a spurt of growth, and any necessary supports are best set in place now so the foliage will grow over and around to hide them. While stakes, canes and pre-fabricated frames can be used, the best and most natural effect is achieved by using twigs and branches. These are easily cut or bent to size without waste.

✔ AUBERGINES Seedlings of the aubergine or egg plant which are to be grown under glass, should be ready for planting. Those raised under glass to be set outdoors should gradually be hardened off for planting out under cloches towards the end of the month. Work a little general fertiliser into the bed and put the cloches in place now to warm the ground before planting.

✔ CHECK PEAS If you are growing peas close to plots which have contained cruciferous plants such as cabbage, check them over and look for mottled sil-very patches on the leaves. If found they are a sign of thrip damage. Although a slight attack is not a great problem, severe infestations can check growth and lead to plants becoming stunted.

✔ STRAW STRAWBER-RIES When flower stems appear on straw-berries, place either clean straw or polythene around the base of the plants so that fruit will be kept clear of the soil as it develops.

✔ LATE GREENS If you missed out on raising cabbage or cauliflower for transplanting, late crops can be had by sowing direct in the bed. Space sow seed three to a station at 40x45cm up to 45x60cm (20x27in) depending on variety. Thin out the weak-est seedlings.

✔ THIN ROSES Following pruning, strong new shoots are pushing forward on roses. Despite careful pruning a num-ber of these shoots are likely to be badly placed and are best pinched out while small.

A Basinful Of Strawberries

Strawberries, that summer delight, will need attention to ensure that you obtain the amount of fruit you require.

Plants which are well established, say over 2 years will need a dressing of fish manure at 4oz (113g) to the square yard topped off with a mulch of decayed compost around the plants.

But before all of this, you need to hoe well between the rows to cut back as much weed as possible.

As soon as any flowers appear, cover the soil beneath the plants with straw and slug pellets or strawberry mats. Opened up black polythene waste bags with slits to allow the plants to

poke through will do very well, held down on the soil by bricks or large stones. Both the polythene and the straw will also help to stop soiling of the fruit by mud splattering during rainy periods.

Later, as runners appear from the plants, prepare to increase your stock, remembering that it is best to replace plants after 3 years.

Where the runners appear with new plants at their ends, sink small pots filled with loamy soil up to their rims and put the plantlets (still attached to the parent plant) in the pot of soil. Then pin down the 'umbilical' (as shown).

After about a month the new plants should be well rooted. They can now be severed from the parent and the pot lifted so that they can grow on their own accord.

Sweet And Pretty

As ever, May seems likely to be one of those "should I or shouldn't I?" months, with more sun and rising temperatures increasing the desire to set plants outside. It would be nice if we could be certain that there will be no more frosts, but history dictates that there will be, especially if a gamble is taken with tender plants and vegetables.

Of course if you grow your own plants from seed, then for little extra time and expense it would have been possible to raise a few extra of each plant with which to gamble. If you have to buy in seedlings or young plants then that is less of a option. Equally, there is little point in buying these too early. Let the nurseryman take the risk; but it might be wise to order in advance for delivery when the chances of frost are slim.

This year I thought to give sweet corn a try again. It does command a chunk of space, as the best results are obtained by growing several rows in a block.

This is because the female plants are fertilised from pollen carried on the breeze. In a single row pollination can be poor and result in badly formed cobs.

Plan to make two sowings straight away. The first can be outdoors, preferably with the benefit of cloch protection to speed things on a little. The second can be under glass.

Outdoors select a plot about 1.5m (5ft) wide, which will allow four rows up to 37.5cm (15in) apart to be sown. Using a draw hoe, take out drills 10cm (4in) deep and place seed in the bottom.

Cover with 25mm (1in) of fine soil and settle in by watering through a fine hose. There is merit in placing two seeds at each station 37.5cm (15in) apart in the row, one of which can be removed if both germinate.

Because of the depth of the drill taken out, the young plants will be growing in a shallow depression.

This allows earthing-up to be easily achieved, improving stability and also acting as a top-dressing for roots developing at the soil surface.

The indoor sowings can be raised in an unheated glasshouse or frame. Sow seeds singly in pots using seed compost. Planting out can take place in June.

Sweet corn appreciates well cultivated ground with a good supply of organic matter to retain moisture. This could be particularly important if we have another dryish summer. It can be further enhanced by a sprinkling of general fertiliser prior to sowing or planting.

With varieties, it's a good idea to try alternatives in successive years; and inadvisable to grow separate varieties close together, as cross pollination may mask and detract from varietal qualities and flavour. There are several to choose from, Kelvedon Glory and First Of All being well tried and tested. Earlibelle gives good crops even in poor conditions and, if you like your cobs sweet, try Candle.

Indian and Japanese azaleas make attractive pot plants during the winter. Most common is the Indian form, which is almost submerged beneath flower in season. The Japanese form has smaller flowers, but tends to be hardier and so can be planted outdoors when you have tired of it in its pot.

In any event, both types benefit from spending the summer months outdoors, where they can enjoy light and air. This is the time to start and harden them off with a view to moving outside next month.

If re-potting is needed it may be done now. Check by knocking the root-ball out of its pot and see how developed the roots are. If a move is needed, go up two sizes and use a lime-free potting compost.

Keep well watered through the summer, and apply liquid feed once a week to build up the flower buds for winter. Ideally, watering should be with rainwater, which is likely to be less alkaline than tap water.

Gone, But Not Forgotten

Some six weeks have passed since my beloved beagle shrugged off his mortal coil. Even now I don't think that I've come to terms with the loss, for he was a constant companion, whether on long walks or just joining in the spirit of things within the garden.Thirteen years is a big piece out of anyone's life and I miss him. The only satisfaction is that now there is a part of the garden that is his.

Somehow such a passing concentrates the mind. Without being morbid, his plot provides the opportunity to make fresh planting which does justice to his memory and provides a daily reminder to the joy he brought. Nobody who has ever had a beagle can forget the mixture of joy and frustration, the sheer emotion that such a character can bring.

So now his part of the garden has spring flowers: fritillarias, primulas, muscari and crocus, together with a fine specimen of Magnolia soulangiana which has flowered well for several weeks. Perhaps its position is a little more exposed than I might have wished, but it will be interesting to see how it performs in future years.

Of course having a dog is part of a way of life and it wasn't long before the family did the rounds of the local sanctuaries. There seemed to be some interesting dogs looking for a home, but also some that seemed a bit iffy with young twins to consider. A visit to nearby kennels resulted in the acquisition of a bearded collie pup.

So far he has settled into the garden well, except for a seemingly insatiable appetite for any plant which finds itself in his path. Woody branches have been chewed and fresh leaves and stems stripped to the ground; and if he doesn't chew it, he will sit down and squash it! Of course he's only a puppy and will soon grow out of it - and grow he does; he seems to double in size every week.

That's not the only problem in the garden. I had thought that I was beginning to overcome the problem of moss in the lawn, but this year it seems worse than ever. I guess the wet spells have leached out food leaving the grasses a little weak, and the general weather that prevailed through winter has encouraged the moss in constant active growth. Add to that the wear and tear of regular use, and it is easy to understand why some additional work is needed.

Moss is indicative of poor ground conditions, and really requires radical improvements if any lasting answer is to be found. Using a moss killer is but a temporary expedient. It's hard to remember how long I've been saying this to myself, and still the moss killer returns with monotonous regularity!

Dampness is conducive to the spread of moss, with moist spring and autumn seasons allowing rapid colonisation. Poor drainage is the main problem.

This can be due to an inherently heavy soil or compaction, and is usually made worse by too much shade. These conditions encourage the prostrate or trailing types of moss whose feathery stems spread across the soil surface.

Moss can also be found on sandy, well-drained soils. Usually it gains a toehold because the grass has been weakened, perhaps through drought or because the land is impoverished. In this case the moss is usually upright in growth, having green leaves at the top and brown leaves at the base.

The third form of moss commonly found are the attractive bright green cushion mosses. These arrive because the ground is uneven and areas or turf are 'scalped' by close mowing, creating an ideal nursery bed for the moss to establish.

Next week we'll have a look at some remedies, but in the meantime it's time to put my boots on. The new pup has just come out of quarantine following his injections, so it's off to the fields for half an hour.

All good fun and not to be missed, though I'm sure there will be three of us on this trip!

Your Gardening Week

 HERBACEOUS CUTTINGS Many herbaceous plants can be propagated by making cuttings of the new shoots appearing now. With those such as delphiniums - which might benefit from a little thinning - the shoots can be inserted in frames or pots. Kept covered for a week or two, they should root readily.

HARDEN CELERY Celery sown in heat will be ready to plant out at the end of this month or early in June. Take all opportunities to harden-off, so minimising the risk of any shock at planting time.

MORE BEANS Scarlet runner beans and dwarf kidney beans can be sown direct into the garden. They are tender to frost, but should be safe in most areas now. Plants raised under glass should not be set out until the end of the month or early June, although runner beans should be given plenty of room to prevent them becoming entangled.

PROPAGATE HYDRANGEAS Given a warm frame, stocks of Hydrangea hortensia can be increased by inserting cuttings, singly, into 3-inch pots and plunging them in the frame. When the cutting is rooted and a few inches high, it may be stopped to encourage the production of sideshoots - which can give up to six flowering heads for next season.

PLANT HYACINTHS Galtonia candicans, the Cape Hyacinth, can be planted now. Put in at 15cm (6in) deep and 30cm (1ft) apart, they will grow to over 90cm (3ft) and look well in a border among low growing shrubs.

SWEDES AND TURNIPS Continue to make successional sowings of swedes and turnips through to July. These will produce crops from August to October. Use the globe turnip Snowball, or the cylindrical Jersey Navet, and the swede Western Perfection.

Climbing Made Easy

For many gardeners, and particularly for those who like to grow climbing plants, such as beans, one of the main difficulties is finding good support for them.

Nets and poles do the job well, but are often subject to unexpected gusts of wind and, invariably, are too tall - particularly for the retired who may find it impossible to reach and stretch for the fruits of their labours.

One of the best ways round this problem is to place poles at an angle and to tie them at the tip, wig-wam fashion (as in the illustration). The poles can be angled to be tied just above your own height, and spaced so as to allow you to get within the wig-wam to give the plants attention.

The arrangement is excellent for beans, sweet peas, etc. Among the et ceteras you might like to include marrows which can be trained up wig-wam poles.

Little Gem is a small fruited variety which can be treated in this way and seeds can be sown outdoors in late May or early June. Choose a sheltered but sunny spot. Sow two or three seeds at each 'station', each seed about an inch deep. After germination, keep the strongest plant at each station.

One of the main disappointments with marrows is the failure to set fruit. The cause is invariably a lack of pollinating insects. You can help nature along here, however, by hand pollinating. Choose a dry day and take the male flower, fold back its petals and push it into a female flower (see illustration). Which is which is easy to remember, for only the female flower bears an embryo marrow behind its petals.

As the fruits begin to develop begin a fortnightly feeding programme, using a high potash content liquid feed. This will help them to produce over a long period, as will the gathering of fruits before they are too large.

Your Gardening Week

Too Many Tiny Feet

Centipedes have the appearance of being dangerous (for their size). They are quick to move when disturbed, whereas millipedes are slow-moving and curl up when touched, seeming to be no threat.

In fact, for the gardener, these appearances are deceptive. The speedy centipede does no harm to plants. It is carniverous and feeds on insects, small slugs and worms. I suppose this is a mixed blessing in that some of its delicacies are detrimental and some beneficial. What I need for my garden is a super-centipede, feeding only on slugs and capable of tackling large ones!

The slow, quiescent millipede is another story, for it feeds on plant material.

There are around 50 different species known in these isles, though many are rare and confined to localised habitats. Most problems stem from two main groups known as the 'snake' and 'flat' millipedes. Just to add insult to injury, they are commonly found to occupy the same territory.

The snake group is so called because the movements and appearance of these many-footed beasts resemble those of a snake. They have a smooth, rounded body made up of 30-60 segments. In gardens and glasshouses the most common to be stumbled across is Blaniulus guttulatus, the 'spotted millipede'. This has a slender body with a row of orange or red spots down either side, one to a segment.

The 'flat' millipedes are most commonly found under stones and surface litter. They have projections on their body segments which create the appearance of a flat back - hence their name. The most common problem species is Brachydesmus superus, which reaches around 10mm (1\2in) in length.

Millipedes often feed on plant tissues that have already suffered damage from some other cause; but they also go for the soft parts of undamaged tissue. The fine roots of many plants, together with bulbs and tubers, may all receive attention. Carrots, potatoes and strawberries, together with the germinating seed and seedlings of peas and beans, are all susceptible and cucumbers can be cut down by the attentions of the glasshouse millipede.

There is nothing particularly distinctive to identify millipede damage, and other organisms can be attracted to the injured tissues, tending to mask the identity of the original perpetrator. All you can say is that if millipedes are around, they must be feeding on something. Equally, the millipedes may have been attracted to an area already damaged either mechanically or by some other pest.

If a serious problem arises there may be a need to consider chemical controls; however, cultural measures can limit the problem. Firstly, being tidy and keeping rubbish and debris to a minimum restricts the places where they can hide. Secondly, susceptible seeds and seedlings such as peas and beans can be started in pots and transplanted, rather than being direct-sown into the ground.

Although sowings should have been made in April to produce crops for harvesting from July, seakale beet or Swiss chard can be sown now to give crops in spring, although cloche protection will be necessary to see them through the winter.

This plant is suited to a wide range of soils, though better performance can be expected from land with a pH around 6.5. Sow 15in (38cm) apart in rows 18in (45cm) apart and set about three seeds to each station, thinning to leave the strongest seedlings after germination.

Water in the form of a pond or stream adds an extra dimension to the garden, with the potential for attractive reflections when it is still and the magic of rippling light when ruffled by a breeze. The best time for planting aquatic plants is from April through to mid-June - a time when they have not made too much growth but when the weather and, consequentially, the water, is warming up.

Kill Moss And Weeds

I have a set of metal pins that I use with string for any marking out that needs to be done. Last autumn one went missing - because the heavens opened, and in my dash for shelter I dropped it.

It fell on a bank of roughish ground where the grass is not mown very often. Today I found it, unfortunately with the mower blade which was bent beyond any reasonable hope of being straightened and remaining in balance! The cost of a new blade seemed nearly enough to ensure the manufacturing industry will climb out of recession before long.

Last week I mentioned that moss was still a problem in some areas of lawn. Besides poor drainage, shade from trees and shrubs is a significant cause of moss growth. I had intended to attack it again and wreak havoc among it - but instead spent some time reflecting. While some areas which are more out in the open do need attention, there are others where the green, mossy carpet, especially of cushion moss, looks perfectly in keeping, and can remain.

Where treatment is needed, the options are to use a dedicated moss killer or lawn sand. I still prefer the latter, which can be applied from mid-April through to the beginning of July.

Lawn sand is a mixture of three parts of sulphate of ammonia and one part of sulphate of iron, carried in 20 parts of silver sand, all by weight. There is a danger that careless application will result in fine grasses being scorched, but only the top-growth is affected and not the roots.

Weighed against this are the advantages that weeds other than moss are controlled and the ammonium sulphate acts as a fertiliser, encouraging a rich, green sward while sustaining the slightly acid conditions that are beneficial to grasses.

Now I know those gallant folk at the met office do their best, but even so, predicting the weather that will affect your garden

is a chancy business. Barometers, pine cones, seaweed and a good sniff of the air are all useful indicators to the imminence of ideal condition for application.

What we are looking for is soil that is moist and a sunny morning, with the prospect of rain within a couple of days. The lawn sand should be applied evenly at a rate which generally will not exceed 136gm/sq metre (4oz/sq yard). The powder clings to the rough and broad leaves of weeds and moss, causing rapid scorch, which results in the demise of the foliage and eventually weakens or kills the plant.

While grasses may be blackened, they soon recover, because the impact is limited as the powder slips quickly from the smooth, narrow stems.

Take care not to retrace steps over treated areas, and do not mow until after rain or water application. If rain has not fallen within a couple of days, give the ground a thorough soaking. After about three weeks scarify the surface to remove debris.

At that point you will have to consider whether further applications will be needed to give satisfactory control. If not, where the grass is sparse, oversowing with grass seed can be undertaken. Where weeds with tap roots persist, they can be spot-treated with more concentrated lawn sand but are perhaps better tackled with selective weed-killer.

If treatment is to be given in autumn, use a proprietory moss killer and liquid selective weedkillers.

I mentioned that the application of lawn sand helps to maintain acidity which is beneficial in discouraging both weeds and earthworms. In extreme cases the ground may become too acid, indicated by the presence of sheep's sorrel, woodrush and moss.

The application of lime is an activity to be approached with care and can lead to a significant deterioration of the sward. If you suspect a problem, carry out a thorough pH test. If the pH is below 5.5, ground limestone - not ordinary garden lime - can be applied in autumn or winter at a rate of 2oz per square yard (50g per square metre). If in doubt - don't.

Your Gardening Week

MORE CLEMATIS Increase stocks of clematis by taking softwood cuttings from now until mid-June.

SUPPORT GLADIOLI Don't allow gladioli to grow too tall before staking them. By the time they have reached (30cm) a foot, a strong stake should be in and the first tie made.

EARTH POTATOES Earth up potatoes as growth is made. If you think they will benefit from additional fertiliser, dust a little along the rows before drawing the soil up.

KEEP TIDY Climbers and wall plants are starting to grow away with vigour. Keep on top of them by tying in the stems before they become entangled and are difficult to manage.

SOW WALLFLOWERS Although coming to flower late, my wallflowers produced another good display. Sowing for next year can be made in late May or early June.

SOW SPINACH Make a last sowing of summer spinach for later efforts are prone to bolting. Perpetual spinach can be sown to give leaves in autumn. New Zealand spinach can be sown outdoors by placing pinches of seed at 90cm (3ft) intervals, though it is better indoors.

CHOOSE YOUR COLOUR Hydrangea hortensia will colour up depending on whether your soil is acid or alkaline. Alkaline soils lock up iron and result in flowers of pink, white or red depending on variety. On acid soils they are blue or purplish red. For a change, on alkaline soil apply ammoniated alum and on acid soil apply hydrated lime.

RHUBARB CARE Apply a handful of fertiliser which should then be well watered in. Break off any flowering stems.

MORE GLADIOLI Finish planting gladioli without delay. Those planted earlier should be showing through.

Don't Play Gooseberry - Pick A Sawfly

Gooseberries are not only one of the easiest grown fruits for the average gardener, but they are also very much welcomed by those who prefer to spend their time in the kitchen (making jam and other sweet delights) or better still, eating.

Gooseberries are easy growers, doing well in virtually any type of well drained soil, and are capable of thriving, be their site in partial shade or direct sun.

There are, inevitably, problems to be on the lookout for. One of the most common is the Gooseberry sawfly, or rather its caterpillars. These emerge this month, and you will do yourself a favour if you pick them off the leaves as soon as you become aware of them. Left for just a short time, they will get to work on the leaves and

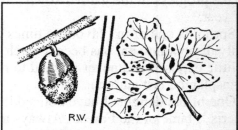

strip the bush. Whilst the caterpillars will not be tempted by the berries themselves, denuding of the plant will weaken it considerably and thus affect the quality of the fruit.

Sprays containing malathion can be used but hand clearing is best, especially where fruit is soon to be picked.

American gooseberry mildew is a fairly obvious condition affecting fruit which are covered with a white powdery growth (see pic left), which later turns brown. This is best controlled by keeping the bushes 'open' and cutting out affected shoots in the autumn. Regular spraying with benomyl or denocap will help control the condition.

Finally, watch out for leaf spot, which also shows itself in May as a series of dark spots on the foliage (see right). If left unattended the condition will get a hold and the spots will become more numerous, eventually turning the whole leaf brown and causing it to fall off. Again, the danger is that the quality of the fruit will suffer from the weakening effect of defoliation. Regular spraying with benomyl is the answer.

Be careful to follow the instructions about gathering fruit.

A Garden Is More Than Just Flowers

O ver the years there has been some fuss made about the May Bank holidays, with arguments as to why some of them should be abandoned. So far as I'm concerned - and it's a selfish view - they should all stay. The fact that many people are out on the road makes a jolly good reason for staying at home, and the long weekend provides an ideal opportunity to make progress in the garden at what is one of the busiest times of year.

Spring is one of my favourite times of the year, and so far my only disappointment has been a batch of wallflowers. They were a little exposed and never seemed to make much growth once transplanted last autumn.

One of the delights I have noticed in a number of places is Pieris 'Flame of the Forest'. Always a good show, it has brilliant red young growths, leaves which pass from red through pink and rich creamy-white before assuming green, and large, drooping panicles of flower. The clarity and strength of the various colours is always impressive, making this most certainly a shrub worth its place.

A second which has impressed is Chaenomeles speciosa the Japonica or Japanese Quince. Having started to flower in March, they continue to provide a show. Being prone to throw rooted suckers, I have harvested many of these over the years so that such plants occupy a variety of positions in the garden. Each seems to perform well, be it in full sun, partial shade, in open border or against a wall. The quality of the soil seems to have only marginal impact. Most varieties are in red and scarlet, but a search may reveal pinks and even white.

A gardener learns patience. A gardener (me) with four-year-old twin girls to accompany him, calls on that patience to grow and flourish. Why is it that the small spades of appropriate size are not attractive for children? Why is it that the wheelbarrow never has a full load of soil, manure or stone? Because it is always someone's turn to ride on top. No matter that weeds grow and jobs go slowly, it is really good fun!

This year they each have two plots - one for flowers and the other for salads. Attention spans can be limited, so in both cases we have settled for the faster-maturing specimens. Thus the vegetable spot will have lettuce, radish, beetroot and French beans.

For flowers, we will be choosing a range of seeds for interest.

Mixed cornflower (Centaurea cyanus) will give a variety of colours. But in these circumstances something like Polkadot, which only grows to 38-45cm (15-18in), and will not need staking is appropriate. Although having similar flowers, Love-in-a-mist (Nigella damascena) is useful. As a contrast to the mixed cornflowers, the clear blue of Miss Jekyll should do.

A dwarf mixed variety of Candytuft (Iberis) should be easy to grow, and then all that is needed is a few Nasturtiums, which will be sown in vacant soil around the garden.

Being in the garden with children reminds me that there is much else to see besides plants. We can recoil from slimy slugs and worms but delight in beetles, ladybirds and spiders running up and down our fingers. We can wait for ages for the grey squirrel to appear or watch the magpies raise a second brood in the top of a Lawsons Cypress. We can see the solitary carrion crow cause consternation as it threatens eggs and chicks and, if we are very quick, see the excitement of mating blue tits.

We (and I mean we) have nearly finished rebuilding a drystone wall about 120cm (4ft) forward from its previous position. Around 25 strides long (25 yards in real money), the wall had obviously provided shelter for a range of fauna from wrens to weedlice, millipedes to mice, beetles to bumble bees. Besides trying to accommodate all these original inhabitants, we have also built in a number of stone chambers which connect to gaps in the wall's courses.

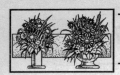

Blooming Marvellous

Following comparatively mild winters that lack the harsher frosts, flower buds can survive and the calm, sunny conditions without too much heavy rain is why the flower has persisted well. Today I was passing close of those electricity generating wind-farms. Of about thirty towers with their shiny, three-bladed propellors, only one was moving, and that very slow.

So it has been that the mass of cherry blossom has fallen slowly in its own good time, carpeting itself over turf below to turn the ground pink and white, rather than being dispersed by wind and spread thinly. While rhododendrons have carried bloom as good as any I can remember.

About this time of year, Chaenomeles speciosa is usually flowering well. That is also true on bare branches in February and should accompany fresh new foliage into June; a good long season. You might call it a Japanese quince or even just Japonica, and, in the strictest sense, both would be wrong, but it doesn't matter so long as you find a space for it or some of its near relatives.

Speciosa itself is a deciduous shrub, well-branched and with hard, almost spiny twigs. The alternate leaves are a dark, shiny green on top and grow to around 10cm (4in).

Flower of scarlet are borne in clusters of two or four along the previous season's growth and can be 2.5-5cm (1-2in) across. They are made up of five rounded petals which form a cup shape.

Growth is reasonably vigorous when they are young, but slows down to produce a rounded suckering bush, broader than it is tall.

Left to it own devices it may reach 2-3m (6-9ft), but when trained against a wall can exceed 4m (13ft).

There are quite a number of cultivars, not surprising since the

type was introduced from China before 1800. However, some tend not to be found in garden centres, though they may still be common in gardens.

'Simonii' is one to look out for. With blood-red semi-double flowers, it is of spreading habit growing to less than a metre in height, but stretching twice that far. It also has a long season, from February to June.

While most tend to be in shades of red and orange 'Snow' is, to state the obvious, white. The flowers are large and the upright bush grows to 1.8x1.8m (6x6ft). 'Nivalis' also flowers white but is larger extending to 3x3m (9x9ft).

'Moerloesii', better known to me as 'Apple Blossom', has flowers of pink and white and grows to around 2.5m (7.5ft); look also for 'Umbilicata' with large flowers of deep salmon pink and 'Geisha Girl' in orange pink. Others worth a mention include 'Atrococcinea' (blood crimson), 'Cardinalis' (deep salmon pink), 'Eximea' (deep brick red), 'Kermesina Semiplena' (scarlet, semi-double), and 'Phylis Moor' (large clusters of pink, semi-double flowers).

Equally attractive though generally smaller are cultivars of Chaenomeles x superba, which is a hybrid formed by crossing C. japonica with C. speciosa.

They tend to form dense, rounded bushes and are more suited to the front of a border.

'Crimson and Gold' has a spreading habit and forms a hummock to around 1x1.5m (3.3x5ft). Flowers appear in February and persist until May, with deep crimson petals and produced in abundance. It looks well trained to a wall, or set on a bank. For something lighter 'Hever Castle' comes in shrimp-pink, and 'Pink Lady' is a clear rose pink although darker in bud.

All are of spreading habit and tend to flower from February or March to May.

Finally there is Chaenomeles japonica itself. It makes a low, spreading thorny shrub with an abundance of bright orange flowers in April and May.

Your Gardening Week

✔ **LIFT BEDDING** Think about lifting spring bedding that will be followed with fresh plants for a summer display. Even though still in flower, delay in dealing with the summer bedding can reduce quality.

✔ **TIE RASPBERRIES** As new shoots continue to make growth on autumn-fruiting raspberries which were cut back in February, they should be tied in.

✔ **MORE SUGAR PEAS** If you made a first sowing of sugar peas during April, follow on now with a second sowing for succession. Sow in double rows and plan for a further sowing in June.

✔ **MOVE HOUSE-PLANTS** Only by sitting near a window for a long time are you likely to realise the amount of heat which can be generated by the sun in May. Most house plants prefer conditions without direct exposure, so move them away from south-facing windows.

✔ **PLANT LEEKS** Leeks for mid-season use can now be planted. Drop them into holes 15cm (6.6in) deep, 20cm(9in) apart in rows 30cm(13in) apart. Trim off the tips of the leaves, as they will undoubtedly wilt and can provide a foothold for disease. Fill the planting hole with water to settle in.

✔ **LET THE GRASS FLY** While dry conditions prevail, allow at least some grass mowings to remain over the lawn by removing the grassbox from time to time. They will provide a mulch to retain some moisture.

✔ **ALPINE STRAWBERRIES** Alpine strawberries can be sown now in a seed bed. When large enough, the seedlings can be set 30cm (13in) apart each way in a prepared bed.

✔ **FUCHSIA CUTTINGS** Take cuttings from fuchsias, to provide a batch of young plants which should flower in autumn.

Trees And Shrubs

By now, most of the early flowering trees and shrubs which have been prolific in their blooming will unfortunately be past their best and they will need attention if, next year, they are to do as well again.

They should not be allowed to set seed and should now be dead-headed. This should always be done by hand, (see left hand illustration), picking off the flower heads as they fade from laburnums, lilac, rhododendrons and azaleas. The heads will come away easily and it is a job which can be done on a daily basic, so as to enjoy the colourful blooms as long as possible.

Buddleia, which does so much to attract butterflies to the garden, will need tidying-up. Using secateurs, take out some of the old stems which have flowered and any others which may tend to make the bush overcrowded.

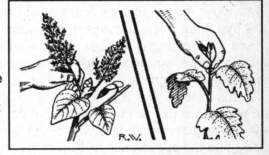

Another favourite that will require attention is the sweetly scented mock orange. Those bushes which may have become too big can be cut back hard after flowering. This should allow you to shape the bush and will induce better flowering next time round.

Of the border plants needing special attention just now are chrysanthemums which were set out last month. You can encourage growth and the production of blooms by 'stopping' them, by pinching out the growing tips within the first two weeks of the month (as in the illustration.

With warmer weather, keep an eye on the moisture requirements of all plants. In the case of chrysanthemums, not only will they require regular watering but also regular weekly feeds of a liquid fertiliser.

On the subject of moisture, to return to the rhododendrons, azaleas and other evergreen shrubs: mulch them with moist peat or well rotted compost. This is best done after a good shower and while the ground is still wet.

Your Gardening Week

Slow Springs Spell Patience

S low springs, when the weather is about two or three weeks behind its usual cycle, can be very frustrating for the gardener, although often the wait will be worthwhile when finally everything comes good.

Recent years have been good for the showy Lavateras; and the relatively mild winters have allowed this not entirely hardy tree mallow to make good growth. I do remember a time, though, when my seven or eight foot beauties had to be cut back to a foot, and still struggled to make new growth.

I suppose the prudent gardener would anticipate such eventualities by taking a few cuttings in mid-summer, keeping them in a closed propagating case until rooted, and providing the young plants with protection through the winter against their being needed as replacements in spring.

At this time of year it is heartening to see so many insects on the wing. Certainly a good number of bees should be in evidence b y now, together with less-welcome wasps. Happily this coincides with the appearance of flower on apples, pears and plums. Their ministration holds promise of a good set of fruit.

Life is a compromise! The back garden is not what it was. Our bearded collie is now some 16 months old, and though little more than a greyhound with long hair, delights in racing around the garden chewing branches and shoots.

Thus the lawn is furrowed and bare in meandering lines. In his favourite places, tree roots stand exposed where the soil has been worn away. That delightful little border that ran alongside the garden path has taken on a rather battered appearance as the dog charges back and forth across it.

The Ligularia Przewalski, which is a plant I thoroughly enjoy, has produced clumps of leaves, but they seem a little small. I'll have to move it before the flower spikes are knocked off. The strong strap leaves of a variegated Phormium tenax are tattered and limp at the ends, and I still await the appearance of Aconitum nappelus, the Monkshood, which may have succumbed to the constant battering of furry paws.

There is, however, one success story. What is a weed? By common consent a weed is a plant growing is a place where you do not wish it to be. Over the years my views have changed and plants which once I would have sought to discourage now find a home.

One such is lamium album, the white dead nettle whose light-green, toothed foliage and whorls of white flowers are not unattractive.

A clump had established in corner of this border and, being in bounds, had been left to flourish. Alongside I had planted Euphorbia griffithii 'Fireglow' whose reddish-orange flowers and bracts appear in April or early may. Spreading vigorously underground the euphorbia had infiltrated the nettles, which now it shows nicely above. Those stems not afforded such protection have again suffered the power of the paw.

Beside being prepared to view nettles as attractive, my real motivation for allowing them to grow is in the hope that they may also encourage butterflies, for the caterpillars of several species find them attractive as food plants.

I've not seen any signs of success, but the clumps I allow are only small. Perhaps is needs everyone to encourage a clump or two in order to create a food supply network sufficient to allow the species to spread.

Tasty Quince

I have already dealt with a number of the flowering quinces (Chaenomeles), but did not mention that the majority produce fruit. They are rounded and greenish-yellow in colour and can be used in wine and jelly, but the flavour is not as good as that of the true quince - Cydonia oblonga.

The quince makes a small tree which can be grown as a specimen in a lawn or in a larger garden as a group. As a standard it can reach to over 5m (16ft), though it may be grown as a half-standard, a bush or even fan-trained against a wall.

In making a decision about this, one of the key questions to be considered is the prevailing climate. The tree hails from warmer climes in Turkestan and Transcaucasia, and has been in cultivation since ancient times in such places as Mesopotamia, Crete and Greece, in which areas the fruits ripen to sweetness and can be eaten raw. Here the ripening process is not completed so the flavour remains acid and the texture rather gritty. Therefore the fruit should be converted to jams and jellies, while the odd slice will bring a little extra life to an apple pie or pudding.

In warmer areas the trees can be grown in the open, but require a sunny, sheltered position. In less favoured areas more protection is needed and the answer may be to try it as a wall-trained fan in a sun-catching corner.

While growing in most soils, the quince prefers a deep, light, fertile and moisture-retentive soil, and is well suited to a position beside pond or stream.

Left to its own devices it will form a deciduous tree with a crooked and irregular mode of growth. When fully grown it will reach around 4m (12ft) with a similar spread. Pruning and training can be difficult, and there is merit in buying a young tree already partly shaped as standard, half-standard or bush by the nursery.

The flowers are quite large, reaching 5cm (2in) across in white

or very pale pink. The bark is a pale grey and the oval leaves dark green, though they often turn to a rich yellow before falling.

Fruits vary and may be apple or pear-shaped, generally with a greyish-white down on the skin. With ripening they become a fine golden-yellow and fragrant.

Bare-rooted specimens can be planted between November and March, though container-grown specimens can be dealt with at any time. When preparing the planting pit, remove all traces of perennial weed and work in a dressing of general fertiliser together with a handful of bonemeal.

While many young trees require support, this is particularly true of the quince because of its crooked growth.

This support will be required during the formative years and until the main stem has gained sufficient strength to support the top growth.

Although one tree should be adequate to meet the culinary needs of most families, (unless into quince wine in a big way), where more than one is planted, they should be set 6m (20ft) apart, half-standards 4.5m (15ft) and bush trees at 3m (10ft).

Regular pruning will be needed up to the fourth year in order to achieve a goblet-shaped tree with a fairly open centre. This is achieved by cutting back half of the previous season's growth on the main branch framework during winter. Leave any outward-facing buds. Any side-shoots in competition with the leaders and any badly-placed or crowding into the centre can be cut back to two or three buds.

After the fourth year, pruning is limited to the removal of over-crowded shoots and any suckers or shoots that appear on the main stem. Fruit is carried on spurs and on the tips of the last season's growth.

A Medieval recipe for quince marmalade required the fruit to be peeled, quartered and boiled in red wine, strained, then boiled again in concentrated honey with added spiced wine and after setting to be sliced and served. Might just be worth a try!

Your Gardening Week

WORK FOR THE WEEK

 CHECK SUCKERS Suckers may start to appear on fruit trees, grafted ornamental trees, rhododendrons and roses. They are best removed when small by pulling away, rather than cutting.

 PLANT BRASSICAS Sprouting broccoli, Brussels sprouts and summer cabbage should all be ready for planting. Discourage cabbage root fly by placing collars round stems as appropriate.

 RUNNER BEANS Runner beans raised under glass can be planted out at this time. Sowings can now be made outdoors. In milder areas a second sowing later in June will provide for a late crop.

 STOP CODLING MOTH If codling moth is a problem, it can be controlled by hanging pheromone traps in apple and pear trees.

PINCH FRUIT Young growths appearing on trained fruit trees can be pinched out at the fourth leaf, though the leading growth at the end of each stem should be left. Plums, gages and sweet cherries will benefit from this attention.

 MORE SOWINGS Make sowings of carrots, turnips, beet, lettuce, spinach and ridge cucumbers.

FORGET-ME-NOT If forget-me-nots have been used in spring bedding schemes, the plants can be lifted and re-set in a spare corner, where they will ripen their seeds and spread them around. Many seedlings will germinate and can be transplanted as required.

 MORE MULCH Continue to apply and refresh mulches to discourage weed and conserve moisture.

FOR THE FUTURE Make sowings of herbaceous perennials to create plants for the future at comparatively low cost.

Water With Care

Providing water for either flower beds or, more particularly for vegetable plots is always a problem, but never more so than after a particularly dry summer followed by a dry winter.

With some parts suffering drought conditions already the warnings are going out. It cannot be too long before we shall be asked to save water and even to recycle it after washing and baths for other uses.

Such shortage is obviously a major concern for those who have vegetable plots. It is necessary to ensure that seed beds are sufficiently moistened to allow for germination. For this

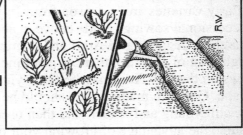

reason try and find shady spots for them, or be able to provide some shade in the form of screens, etc.

Give seed drills a good soaking from the watering can (see right) so as to get them off to a good start.

Again, when putting in young plants, soak the holes that are made for them and try to conserve moisture by shading them with covers of newspaper or upturned pots.

Before watering in general, hoe the area lightly between the plants (see left) firstly to keep weeds down (thus denying them the need for water) and to break up the top soil to allow water penetration. Application of the water is obviously best left till the evening or cooler part of the day, so as to lose as little as possible by evaporation.

Apply by a fine spray with not too much force and over a period (which may mean using one of the patented sprinkler units which sit on the ground) or by arranging for the hose end to be held perhaps in the handle of a fork. The idea is to simulate gently falling rain. Short, sharp bursts of water really do little good for the plants.

Turnip Time

I guess turnips are not as popular as they used to be; probably because there is such a choice of home-grown and imported vegetables available. These, having brighter colours and a less earthy appearance, are more likely to attract the impulse buyer. For me, it and the swede are two vegetables I would not do without - especially in stews and soups.

Turnips fall into two categories from a seasonal point of view: the early varieties, which do not store well; and the maincrop varieties, which can be lifted and stored.

Early varieties are in season from July to October, raised from successional sowings made between about the third week in March or beginning of April and continuing through to the beginning of July. So, there is just time to get a couple of short rows on the go! They may be flat, cylindrical or globular in shape. Quick to mature, they should be pulled while the roots are still young and tender, and then used within a few days. Of course the advantage of growing your own is that they can be pulled as needed.

Germination should be complete within ten days, with maturity reached anything from 6-11 weeks later depending on season and variety.

To follow on, maincrop varieties are sown, again in succession, from late July through to mid-August. Crops from these sowings will be ready for use or storage from the middle of October. While they may be left in the ground, in cold and wet areas it is advisable to get them into store by early November.

If, as I expect, you wish to make the most of the crop, then to ensure tender flesh and good flavour fast growth is essential. To achieve this the ground should be well manured and in good heart. In addition it is worth checking the pH and, if needed, liming to achieve a reading around neutral.

If by any chance the ground has not been prepared well in

advance, don't be tempted to embark on cultivation shortly before sowing. Turnips are brassicas, and like their relatives require firm ground, so at this stage make the best of what you've got. Just rake over the ground to create a tilth and work in a dressing of general fertiliser.

Sowings can be made in drills 37.5cm (15in) apart, though for earlies they can be brought a little closer. Once the seedlings are large enough to get hold of, start to thin, doing the job in stages until the earlies are 15cm (6in) apart, and the maincrop twice that.

A constant supply of water is essential to ensure steady growth, and in particular make sure they don't go short in dry spells. If these are followed by heavy rain, the roots may split.

Maincrop varieties to be stored should have the leaves twisted off and, after cleaning, can be set in boxes of sand. Kept like this in a dry shed, they can be drawn on through to March.

Swedes require similar conditions but are sown in early May in the North and late May in the South. Hardier, they can be left in the ground and lifted as required from October to March.

On turnips the small, black, jumping flea beetle can be a problem with an appetite which may decimate young leaves, particularly during periods of dry weather. Clubroot is also commonly found and mildew can appear in autumn.

Swedes are also affected by diseases common to brassicas and also suffer from brown heart, a condition caused by boron deficiency.

For early varieties of turnip, Purple Top Milan and Snowball are fine. The former is flat-rooted while the latter, as you might expect, is round with white flesh. It has a very acceptable flavour.

For maincrop, Golden Ball is a good all-round performer with compact roots of tender yellow flesh, good flavour and good keeping qualities. Green Globe has round roots and white flesh. Sowings of this variety can be made in August and September to provide 'greens' in March and April.

Hoe And Sow

A walk around the garden in the evening is a regular part of the daily ritual. Generally I am accompanied, if only by a hoe. It is easy and quite relaxing to disturb odd weeds in the borders, or run along a couple of rows in the vegetable plot. Doing it a little at a time like this prevents the job turning into a chore.

When the time comes to give plants a boost I apply a dressing of general fertiliser before wielding the hoe, taking care that none touches the foliage or stems of growing crops. That's feed and weed dealt with at one go.

There is always competition for a place in the sun, so crops which will cope with some shade are useful to have. While early radish and lettuce do better in an open position, as the summer matures, successional crops can be moved to more shaded zones. In the middle of summer the lettuce will be softer and fresher and the radish less stringy.

Many herbs will tolerate shade, especially mint. Sage and thyme like the sun but will do reasonably well in shade, while some of the medicinal herbs like balm and hyssop will also succeed.

Spinach, spinach-beet and rhubarb will all do reasonably well in some shade. They also seem less prone to run to seed in such situations.

Of the cabbage family, winter greens such as sprouting broccoli and kales will be quite successful.

They do not have to heart up, only producing edible shoots and leaves. Cabbages proper may form soft, loose heads, but be quite useful for cooking. Heading broccoli and cauliflowers on the other hand are unlikely to succeed, as they need good light to develop good, firm curds.

Beetroot is still one of the most popular of crops. It can be sown over a long period from early spring through to July.

Whether stored dry for cooking or pickled, it has a long availability for use.

Crops should be raised on ground which was manured for the
previous crop - fresh manure could cause fanging. While the
crop should thrive on the majority of soils, a pH of 6 to 6.4 is
ideal. Fertility can be boosted by applying a dressing of fertiliser.

Beet seed is peculiar in that it is made up of a cluster of several seeds, held in corky tissue. This means that they are easy to
handle and can be space-sown; but before doing that, soak the
seed overnight. This enables moisture to reach the seeds and
start germination more readily than if they are sown when dry.

Take out drills 25mm (1in) deep and 20-30cm (10-12in) apart.
Where the ground tends to be dry, the drill can be made a little
deeper and if needed can be watered along the bottom before the
seed is sown.

Space the seeds 7-10cm (3-4in) in the row. Given the make-up
of the seeds, more than one seedling may arise at each location.
These can be thinned when large enough to handle, leaving the
strongest to grow on.

Further thinning is achieved by removing and using alternate
roots when they reach baby-beet or golf-ball size. These young
roots have the best texture and taste. There is an argument for
increasing the number of successional crops and harvesting them
all at this sort of size.

Besides the traditional deep-red varieties try one of the golden-
fleshed ones for a little extra interest. These have the additional
advantage that the leaves may also be harvested and used like
spinach. A further advantage from this is that while the roots
themselves are a source of vitamin C, the leaves and stems contain both A and C.

The leaves can be harvested in the same way as spinach by
taking a few at a time from several plants. But don't jump in too
early; the plants need time to establish and be growing away
strongly first.

Your Gardening Week

 HARDY PRIMULAS Many of the hardy primulas can be raised from seed sown from now through to the end of the month. Germination may be erratic, but a little care and patience will provide plenty of plants for flowering next spring and summer.

 REMOVE FLOWERS If you have the time, patience, and can reach, there is merit in removing rhododendron flowers which have passed over, so that energy is not wasted in the production of seed.

 MORE ANNUALS The early season means that many annuals will pass their best earlier than in an average year. So make sowings of fast growing types which can be planted out as needed.

 PLANT DAHLIAS Dahlias raised from cuttings can now be planted out, provided they have been adequately hardened.

 PICK GOOSEBER-RIES Treat yourself by taking a few small gooseberries for an early pie. Select them from all over the bush, so that the exercise amounts to thinning and will encourage the remaining fruits.

 EARTH POTATOES Continue to draw earth around potatoes planted during March and April, aiming to complete the job by the end of the month.

 MULCH PARSNIPS Apply a mulch to the shoulders of parsnips to prevent the flesh from shrinking and cracking. This will reduce the chance of infection by canker.

 REMOVE SEEDLINGS Spring proved ideal for seed germination, and has resulted in the appearance of many seedlings. Often the tougher ones - trees for example - become established in places where the hoe will not reach, so do your best to pull them out before they become large and more difficult.

A Plant For Starters

Of all the summer foods, salads are undoubtedly the most popular even if only for their slimming attributes.

Salad plants help to make excellent starters (for those who don't have to watch their waistlines, too) whilst radishes are the salad plant which make excellent starters for even the most inexperienced of gardeners.

You do hear it said that some folk just cannot grow them-but even they will gather a goodly crop provided that they plant neither too deep nor too thickly. For summer choose either the traditionally shaped scarlet Glove, illustrated in the sketch, or the long white Icicle.

However, you do not need much space, for you can even grow them in the flower border, dotted amongst the perennials.

All you need is an area or patches of fine soil. If yours is on the sandy side, then turn in some peat or leaf mould to help

retain moisture, which is a prime requirement for radishes.

Choose a nice shady position where you can take out a drill or two, o where you can find space to 'station seed' and sow thinly, no more than half an inch deep.

Another method is to sprinkle the seed on top of the soil and then to gently rake them in. Finally, water them well.

Given that you have scattered the seeds well, there should be no need for thinning, but do so if they are less than an inch apart.

Then, to assure that you can keep pulling the crop over a number of weeks, continue sowing some of the seeds at then day intervals throughout July and August.

There is not a lot that can go wrong with radishes and they grow at a fast rate, so that within six weeks you should be pulling them and cutting them up for the salad bowl.

Kill Or Cure?

Last year I cleared out a good half of the strawberry bed and planted new stock taken from runners. The young plants settled in and have grown well to produce sturdy specimens which, during late May and early June, were clothed with plenty of flowers.

To ensure that there is some good quality fruit, I pinched out a few flowers on a number of plants so they would not be overloaded. They and the rest are now producing swelling fruit. The only problem now is to see them through to full ripeness.

There are always those who would get there before me. While I don't mind a few losses in the interest of nature conservation, damage has to be kept to a reasonable minimum.

As the fruit swells and increases in weight, it gradually pulls down the stems until, if not prevented, the fruit will touch the ground where it may be dirtied by splashes of mud sent up by heavy rain or - worse still - damaged so that a lesion is made which can provide a breeding ground for botrytis.

The way to prevent this is by spreading a layer of straw beneath the foliage of the plants, providing a cushion on which the fruit can rest. Before doing this, it's a good idea to spread slug bait around the bed. If left to their own devices, slugs will surely find a way to the crop.

Birds are also a potential problem, especially blackbirds who start sampling the fruit long before it is ripe. The only way to stop this is with netting. In the past I used to lay light netting loosely along the rows of plants. Birds could still reach the fruit if they tried hard enough and then, in their excitement, become entangled in the netting. It was a regular and time-consuming job to try and free them without damage.

Now I make a low framework over the bed and stretch the netting quite taught, making sure there are no loose edges where they may try to find a way in. By and large this cures the problem; but I also set a few bird-scarers of foil tied to canes, in an attempt to keep them away.

Kill or cure; that is what water can do. Giving the right amount of water to keep plants and crops in the best of condition is probably one of the most difficult tasks that any gardener faces.

Although things have improved in recent years, with greater emphasis on standing pot plants on trays of pebbles and the like, there is little doubt that the majority of them in home and glasshouse are killed by kindness. Too much water produces sodden compost with little or no air. This causes the leaves to flag, and it is not difficult to convince yourself that these symptoms indicate drought - and so more water is given. The result of this deadly cycle is suffocation!

Make sure you check the state of the soil before giving water, then give a good soaking. Allow the excess to drain away freely, and only water again as the pot begins to dry out. This will ensure plenty of opportunity for air to permeate the soil.

The same general rule applies outdoors. Don't give small amounts of water regularly. When water is needed, thoroughly soak the ground, creating a deep reservoir of moisture which will attract roots to grow down into the ground. Light watering which does not penetrate deeply will encourage shallow roots to develop.

These will be prone to damage when the sun appears and dries out the soil surface.

Your Gardening Week

It's Mulching Time

Mulching is a practice that seems to have grown in popularity and with good reason. It has a number of benefits in the garden by supressing weed growth, restricting water loss through evaporation and, if organic material is used, increasing soil fertility. It also has the fringe benefit of reducing the amount of work needed to keep the garden in good order and, depending on the materials used, can produce an attractive and tidy finish.

Traditional mulching materials are straw, strawy manure, leaf mould, lawn mowings (provided the lawn has not been recently treated with chemicals), peat and similar organic materials, not to mention the product of the compost heap. I hesitate to mention peat, not only because of concerns about the effects of removing the peat on sites of ecological importance but because, in this context, it is quite expensive. At least the other items can be considered to be recycling or come from a renewable source.

Wood chippings or bark are also useful. Their popularity is certainly in evidence on new local authority planted areas, generally I guess to suppress weeds and limit the amount of weedkiller application by your environmentally friendly council. Not only that, but chemicals tend to be expensive. I invested in a reasonably robust chipper last year, and so produce some of my own, but a big heap of prunings only seems to go a little way when reduced to chips, and processing takes quite a long time. Perhaps a better bet would be to get together with a group of other users and purchase by the wagon loan.

Polythene sheeting has found a niche for this work, but can become unsightly and in my view is best restricted to the vegetable plot. Black polythene is suitable. Sheeting that is black beneath and white on top has the benefit of reflecting light back onto the plants, while keeping the roots cooler to some extent.

If suitable material is difficult to come by, old carpeting, card-

board or even papers can be pressed into service, but the decorative impact does perhaps need to be taken into account.

Before applying any mulch, there are three principles to consider.

The first is that the ground should be well soaked in advance. This is because besides helping to retain water in the ground by limiting evaporation, the mulch will also restrict penetration by fresh water into the soil beneath.

Secondly, the soil should be cleared of weeds, for even small weeds compete for water. Any that are well established and tough enough may grow through the mulch, at least partly defeating the object.

Thirdly, the year should be sufficiently advanced for the soil to have warmed. Certainly it should not be frozen, and ideally it will have had a fair amount of sunshine to raise the temperature. If a mulch is applied when the ground is cold it will act as a thermal blanket and keep the heat out, reducing beneficial activity within the soil.

Despite the mulch, the need to give water may well arise. If the mulch has been dry for some time it may well form an effective crust. This has to absorb water itself before allowing water to penetrate through into the soil. The by-product of this is that a chain of water has been set up through the mulch and will allow some evaporation before the dry layer is formed again.

I have employed two methods to work round this problem. On crops like raspberries I've used the lay-flat type of hosepipe, which is full of holes and allows water to dribble out along the rows. By laying it along the row before setting the mulch in place it has been an easy matter to connect a perforated hosepipe to the end of the row and water all along at one go.

Secondly, with specimen plants that have a root system which penetrates the ground more deeply, a suitable large plant pot sunk into the soil within the root run, provides an easy and fast receptacle to take water from either hose or can. The water then enters the soil from the reservoir at its own pace.

Your Gardening Week

WORK FOR THE WEEK

 ASPARAGUS AND ARTICHOKES While the harvesting of asparagus should have ceased, in order to give foliage a chance to develop and so feed the roots for next year's crop, globe artichokes should be harvested before they begin to flower.

 TOP-DRESS CUCUMBER As the roots of indoor cucumbers grow through the mound of compost on which they are planted, apply extra sustenance by applying about 5cm (2in) of top dressing.

 SOW COREOPSIS There is just time to make a sowing of hardy perennial varieties of Coreopsis in a seed bed, prior to planting out in autumn.

 VARY SPRAYS If you have to resort to chemical sprays to combat pests or disease, try to introduce some variety. Repeated applications of the same chemical may hasten the build-up of resistance. Good cultural practises which reduce the need to spray at all, should obviously be a priority.

 CLEAN LUPINS As lupins pass out of flower, cut off the faded blooms. This prevents them setting seed, conserves energy and reduces the chance of the crown dying out - which often happens with the best varieties. Once the flower has passed, lupins leave an empty space. Consider growing them as annuals and replace after flowering among later-flowering bedding plants.

 SOW SEEDS Swedes sown now will provide a crop from October through to March. If club root is a problem, choose a resistant variety.

MORE CARROTS This is about the last chance to sow intermediate or long-rooted varieties of carrot to harvest in September or October.

 LATE RUNNERS In milder areas, a late sowing or runner beans can be made for harvesting through to the end of October.

Summer Veg Sowing

Any space left now in the vegetable garden is pretty valuable, for there are several crops which you can sow now to mature for autumn and into winter.

The first thing to remember when sowing seeds for such crops, is that by the time they are beginning to mature, weather conditions will be very much different, with shorter days and less sunshine. Try, then, to put them where they will get the maximum benefit from the shorter hours of sunshine but where they will find some protection from winds.

The main thing to remember about sowing at this time is

that the main requirement of the seeds is moist conditions in which to germinate. Never let them dry out and, to ensure that they get off to a good start, hoe in a light dressing of Growmore or fertiliser of your choice.

One crop you can start now which is somewhat different is radishes for the winter. They are certainly different in appearance to the summer crop, with roots which can in some cases weigh up to 11lb (5kg). Black Spanish (above). is one such radish. It is a hardy radish with white flesh and a good flavour. This really is very good with either meat or salads. You can leave them in the ground and lift as required from the autumn, or store them in sand.

Greens are always welcome in the kitchen. One you can plant now is Celtic Hybrid (pictured right), a ballhead which is rock firm and which can be left standing until February.

There are many others of course; you can make your own choice, based on your table needs and cropping requirements by going through your favourite catalogue. Do remember that whatever your choice, water will be a prime requirement.

Your Gardening Week

The Bells, The Bells

I've a hunch that most gardens would benefit from a few clumps of bluebells. Glorious in natural settings, they are an essential component in our countryside, bringing joy to spring walks. Equally they add to the garden scene, but require an informal setting to be at home.

Fortunately the name bluebell is well recognised, for in the botanists' world they have experienced a number of re-classifications. Starting out as Scilla - a nice, simple and easily remembered name - they changed to Endymion, and now have become the less appealing Hyacinthoides. All this is truly academic, for the plant we have is constant.

There are two types in widespread use: H. non-scripta, our own native form, and H. hispanica, still to me the Spanish Squill. Both grow to 30-45cm (12-18in) and are to be had in blue, pink and white. The Spanish form sports larger bells and stouter stems.

While they may be grown in a border, if the situation is available, they naturalise well beneath the dappled shade of trees and look well among ferns, where their flowers occur before opening of the fronds. They thrive best in a heavyish loam or even clay soil, provided it does not become waterlogged.

Planting can take place in autumn, with bulbs set 75-100mm (3-4in) deep. They should generally be left undisturbed, but once thick clumps have formed they may be lifted and divided.

Mention of ferns reminds me that there are many different forms in cultivation. In areas of my own garden they provide interesting and in some cases substantial elements, which generate a restful green background to complement more colourful plants. Again the botanical world of ferns has seen many name changes, but so far as I know those to come are current. Like so many groups within the plant world, there are more to choose from than you might imagine and there is a distinct danger of becoming a collector.

Dryopteris provides a large genus of ferns, some of which are native. D. filix-mas has feathered and crested foliage which grows to 30-90cm (2-3ft). It is variable in form, and has given rise to many named cultivars and varieties in common use. Its common name of "male fern" is due to its robust appearance rather than any particular proclivities. D. austriaca spinulosa - the broad shield or broad buckler fern - has finely cut fronds often used in floristry.

Benefiting from a shady position, planting should take place in March or April before the fronds unfurl. A light, moist soil with plenty of leaf-mould is ideal and an annual top dressing of leaf-mould will help.

Osmunda regalis, the Royal Fern, is one of the largest in the world with fronds growing to 60-360cm (2-6ft). Interestingly, its name may be derived from a Saxon word meaning strength, or from osmunder, one of the names for the thunder god Thor. It needs moist, acid soil conditions and can be grown in sun or shade. The fronds colour well in autumn, and the roots are the source of osmunda fibre, used to grow orchids.

Having mentioned the male fern I'll also include Athyrium, the Lady Ferns, not because of any non-discrimination policy, but for their attraction. In this case the common name is a reference to the soft appearance of the fronds which come in delicate, finely divided forms.

A. filix-faemina, in its various forms, is probably the most common fern to be found in northern temperate regions. Fronds vary from 60-90cm (1-3ft) in length, and may be 30cm (6in) across. Of the forms A. f-f. Corymbiferum has striking fronds, while 'multifidium', 'plumosum cristatum' and 'Victoriae' are all worth looking for. This latter cultivar is unusual in having narrow, dainty fronds, the pinnules or leaves of which criss-cross one another to form a trellis pattern.

Choose a moist, shady border for these, and a soil with plenty of leaf-mould.

You Can't Grow Onions There

While spring is often a riot of bloom and colour in the garden, there is often a lull or reduction in the display as early flowering trees and shrubs in particular, shed their petals and don their less colourful leaves.

Spring is also accepted as the time for bulbs and traditionally we plant masses of them, looking forward to the time when their appearance heralds the passing of winter and the start of a new growing season.

But there are other bulbs; bulbs that provide a continuity of flowering through the summer months and which, I am sure, deserve to be more widely planted.

While this is not the season to be planting them, it is a good time to see them in bloom, to make notes and resolve to plant some in autumn or spring.

Alliums, the decorative flowering onions, probably suffer from their association with their vegetable-plot relatives with whom we spend time trying to discourage bolting to flower. Yet these bulbs provide a range of attractive plants in a useful variety of sizes and colours.

Conversely, every garden has a space or place in which an allium will grow. Their value in the vegetable plot in the form of onions, chives or shallots is easily matched by their presence in the flower garden.

Alliums carry their flowers in spherical heads held aloft on smooth, bare stems, opening up the possibility for interesting associations with lower-growing plants.

While many come to flower in June and July, a broad selection can produce a succession of displays stretching from April through to September.

As its name suggests, Allium giganteum is a big 'un, achieving

heights of 120-180cm (4-6ft) depending on the situation. Its heads are a tight mass of mauve or pinkish purple flowers, held in a ball around 12.5cm (5in) across.

They appear in mid-summer at a time when the foliage is dying back, so it is a good idea to plant behind some lower plant, to blend the stems to the ground. It needs a light soil, otherwise the bulbs tend to rot in winter.

Allium afflatuense flowers more freely and is cheaper to buy. Growing to 60-90cm (2-3ft), its flowers are rosy-purple in May and early June, with dense round umbels which persist and later fade to the colour of straw and may be cut.

Allium christophii (syn. A. albopilosum), grows only to around 60cm (2ft) in height, but then there are the flowers. These, appearing freely in June, are stiff-petalled, star-shaped, rosy-mauve and are carried in umbels 20-30cm (8-12in) across. These die and dry on the plants, persisting into autumn but may also be harvested for use in floral art.

If you are happy to live with a plant which establishes rapidly and has a predisposition to spread, then A. moly is ideal. Commonly known as the Golden Garlic, it grows to 20cm (8in) with upward-looking branches of bright yellow flowers which appear in May.

Another fast increasing species is A. caerulium. While less imposing in stature than many of the others, it gives a good quality blue flower in July. Somewhat variable in height, it may carry flowers on 10cm (4in) stems or yet again attain 30cm (1ft) or even more.

There are many other species to choose from and some hunting around may be necessary to find a supplier for a particular one, but the reward is worth the effort.

Most are fully hardy, but odd ones may succumb in a bad winter.

All-in-all they offer a range and diversity to satisfy any taste and need only a minimum of attention. Give some a try - you could become hooked.

Your Gardening Week

✔ **TIME TO PRUNE** Early-flowering shrubs which have finished their displays such as lilac, diervilla, forsythia, deutzia and so on can be pruned if required. Remove weaker growths first, and then any which are overcrowding or invading space where they are not wanted.

✔ **PANSIES** Make a sowing of winter-flowering pansies for a display next winter/spring.

✔ **RASPBERRY BEE-TLE** If raspberry beetle is an expected problem, it may be controlled by dusting the fruit clusters with derris some ten days after the flowers have gone over. Never dust open flowers which are still being visited by bees.

✔ **GOOSEBERRIES** Gooseberries in full fruit should be picked over. Remove young green berries for cooking or preserving; but leave an ample number to mature for dessert. I would normally advise watering in hot, dry periods and feeds with liquid manure, but hesitate to do so in current circumstances. By the time you read this it'll probably be pouring!

✔ **PINCH PEAS** Remove the growing points from early peas which have finished flowering to concentrate energies on pod production.

✔ **BOOST GLADIOLI** Better blooms can be expected on gladioli if they are boosted with a programme of liquid feeding. From now through to the first appearance of flower, make an application every 10-14 days.

✔ **LATE RUNNERS** It seems but a moment since the season for sowing runner beans started, and yet already it is at an end. A final sowing can be made in milder areas, to produce crops until the end of October.

✔ **FEED ANTIR-RHINUMS** Antirrhimuns can be improved if weak liquid manure is applied at fortnightly intervals.

Wish You Were Here

For many - particularly those with children at school - this is the time when thoughts turn to holidays.

If you are a gardener too, whether it be indoor or outdoor, there really is quite a lot to do before you take the pet to the local animal hotel and close that door behind you for a fortnight away.

Outdoors you will need to give a good general tidy-up; dead head flowers in bloom (particularly roses) and keep a wary eye open for aphids and other bugs, which should be sprayed before you go and immediately upon you return.

Grass, which needs regular weekly cutting now, should be trimmed - probably the last outside job you do before you go away.

If you have a glasshouse, then leave vents open, for a good circulation of air is necessary to reduce temperatures on sunny days and to ensure the plants remain healthy. Shading, too, will help to reduce scorching temperatures, either by painting the  glass with a propriatary paint, or by fitting, (albeit temporary), blinds.

A major worry for holidaymakers are house plants. Obviously they should not be left on windowsills where they will receive the full heat of the sun. Best to remove them to a cool shed, or garage. Failing that, stand them in the bath or on the sink draining board.

Left in wither position you can rig up a simple watering device, which should see them through adequately until you return.

Place the pot plants around a bucket filled with water and connect each plant to the water supply by water-drenched wicks or woollen cords. A bucket of water should meet the demands of three or four pot plants (pic left), especially if they are left in a shaded place.

Another method is to put them outside in a trench cut in a shaded area of the garden (pic right). When you have placed the pots in the trench, fill around them with peat which should be soaked with water.

If you can't get a neighbour to give them a look now and again, either method should keep them happy. After all, they can't drop you a card saying "Wish you were here!"

Your Gardening Week

Hoe And Grow

With a mixed bag of weather, the rain accompanied by strong breezes will be sufficient to remove a fair number of smaller branches from trees, contributing to nature's regular pruning cycles.

Then the thunderstorms, full-flushed with downpours enough to top-up any number of expectant water-butts. While the rain is to be welcomed, its force can be sufficient to put a quick end to loose-petalled displays on the likes of cherries and early- flowered roses. But then the sun can be of a strength that causes this sometime 'mad dog' to limit exertions on some days to early morning and late evening.

These alternating conditions mean that one tool - the hoe - will be in regular use to take threefold benefit of its action. The most obvious of these is the prevention of weed growth, which reduces competition for nutrients, light and water among growing crops. Its use for purely cosmetic purposes in established borders is, however, to my mind, an indication that more planting is needed to cover the ground.

The second job accomplished by hoeing is water conservation. Rain, having percolated through the ground, is available at depth in the soil, and finds its way both to plant roots and back towards the surface, by the process of capillary attraction through the small air-spaces in the soil structure. The process is driven to some extent by wind and sun causing evaporation at the surface. This draws more replacement water from lower down, thus depleting reserves. By using the hoe to destroy soil structure at the surface, capillary chains are broken and a 'dust mulch' is formed.

I think this action has a further benefit, in that when sun follows rain the loose, moist soil can bake and form a crust. When subsequent rain falls, this can cause a degree of run-off rather than percolating into the ground.

So hoeing to meet these changing conditions, besides being a pleasurable task that takes you to all parts of the garden, has a variety of benefits. However care must be taken in the vicinity of shallow-rooted crops, where a mulch is a better proposition.

While we are well into the season for harvesting crops, remember to keep clearing ground as the opportunity arises and make further successional sowings. Lettuce, carrots, chicory, beetroot, radish and spinach can all go in now and for the next few weeks.

Most maincrop varieties should already be on their way, and now I choose small plots and broadcast quicker-maturing varieties of carrot, beet and radish. Sown thinly, they can be pulled when they are still young and tender.

French beans will perform well in warm, moist conditions and successional sowings may continue through to mid-July. The latest sowings will need cloche protection in October, but should continue to crop until the end of that month.

If you have not finished planting winter greens, make the job your highest priority. Broccoli, Brussels sprouts and cabbage should all be in about now, together with autumn-maturing varieties of cauliflower.

As July approaches, have spring cabbage varieties ready for sowing from the middle of the month through to mid-August. They will be ready for planting out in September/October.

Leek planting is a job I find I enjoy. Rather than pulling out drills or making planting holes with a trowel, it's easy to make rapid progress by making 15cm (12in) deep holes with an old spade-handle dibber.

Dropping seedlings into the holes and settling them in with water rather than having to backfill and firm, is quickly achieved.

Fresh peas straight from the pod take some beating. An early, wrinkled variety such as Kelvedon Wonder can be sown through to mid-July and should follow on from the maincrop by coming into season during September and early October.

More Summer Bulbs

The choice of summer-flowering bulbs is far wider than we have touched on, and the names a little more complex.

Here is one to chew on - Ornithogalum. Perhaps the best known of these is O. umbellatum, the Star of Bethlehem, which flowers in April and May, but whose white and green petals only open when the sun is shining. While it is hardy, the same cannot be said for O. thyrsoides (or O. lacteum), which will not survive the winter. Known delightfully as 'Chincherinchees' after the noise made by dry flower stems rubbing together in the breeze of South Africa, its bulbs can, however, be planted in March in light soil and a sunny position, where it will first bloom in July and continue in succession until autumn.

Stems, of which as many as three may appear from each bulb, vary between 40-75cm (16-30in) in height and carry dense spikes of cup-shaped flowers in white and with yellow stamens. These can be picked while still in bud and will stand for weeks in a vase, provided the water is changed regularly.

Because the growing season is shorter than in its native climate, the leaves fail to develop fully and are unable to build up the bulb for flowering in successive years. This can be remedied by growing in a frame or cool glasshouse.

Ornithogalum arabicum (or O. corymbosum) is reasonably hardy, but may require winter protection. This, however, is a precaution worth taking, for it is among the most handsome of the species. Growing to 40cm (16in) or more, the stems carry a corymb of around a dozen flowers in shining white and with a glistening black ovary in the centre. Saucer-shaped, each will be 5cm (2in) across and scented.

I won't mention summer flowering lillies on this occasion, but from the same family comes Camassia, whose name derives from the North American Indian word 'Quamash'. While apparently the Indians used to gather the bulbs of some species for

food, I don't know which they were. However, it would be a shame to lose out on the opportunity to enjoy the tall stems and loose racemes of flower which are graceful in a border or naturalised in a woodland setting.

Cammassia leichtlinnii is a strong grower and attains 60-90cm (2-3ft), with rosettes of 30cm (1ft) long leaves from which arise the stems bearing long spikes of flowers in deep mauve-blue or purple. The variety 'alba' has creamy white flowers and glaucous foliage and there are double forms available.

C. quamash (or C. esculenta) is shorter to 45cm (18in) with variable violet-blue flowers.

Choose a moist soil in sun or dappled shade, and plant 75mm (3in) deep in autumn. Once established seed may be produced which can be sown in March, or extra stock may be had by lifting every third year and detaching the offsets.

The genus sisyrinchium affords us a number of plants of interest. Related to the iris they produce tufts of narrow leaves which die back after flowering. For preference the soil should be a sandy loam enriched with leaf mould in a sunny position.

Sisyrinchium brachypus reaches 15cm (6in) with flowers of buttercup-yellow from June to August. S. iridiflorum has narrow leaves to 37cm (15in), topped by flowers in white, each enhanced with a purple centre and purple stripes on the outside. These appear in succession from June to October. S. straitum grows to 60cm (2ft) with masses of straw-yellow flowers striped purple on the back and in season from June to September.

When someone mentions scilla, a normal reaction would be to think of blue flowers in spring. Again there are species for other seasons.

One such is Scilla peruviana, named by accident after the ship Peru which brought it to these isles, rather than its area of origin in the Mediterranean. Growing to 15cm (6in) or more, it blooms in May-June bearing up to a hundred star-shaped flowers of variable blue held in a dense pyramid. The large bulb, best grown in a warm sunny position, may need winter protection.

Your Gardening Week

WORK FOR THE WEEK

 CYCLAMEN Make a sowing of Cyclamen persicum for flowering in 15-18 months.

 SOW CHICORY Chicory can be sown now for harvesting in October/November. Sow thinly in rows 30cm apart, and thin to 25cm after germination

 LAST RUNNERS In milder areas a last sowing of runner beans can be made around now. On more advanced crops, prepare to apply a mulch and embark upon a programme of liquid feeding during July and August.

 NEW RUNNERS Strong healthy strawberry runners can be selected for propagation. Plunge a small pot for each runner to root into, taking not more than four from reach parent plant.

 HOUSE PLANT HOLIDAY Many house plants will benefit from being moved outdoors for the summer. Where they are in ornamental containers take extra care to see that these are not broken.

 SOW TURNIPS Sow turnips for an October crop, and then delay sowing until late July for maincrop varieties.

 TOMATO MULCH Recently planted outdoor tomatoes will benefit from a mulch of manure or compost over the roots.

 STOP MELONS Melons growing in frames need stopping when the stems have reached the sides. The flowers need careful pollination to develop properly, and all on a plant should be dealt with at the same time.

 LEAF CUTTINGS African violets, begonias, gloxinias, peperomias and streptocarpus can all be propagated now by taking leaf cuttings.

 MORE ANNUALS Sow quick-maturing annuals such as clarkia, candytuft and cornflower to fill any gaps you might have in borders.

Dahlias By The Dozen

One of the most colourful of summer flowering plants for the border is the dahlia. They come in a mass of different colours from pure white to the deepest of purples with full rainbow of colours in between, augmented by bi-colours.

Even then there are so many variations in the shape of the flowers from the ragged looking cactus type to the delicate, quilled pompons and "decorative" (see left illustration).

To grow them well, the basic work has to be done in the autumn, of course, with deep digging, the introduction of manure or compost and a dressing of bonemeal.

Given that sort of start, by mid-July, depending on type, the plants could have reached anything up to 60cm (2ft) in height.

Check, as they grow, to ensure that they are well

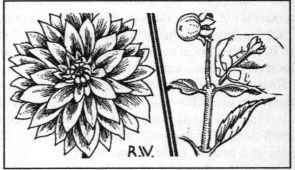

tied to stakes and feed them every fortnight with a liquid feed applied, preferably, when the soil is damp after rainfall, or after watering by hose.

Dahlias are loved by flower arrangers who will be even more delighted by blooms carried on long stems. You achieve this by disbudding.

The form of the plant is that a flower bud is carried at the top of the main stem, whilst beneath this you will notice two smaller buds growing from leaf axils. These two buds should be removed by pulling them with the fingers (see right illustration), allowing the remaining bud the benefit of food and water taken in by the plant

Once flowering is in progress keep dead-heading to prolong the flowering period.

Plants For A North Wall

With the number of bright, sunny days in the run-up to summer, it is easy to forget the shadier parts of the garden; especially walls and fences with a northerly aspect. Yet if you have such a position, it presents a further opportunity to add interest and soften a stark feature.

Of course walls vary, in that one with an open aspect might pick up a deal of reflected light. One facing another wall at close proximity may be very dark, and have the additional disadvantage of creating a wind-tunnel. So here my thoughts are of a north-facing wall with a generally open aspect, but some shelter from the worst of the cold winds and frost. I suppose the options lie between choosing something ornamental and something productive, or even a combination of the two.

Roses normally prefer a reasonable amount of sun, but ramblers will do quite well in such situations. With a little patience, climbing roses - as opposed to ramblers - can be encouraged to reach the top of the wall, where they escape the shaded conditions and benefit from further light.

One of the showiest of climbers for a north-facing wall is Hydrangea petiolaris. Although it may be grown as a shrub, more commonly it is chosen to cloth walls, fences or even trees. In these situations its vigour and self-clinging ability may cause it to spread to 20m (70ft). While young shoots are a refreshing green, with maturity the older stems have attractive, peeling bark. The leaves are sharply toothed and a vivid green, smooth on the upper surface with down on the veins beneath.

Hydrangea petiolaris can be slow to establish and so is best planted in a prepared plot. It may also require a little guidance and support until it becomes attached to the wall. New plants may be had from layers or by taking half-ripe shoots in early July. I have found that the cuttings can be a little difficult, but by taking more than you need and setting them in a frame an adequate proportion will root.

Clematis are a bit of a gamble, and the likelihood is that you will only establish by trial and error what will do in your situation. Most will bud up without the benefit of direct sunlight, but in colder areas montana and alpine types are likely to be safer. Of the large-flowered hybrids, the ever useful Nelly Moser is worth trying. A vigorous grower to 3.5m (12ft), with flowers 17cm (7in) across in rosy-mauve with a carmine bar, she does tend to bleach in the sun and so a shady position is beneficial in this respect. Comptesse de Bouchard, in bright mauve-pink, is also vigorous but less tall.

One of those plants that I have always admired for its presence, that indefinable something that suggests quality but without ostentation, is Garrya elliptica.

The genus contains a number of species, each of which is dioecious, which means to say that the male and female flowers are borne on separate plants. The male plant of G. elliptica is a magnificent evergreen, handsomely furnished with shiny, dark green, wavy-edged leaves of elliptic shape. During January and February the plant is draped with a profusion of silky, silvery, grey-green slender catkins. The female form is less commonly found but should not be discounted. While less attractive at catkin time, they do have the merit of long clusters of deep purple-brown fruits in autumn. Bear in mind it will be necessary to have both male and female forms close to one another or fertilisation will not occur, and fruits will not form.

Apparently succeeding in all types of well-drained soil, this Garrya is ideal for a north-facing wall. Its only weakness is the need to be protected by trees or other buildings from the full effects of icy winds. Young plants can improve in form if shoot tips are pinched out to encourage branching.

Propagation is effected either by making 10cm (4in) cuttings from mature wood in August and inserting them in a coldframe with sandy soil, or by pegging down and layering shoots in September.

Sow Herbaceous Perennials

The season is moving on, but there is still time to get stuck in and sow many of the herbaceous perennials. Much of any seed catalogue is made up of annuals, the plants that have to be grown afresh each year; but for me the real value is in hardy herbaceous perennials, which repay the investment in them time and time again.

The description is generally given to plants which die back to ground level each winter and then reappear from a perennial root system the following spring. Many of them, such as delphiniums and paeonies, do this naturally while others, such as romneya, are cut back by frost.

While there is merit in growing them in a special herbaceous border, the average garden is too small to justify this. In these circumstances I feel that they are best incorporated among shrubs and associated with annuals so that a mixture similar to that found in nature is created. While maintenance may be easier in a dedicated border it has the disadvantage of looking bare through the winter months. However it can be brightened up by interplanting with bulbs or spring bedding plants such as wall-flowers and forget-me-nots. These will augment early-flowering herbaceous plants such as helleborus and bergenia.

I've preached before that tidy, bare earth is a sign of wasted effort and the same is true of bark or woodchip mulches, except while new plantings grow to fill their alloted space. While ground cover plants may be considered a good option - for they require little maintenance once established - the majority have nothing like the same impact as a good range of herbaceous plants with variety in colour, foliage, form and season.

General practice is to buy full-grown plants from the nursery-man but, when bought in numbers sufficient to cover ground quickly, the cost soon mounts up - so try some seed! A little patience and a little satisfying work will soon produce more

plants than you can cope with. The only drawback being that some of the more popular varieties will not come true from seed. On the plus side, plants grown from seed have hybrid vigour and are generally stronger than those produced vegetatively.

Ideally, sowing should take place straight away, so there is little time for advanced planning; however, there isn't much that cannot be found at home. Depending on the amount of time available for maintenance you might like to select newer varieties of popular forms which require little staking and tying.

Seed can be broadcast in boxes or set in shallow drills in a nursery plot. In either case it should be sown thinly. In boxes use your usual seed compost. Outside, prepare the seed bed by creating a fine tilth and applying general fertiliser at 113g (4oz) to the square yard before the final raking. As a rule of thumb cover the seed to its own depth.

What to look for? One favourite which always does well in my garden is Echinops ritro, the 'Globe Thistle.' Its name is derived from the Greek echinos, a hedgehog, and opsis- an apt description for the flower heads which resemble a rolled-up hedgehog! The violet globular heads grow on stems which reach over a metre and open into a mass of small flowers. For added interest they are also popular with bees.

The 'Midsummer Daisy,' Erigeron speciosus, grows to 45cm (18in) with typical composite flowers of violet-blue with a yellow centre appearing in summer. Perhaps not for connoisseurs, it nevertheless is a reliable space-filler. Of greater interest is the 'Blanket Flower', Gaillardia, which is normally available in mixed varieties. The flowers, though composite again, puff up to form bright balls of colour and are useful for flower arranging.

One garden plant which has become naturalised in some parts of the country is the Valerian, Centranthus ruber. Growing to 75cm (2.5ft) it has reddish-pink flowers held well above the foliage on slender stems, and you may come across a white form as well. Where new plants establish from self-set seed they seem to like the crevices of stone walls as a foothold.

WORK FOR THE WEEK

 LIFT BULBS Spring bedding bulbs, such as tulips and hyacinths which were set in nursery rows to complete their growth, should be about ready for lifting, cleaning, drying and storing.

 SUMMER PRUNE Wall-trained plums and cherries, with the exception of Morello, can have side-shoots which made growth over the last couple of months, shortened back by a third. Spread the work over several weeks.

 SOW PARSLEY Parsley to stand the winter should be sown now. In colder areas it may be transplanted to a cold frame or given cloche protection. Make a further sowing in three weeks.

 GIVE SHADE Newly planted crops such as brassicas will benefit if shaded from hot sun until they establish.

 TOP-DRESS TOMS Where roots are exposed due to watering, apply a topdressing of Number 3 compost to tomatoes.

 ENCOURAGE CLEMATIS Clematis in flower can be encouraged to flower again in late summer by applying a little fertiliser or liquid feed.

 PATCH AND PAINT Take advantage of good weather to patch and paint glasshouses and frames. Warm conditions allow plants to be moved outside while the work is done.

 MAKE A FRAME If you have no frame, it is useful to construct a temporary one at this time for propagating alpines and shrubs through July and August. Ensure good drainage at the bottom and good compost at the top. Shade during strong sunlight, and keep close until the cuttings commence growth.

Natural Bulb Planting

With the summer still (hopefuly) blazing down on us, it hardly seems to be appropriate to the thinking of planting for results to be seen after the frosts and snows of winter. We should however, not only be 'thinking', but getting down to the 'doing and planting out bulbs for the first flush of flowers next year.

Perish the thought, indeed, of winter to come; but the promise of spring is a delight, with fresh foliage and the brilliant colours of early bulbs.

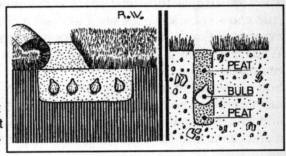

This first show needs to be as natural as possible and for that reason, bulbs always look best 'naturalised'. Remember, too, that since they will be left in place after blooming, they need to be in a spot which is rich in food, so that they can build up supplies for flowering in future years. Under trees is the place, for there they will benefit from falling leaves.

Scatter daffodils and narcissi before planting in holes about 5 inches (2cm) deep. These can be taken out with a bulb planter, the plug of soil being replaced on top of the bulb.

Smaller bulbs, such as crocus, which look superb planted in drifts of separate colours under trees, can be planted in two ways.

You can either cut areas of grass on three sides with a spade, and then roll it back to plant the bulbs underneath the turf (as pictured left); or, better to my mind, by making holes with a crowbar, again at points where the bulbs have fallen naturally. Fill the bottom of the hole with a mix of sand and peat or just peat, and place the bulb on top (see illustration right), so that its top is about two inches below the grass level. Then top-up with peat. The grass will grow over the holes quite quickly, with a transformation due in the spring.

Prepare For Holidays

We have already dealt with plants for a north-facing wall. Besides being useful for ornamental purposes, such an aspect can also be persuaded to provide delectable fruit.

The standard recommendation is to grow a Morello cherry. It's certainly worth a try, because when fully ripe, the cherries are pleasant for dessert.

They are also useful where space is at a premium, being self-fertile and so obviating the need to plant a pollinating variety. Having said that, a fair amount of room is required.

When trained as a fan, the branch framework can extend to five metres.

Soil should be in reasonable condition, and will benefit from double digging and the incorporation of well-rotted manure or compost. Choose a maiden tree, or if you wish to take a short-cut and can afford the extra cost, select a partially trained specimen.

Other types of fruit can be grown including blackberries, loganberries, tayberries and the like. Tree or bush fruits can also perform reasonably, but it is normal to train them as cordons or espaliers.

With some forms it may be necessary to provide protection against frost when blossoms appear.

The main holiday season approaches, and there are always things to be done in the garden before we can go away. Plants, lawns and weeds do not stand still in our absence, but keep on growing.

Provided most jobs are in hand, a last minute sortie - clipping, mowing and trimming - should give a head start, so that when you return it has not become a major job to put things in order again.

General work with a Dutch hoe will loosen the surface of beds and borders and destroy incipient weeds. The lawn can be cut closely, the cutting cylinder being set a little lower than its normal height. Hedges can be given a quick clip as well.

The fruit and vegetable plot is a different matter. Here longer-term planning is needed, with either your holiday planned around your garden, or your garden planned to anticipate your holiday!

There is nothing worse than seeing strawberries start to colour as you leave, and returning to find that they have gone over. Having said that, controlling maturity precisely is not possible. Seasons affect development.

However, varieties can be chosen with a resonably fixed period of development, and sowing times can be regulated to control the cropping period to some extent.

While missing the best of an outdoor crop may be sad, the biggest potential problem is in the glasshouse, where plants could die. To counter this, the best cultivation is of a friend or neighbour who is prepared to pop in on a regular basis.

Failing this, I would advise protection using the green shading materials available at nurseries or sundries shops.

This should be augmented by watering well at the last available opportunity, damping down walls, paths and benches, and leaving containers from which water can evaporate to contribute to humidity.

Special pot plants might be stood in containers of water to half their height, or have wicks attached to an appropriate reservoir of water.

Otherwise they might be moved outdoors to a shady position, where they would also have the benefit of any rain which occurs. Better still, they could be plunged in the ground or in well-watered ashes.

House plants should be set away from windows, preferably in a cool and shady room.

The compost can also be covered with such as moistened leaf mould which will act as a mulch and limit evaporation.

Shady Characters

S o many of the attractive plants available to us come with instructions to plant in full sun. Often they are showy and so catch the eye in garden centre display or catalogue. This can lead to a situation where parts of the garden which are affected by shade become relatively neglected; so wasting the opportunity to take advantage of many useful specimens.

Garden shade can vary considerably in its density and persistence. Some areas will be in partial shade, such as those facing east or west, which do benefit from sunlight for at least part of the day; others may be hidden beneath the canopy of large matured trees, which allow greater or lesser degrees of dappled light.

Whatever the feature which creates the shade, it will influence other aspects of the microclimate. In some cases beneficially by creating a windbreak, in others by competing for moisture and leading to dryness. In extreme cases, even plants recognised as shade-tolerant will struggle and it may be necessary to undertake judicious pruning and thinning or accept a degree of bareness.

In deeper shade, one plant which may stand a chance is Ruscus aculeatus, the Box Holly or Butcher's Broom. This is a native shrub growing to around 1m (3ft) with stiff, erect stems which branch near the top. What appear to be leaves are, in fact, flattened stems known as cladodes. These are small, tipped with a spine, and appear densely packed on the upper stems. Flowers are relatively inconspicuous, and if fruits are to be produced both male and female forms must be planted. When they do appear, the fruits are cherry-like and bright sealing-wax red.

More suited to ground cover is R. hypoglossum, which grows to 30cm (12in) with green, arching stems bearing spineless, leaf-like cladodes which, in turn, bear tiny green flowers and - with luck - red fruits again. Ruscus are undemanding, growing in soils ranging from chalk to heavy clay. They can be planted in

autumn or spring, and stock is increased by sowing seed which
has been stratified through the winter, or by division in spring.

A near relative you may discover is Danae racemosa also
called Ruscus racemosa or Danae laurus), the Alexandrian
Laurel. This shade-tolerant evergreen forms a charming small
bush growing to a metre with graceful, arching branches of narrow shining green leaves. Although the flowers are inconspicuous, after a good summer they will be followed by red berries in
autumn and provide ideal cut material for floral arrangements.

Sticking with laurels, the common laurel and Portuguese laurel
are among the evergreens most tolerant of shade and water run-
off from overhanging trees. They can grow quite large, but
respond well to pruning aimed at keeping them in bounds.

Prunus laurocerasus, the Common or Cherry Laurel, is a vigorous, wide-spreading shrub with large, leathery, dark shiny leaves
which will grow well on all but shallow chalk soils.

Prunus lusitanica, the Portuguese Laurel, is happy even on
shallow chalk, and makes an imposing shrub or small tree if
allowed to develop.

While they may be criticised as not being the showiest of
shrubs, the deepness of their glossy leaves provides a useful
background to other flowering or lighter-foliaged shrubs. Both
can be used as hedges, screens and windbreaks.

One of the general-purpose shrubs which I feel deserves to be
more regularly planted, is Aucuba japonica. Widely used in the
past it will thrive in sun or shade, stands up well to pruning and
is attractive as well. What more could you ask for?

The type has glossy, green, oval, leathery leaves, and there are
many forms, each with its own attractions. 'Crassifolia' has
broad, deep-green leaves, toothed in the upper half. Crotonoides
is perhaps the best of the variegated forms, with large leaves
spotted and splashed with gold. Look out for 'Fructo-alba', with
whitish berries; and 'Fructo-lutea', with yellow berries; and, if
you want a little history, plant A. japonica 'variegata' - the form
which was first introduced from Japan as long ago as 1783.

Your Gardening Week

✔ **WINTER SPINACH** Buy winter varieties of spinach, which can be sown in August and September to crop between October and April.

✔ **TRANSPLANT WALLFLOWERS** Wallflowers sown in May or June should be large enough to transplant into rows 30cm (12in) apart, leaving 15cm (6in) between the plants. Beside giving more room for growth, transplanting breaks the tap-root and encourages the formation of a branching root system - which is more amenable to being moved when the plants are bedded out in October. Rake in a dressing of hydrated or carbonated lime before lining out.

✔ **TREES AND SHRUBS** Often this is a good time to select the types of trees and shrubs - not to mention roses - you may like for future planting as you spot them on your travels. Place orders as soon as possible for autumn delivery.

✔ **WINTER COLOUR** Extra colour under glass in winter can be had by sowing the likes of ten-week stock, larkspur and salpidlosis.

✔ **AFRICAN VIOLETS** African violets can be propagated by inserting leaf cuttings now.

✔ **GRASSES** This is a good time to collect grasses suitable for flower arrangements.

✔ **ROSES** Pinch off faded rose flowers. Cut a length of stem with hybrid teas, as this encourages more shoots to produce flower later.

✔ **FEEDS** Feed onions, leeks and celery on a regular basis.

Tidying Up The Apples And Pears

Recent years have seen so much work done in the field of fruit trees that, however small one's plot, it is possible to grow your own apples and pears. Indeed, you only need to have space for one fairy small tree and you can grow a number of varieties on one stock (the so called family tree).

The main need for the average plot at the rear is to restrict the growth of the tree. To keep the size manageable, and yet encourage new growth for fruit production, you'll need to do some summer prun-
ing.

But let's take pruning in the correct order. First concentrate on this year's fruit. As soon as the summer drop has finished, reduce the number of fruits to one per cluster (see left illustration).

Then it's on to pruning, tackling espaliers and dwarf pyramids first. The pears will be the first ready for treatment. Cut back this year's wood to about five leaves (see roght illustration). Leave leading shoots and those set aside to extend the plant, until they have filled the space you intend for them.

Trees which have been trained will need a thorough ties check, to ensure that they are not so tight as to bite into the wood. Loosen off, or replace, if necessary.

If, now that growth has slowed down, you are tempted to summer prune larger trees, remember that the aim should be only to open up the tree, so as to allow light and air in to the fruit. Do not, especially with healthy trees, attempt anything more drastic.

Where you are lucky enough to have a heavy fruiter, give the tree some help by propping up branches which are so heavily laden as to be in danger of breaking — or support them with ties attached to a tall pole, set alongside the trunk.

Some Traditional Plants

The genus dianthus has given us many attractive garden flowers, among which is one always to be found in old cottage gardens - and that is Dianthus barbatus, the Sweet William. It is one of our best flowers, and the strains and varieties available make it more useful still.

The fragrant single flowers are held in tight bunches atop sturdy stems and are ideal for cutting. Scarlet Beauty and Pink Beauty are good self-colours, while many of the mixed strains have combintions of colour in their flowers.

Sweet William is at its best in June, and though the plants will live for many years they are often scrapped after flowering to be replaced by new stock. So, though not truly biennial they are usually treated as such. Seed is sown in frames, boxes or on a prepared bed during May or June, although I would still risk a batch now.

When the seedlings are well through, they can be pricked off into a frame or nursery row or transplanted directly to their flowering position. Those pricked are moved in October.

If any particular plant is highly thought of, it can be propagated by cuttings. Suitable sideshoots detached in July can be set in sandy soil, under glass, until rooted.

Another old-fashioned flower which I still enjoy is Pyrethrum roseum (or Chrysanthemum coccineum). Reaching to 60cm (2ft), their large, daisy-like flowers are held on long stems above the foliage and their strong colours stand out well. Coming into season in May and June, they help to bridge the gap between spring flowers and summer blooms.

There are many fine varieties in both single and double form. Of the singles 'Avalanche' is pure white; 'Brenda' bright carmine, and 'Kelways Glorious' glowing scarlet.

The doubles include 'Carl Vogt' pure white; 'Lord Roseberry' red; 'Madeleine' lilac pink and 'Yvonne Cayeux' in pale sulphur-yellow. Suited to a well-drained loamy soil and a sunny position, they will also perform well on chalky soils. Ample moisture is needed during the growing and flowering seasons.

Transplanting can take place after flowering and through to September, allowing time for the roots to re-establish in the warm soil before winter. Alternatively, planting can be left until March.

After three or four years the plants will start to deteriorate, with flowers becoming smaller and fewer in number. Re-vitalisation can be achieved by lifting and dividing, in the process discarding old woody pieces.

Opinions vary as to whether this should be done in September or March, so experiment to find which suits your conditions best. Each year cut the plants hard back after flowering. This may result in a second flush of bloom in late summer or early autumn.

Violas and pansies are another joy. While seed can be sown in February or March, I like to raise plants from summer sowing. Such can be made from now through August, and have the effect of treating the plants as biennials in their first year, giving them the chance to become sturdy before flower is produced.

Nevertheless they remain perennials, and once established provide flower over a long season. They can of course be treated as biennials and used in bedding displays, being discarded when the season is over.

In my case 'discarded' means finding a bit of space elsewhere and squeezing them into borders!

There are many varieties to choose from to meet your own taste, and seed can be sown outdoors in shallow drills or in boxes placed in a shady cold frame.

Seedlings are pricked off into a frame or nursery row, and planted out in September or early October.

However, if ground conditions are heavy it is advisable to delay planting until the second half of March, although this may slightly delay flowering.

A Show In The Shade

Essentially a shrub for the larger border where it will attain a height and spread of around 3 m (10ft), 'Crotonoides' or 'Crotonifolia') responds well to pruning. Where smaller size is needed, each year I prune out the topmost canopy, cutting the stems right back in the centre. This encourages a new flush of growth, and the cycle continues.

Because the stems are long and flexible I also set one or two layers so that there is always new stock to hand. New plants can also be raised from seed - sown in a cold frame in October, or from cuttings or small branches. These may be set in a frame or put directly into a sheltered border during autumn.

I should mention that many of the forms of Aucuba are of single gender, and so if berries are wanted it is necessary to plant both male and female types.

It isn't only shrubs that we need for shady places. As you might expect with a name like Wood Lily, the genus Trillium, which contains some thirty species, has much to offer. Probably the most handsome and widely grown is T. grandifloru, the Wake Robin. This has large, tri-petalled, snowy-white blossoms set above fresh green foliage, and grows to 30-45cm (12-18in).

Of the other species of Trillium, T. stylosum flowers pink, while T. sessile has smaller flowers of crimson. T. luteum grows to 15-30cm (6-12in) with strongly mottled foliage and lemon-yellow flowers appearing in early spring. Known as the painted trillium, T. erectum is very variable with colours ranging from white to deep mahogany. T. undulatum, growing to 30cm (12in), has slender, pointed, coppery-brown waved leaves and flowers of white striped with purple at the base.

Trilliums are ideal for dappled shade, and should be planted in August or September. Once established in a dense mass, the tuberous roots can be lifted and divided to extend the planted area. New plants can be raised from seed sown in pans of sand

and peat and placed in a shady cold frame, though the resultant seedlings will not make flowering size for about five years.

Requiring similar treatment both for planting and propagation is Sanguinaria canadensis. It is known as the North American Bloodroot because of the colour of its sap, and also as White Burnet. There is only the single species in this genus but it does have a double form 'flore pleno'.

Growing to just 15cm (6in) the tuberous-rooted plant has pale grey-blue, kidney-shaped leaves and creamy-white flowers appearing in April. Once established it is best left undisturbed, though division can be undertaken during March with a degree of care.

If you can add a reasonably moist soil to the shade, then Rodgersias are worth considering. While suited to shade, the need to fill a shady spot should not dictate their choice. They are a valuable addition in their own right, and in particular look well alongside water or in a wild garden. There are several knocking about in our garden and I find the foliage striking and attractive. The genus contains six species of hardy herbaceous perennials with thick, knobbly rhizomes which grow to form a clump.

Rodgersia aesculifolia grows to just over 1m (1yd), with deeply cut foliage similar to that of the chestnut and up to 45cm (18in) across. The flowers of white, with a tinge of pink, appear in July.

R. pinnate has cultivars with flowers in white, pink and deep pink. It attains 1m (1yd) and its handsome leaves are five-lobed and tinged with bronze or crimson. Of the others, R. podophylla grows to similar size, with palmately lobed leaves and buff-yellow flowers which are held in drooping panicles in early summer. R. sambucifolia grows smaller, with pinnate leaves and dense panicles of white flowers.

A contrast to the digitate or palmate foliage of those mentioned is provided by R. tabularis. Here the leaves are circular and umbrella-like, in shades of apple-green. They are held on stems a metre high and topped by spikes of creamy white flowers.

Your Gardening Week

 THINNING Rows of seed sown in June will need thinning. Carrots, beet, turnips, lettuce and the like will be ready. Water after thinning to settle those left back in place and avoid a check.

 HARVEST HERBS Foliage of many herbs is now in its prime, and can be gathered for storage.

 PRUNE WISTARIA Wistaria have done well this year, and this season's lateral shoots can be cut back to 15cm (6in) now and then taken back to two buds in December.

 LIFT ONIONS Autumn-sown onions can be lifted when growth is complete and the bulbs are ripe. Allow to dry before storing in a cool and airy place.

 DELPHINIUMS As the display fades on del-phiniums, they can be cut hard back to encourage new growth and the chance of a second display.

 BUY CABBAGE Obtain cabbage seed for sowing later in the month or in early August, to provide crops next spring.

 KEEP CUTTING Sweet peas throw a mass of flowering stems. More are encouraged if flowers are cut regularly.

 AZALEA CUTTINGS My Indian azaleas are plunged outside for the season and are growing away well. I'll be taking cuttings which, when set in a shaded cold frame, should root within the month.

 GLOXINIAS When gloxinias finish flower-ing, take off the faded blooms and gradually withhold water until the leaves wither. Then stand the pots in a dry position where the bulbs will rest until urged back into growth next spring.

 SCHIZANTHUS Buy seed of schizanthus, the Butterfly Flower, for sowing in August and September to produce displays from April to June next year.

Cut And Come Again

Despite their longevity, their evergreen quality, or their ability to flower in profusion over many years, many consider that the costs of shrubs is rather on the high side.

But take just the first of these qualities into account and it will be apparent that they are truly good value. Add to that the ease with which so many of them can be propagated and they are really a bargain.

If you have not tried — or perhaps you lump yourself among those who 'can't do anything with plants' – have a go at increasing your stock, for you'll be surprised how easy some of them are.

Take hydrangeas for a start: Take a ripe shoot (that's one with a brown tinges to the green of the shoot) which hasn't flowered. It should be about three inches long and be cut cleanly below a leaf joint.

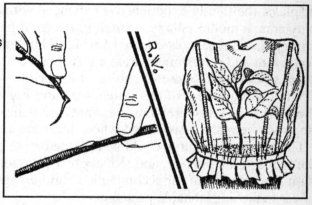

Remove the lower leaves and insert the cutting into a 3 inch pot of seed and cuttings compost.

Other popular shrubs you may like to tackle include viburnums, escallonias and lavateras. Just pull off shoots about three inches long, so that they take a 'heel' of the old wood with them (see illustration left). Remove the lower leaves and push them into a pot of cuttings compost, say three around a three inch pot. Water and ten cover with a polythene bag, supported by pieces of cane and held firmly around the pot by a rubber band (picture right). When the cuttings show signs of new growth, they may be carefully transferred to individual pots of compost. Other 'easy' ones you may like to try include cistus, cotoneaster and euonymus.

A Botanical Delight

If you happen to be in the vicinity of Harrogate, make sure you have a day to spare - and keep your eyes open for the signs to Harlow Carr.

Harlow Carr Botanical Gardens are only a couple of miles from the town centre just off the B6162 Harrogate to Otley Road; and are the home of the Northern Horticultural Society. Extending to nearly seventy acres, they are open all the year from 9.00am to 7.30pm - or dusk if that comes earlier.

While the main reason for a visit will be the interesting plant displays, the family experience is enhanced with a children's play area; a model village; a small museum of gardening containing a range of tools - some of which I had not seen before; restaurant and refreshment area; a gift shop and plant centre, the latter stocked with a useful choice of material.

While not all areas of the garden are currently accessible to those with mobility problems, attempts are being made to improve the path network and wheelchairs are available.

The admission charge could be regarded more as a donation to the work of the Society, and reductions for senior citizens taken with free admission for accompanied children aged sixteen or under make a reasonable package.

I've made a few visits over the years, and always find plenty of interest. Alpine plants are displayed in a range of raised beds and troughs, allowing the sometimes tiny specimens to be inspected at close quarters.

These are complemented by a succession of small rockeries containing not only an interesting range of plants, but demonstrating the attributes of differing types of stone - including artificial hollow ones which are comparatively light and easily handled.

In this general area, the plant which makes the most impact is Hypericum olypicum.

In full bloom and reflecting back the brilliant sunshine, it has self-set in many nooks and crannies to unify the different elements of the display - a feature which could be useful to emulate in many gardens - while the bright strong yellow of Calceolaria polyrrhiza is a dainty reminder of the attractions of the slipper-worts.

Bolax glebara (or Azorella trifurcata) is gently contorted to form a dense mass of hummocks, although its basic height is but 75mm (3in).

During May and June the glossy, light green leathery leaves sport minute yellow flowers, though even without the benefit of these it looks interesting.

Nearby, two borders alongside a path contain a range of shrub roses.

While it was nice to get in among these and search out the ones with fine scent, the path itself is a potential ankle-twister; a good indication of a design to avoid.

The path is the width of two paving slabs, and these are laid alternately to each side, the resultant rectangular spaces being filled with gravel. While it appears attractive, and doubtless looks good on a plan, the movement of the gravel compared with the solidity of the paving makes it a hazard and a distraction from the blooms.

The foliage garden is a pleasant area for rest and reflection, having both seating and a water feature. Many of the plants are variegated, and in this context even the multi-coloured form of the Oval-leaf Privet looks well.

Arundinaria viridistriate is a very hardy species of bamboo, with longish leaves striped in dark green and rich yellow. It can grow to a couple of metres (6ft), but stays smaller in shade. Cutting back to ground level in the autumn encourages the production of new canes with bright foliage.

Philadelphus 'Innocence', the purity of its many white, fragrant single flowers living up to its name, is also impressive with creamy-white variegations throughout the foliage.

Don't Panic - Do Paniculata

Mention hydrangeas, and I bet the majority of people produce a picture in their mind of mop-headed or hortensia types. But there are other forms which, though less commonly grown, are deserving of a place in gardens with a little space to spare.

The first of these to come into my mind is Hydrangea paniculata which, due to its hardy character, is probably the most widely grown hydrangea in the colder districts of the nation. Native to Japan and China, the appearance of the basic species can vary quite considerably in its home surroundings. However, selection and breeding have produced forms which are generally attractive in the garden.

The most common of these must be H.p. 'Grandiflora', which is among the showiest of the larger shrubs. If it has a fault it is the fact that the stems tend to be a little weak for the weight of flower they are expected to carry. These flowers are carried in large panicles which can be up to 45cm (18in) tall and 30cm (12in) across at the base. In order to achieve a satisfactory display and with the side benefit of keeping the shrub to a size which most gardens can accommodate, annual pruning is required.

Left to its own devices, the shrub will probably settle down at around 3m (10ft). By pruning back in March to within 7.5cm (3in) of the base of the previous year's growth it can be made attractive with gently arching shoots bearing the terminal, cone-shaped panicles.

If larger panicles are your aim, then some additional thinning can take place.

Flower appears in August and persists through autumn. What opened as white gradually fades to pink, and is none the less attractive for that.

They can be cut, and they keep well for use in floral decora-

tions during winter.

Where to plant is one of those pleasing dilemmas. This plant will serve as one among others in a mixed border. Also, it has sufficient character to stand alone as a specimen; or to make a focal point against a contrasting background.

Happy in an alkaline soil, results are dictated by the richness of the earth in which they grow and its ability to maintain a supply of moisture to the plant. As with all other hydrangeas, dryness at the root will have negative effects.

Although hardy, a sheltered position is preferred together with a modicum of shade. Then all that is needed in addition to the pruning, is a regular mulch with well-rotted manure to keep a bit of body in the soil.

A further variety is 'Praecox' which has shorter, smaller and less dense panicles of flower, but is possesed of considerable hardiness and vigour.

It has the additional benefit of coming to flower in July, so extending the season. It will come true from seed and has a scent which I have described as a mixture of horse and Chanel No5 - a heady combination indeed.

I'm not sure how many species, varieties or cultivars of hydrangea there are, but it must be a considerable number. For the majority of gardeners there is perhaps a tendency to select those such as the hortensias or H. paniculata, which have the undoubted ability to provide impact with their large and colourful displays.

For those who have the space and are prepared to appreciate the more subtle impacts of other forms, there are plenty to hunt for which are ideal in terms of scene-setting and atmosphere creation.

However, selection can be a chancy business for nomenclature is variable and, as with H. paniculata, there can be significant variation within a described type. The answer would seem to be to talk with your supplier and to try to see established plants, before taking the plunge.

Your Gardening Week

 REPLACE STRAW-BERRIES Ideally, strawberry beds which are three years old should be replaced once the crop has been harvested, as output will go into decline. Plant the vacated ground with winter greens and make a new bed in another part of the garden.

RAKE LAWNS While some turf areas have shown themselves to have access to water by remaining green even in the dry spells, others have turned to golden brown and raised worries over their future. History suggests that while the top may die, the roots remain alive and quickly recover following rain. In bad cases there may be merit in raking dead growth from the surface, where it will impede new growth.

ROCK PLANTS Rock plants such as helianthemum, aubretia, alyssum, phlox, thyme, dianthus and so on can be increased by cuttings now. Set in pots or boxes, and place in a north-facing frame to avoid full sun.

THINK SPRING Start to think about your bulb requirements for spring bedding and pot-work, with a view to ordering early.

POT FREESIAS Obtain freesias and pot them in succession through August. Set several fairly close in a 125mm (5in) pot, and stand outside in a cool and shady position to allow root development.

NEW FOR CHRIST-MAS Save a few new potatoes to plant for a fresh crop at Christmas. Expose them to the light for a few days until they become green all over. Either plant in a container so protection can be given when the weather turns cold, or be prepared to cover the ground with straw once the foliage has been killed by frost. This should protect the crop until needed.

PINCH DAHLIAS Check over large-flowered varieties and pinch out any weak shoots.

Watering Veg

Providing water for vegetable crops poses problems for quite a number of gardeners, but most particularly for those new to the growth area. Summertime is, of course, the time when water needs are greatest — and for humans too! Then, invariably, we are faced, at least in some parts, with bans on the use of hoses.

The need is to ensure that the best possible use is made of water during the summer; to make sure that any delivered to plants is used to their benefits.

If you are planting seeds, or transplanting young plants, make sure that drills and planting holes are well saturated (see pic left), and that the surrounding area is well watered in advance. Drying out of the soil in the early stages will undoubtedly prove the end for even those that looked the healthiest.

If you are watering with a hose, aim to simulate nature, holding the nozzle upwards, so that the water drops onto the plants, and use a fine spray.

A cursory watering of the ground and plants will do more harm than good. You must get the water down to the roots. So water on top and near to the root areas.

If the climate has been particularly dry, the immediate effect of watering will be its running off, often away from plants. Best, therefore, to make sure that the soil is open enough to take a deluge and, where the ground has become compacted near plants, to gently hoe around them (see pic right).

Remember to aim at thoroughly soaking the soil, and try to do it as late in the day as possible. This will first ensure that the plants aren't getting hot water to drink; secondly it will save scorching of the foliage and, finally, it will ensure that what is delivered is not lost by evaporation.

Cutting Your Favourites

Many favourite pot plants can be increased in number, or replaced by new young plants, if leaf cuttings are taken from now through to August or early September. Naturally leaves vary in their shapes, and to accommodate this, slightly different methods of making the cuttings have to be used.

Probably the most natural thing to do is detach a leaf complete with its stem. This method is suitable for Saintpaulia, Gloxinia, Streptocarpus, the majority of Peperomias and some Begonias. All that is needed is to make a clean cut across the stem about 2 inches (1cm) from the leaf blade, dip the end in rooting powder, insert in compost – and firm in.

If you are only dealing in small numbers, the cuttings can be set round the top of a pot; but for larger quantities boxes, or even a frame or large propagating case can be used.

With more succulent plants the leaf stem is not available; so for Crassula, Echeveria, Sedum and the like you can only make use of the leaves.

Pull away mature, fleshy leaves and allow them to stand for a couple of days until the base becomes dry. Then prepare containers with compost, over which a layer of sharp sand should be spread.

Just push the base of the leaf into the compost, and away they should go. With smaller leaves, you may find difficulty inserting them; so they can be laid flat on top of the sand and pressed down lightly to ensure contact without damage.

Finally, you may use parts of leaves, and this system is suitable for many of the plants with larger leaves such as begonia rex, Begonia masoniana, Streptocarpus – if larger numbers are required – and Sanseveria.

Probably the crudest method – though nonetheless successful – is to take the large leaves of the begonias in their entirety, with a piece of stem attached. Insert the stem into the compost, and spread the leaf over the surface.

The chances are that it will not make contact over its full area, so pin it down with bent pieces of wire. Then, using a razor blade, make cuts across some of the larger veins. Streptocarpus can be treated in a similar manner, but only make cuts across the mid-rib.

A more dainty method with the Begonias is to cut the leaves into pieces about an inch square and lay these on the top of the compost. If triangles take your fancy, they can also be cut and inserted with one point into the compost.

Streptocarpus leaves can be cut into strips across the mid-rib and these are then inserted along one edge. That old favourite, the Sansevieria or 'Mother in Law's Tongue', is treated in similar fashion.

The only problem you will find is that cutting taken from plants with variegation in the foliage will only produce new plants which are all green.

If you wish to perpetuate the variegation, then knock the plants out of their pots. You will see that they throw suckers, and any with roots can be detached with a sharp knife and set in 3-inch pots.

If you have no propagating case, then set the leaf cuttings round the rim of a pot and, after watering in, place three or four canes in the pot so that they stand well above the cuttings. Place a polythene bag over the canes, and secure it part way down the outside of the pot using an elastic band. This way you can provide the humid atmosphere which will keep the leaves bouyant until roots have formed.

While such conditions are important for most cuttings, they should be avoided for cactii, succulents and geraniums – all of which should be exposed to air circulation to lessen the chance of rotting.

In all cases the cuttings should have ample light, but direct sunlight must be avoided.

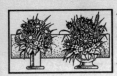

Home-made composts

When I'm moving small tubers or plants raised from seed into their final pot for the first year, I like to do a little recipe-making.

John Innes Nos 1 and 2 composts would be adequate, but when I want to do the job a little bit better still I make up my own mixture, consisting of loam, leafmould, well-rotted manure and silver sand in equal parts by volume.

As the plants grow they need some support. This can be achieved with the judicious use of small canes and raffia or green twist. The flower stems in particular merit attention, for they will have to carry the burden of comparatively large and heavy blooms, and without help will sag and not display to best advantage.

There is always an air of expectation and wonder as we wait for seed to germinate or flower buds to open. In this case, have a little patience and do some disbudding to ensure that the plants have made good growth and are well established before showing bloom.

When eventually you allow the flowers to open, you will see that they are carried in threes. While the majority of plants bear flowers which are hermaphrodite - having both male and female characteristics - this is not true of the begonia.

It has separate male and female flowers on the same plant. The central one in each group will be a double male, and the two outer ones are less spectacular single females.

Unless you intend to harvest seeds, these two outer flowers can be pinched out, leaving the double flowers to develop to their peak - and improve the overall appearance of the plant.

In subsequent years, or if you have purchased larger tubers, plants will probably require a further potting-on into 7.5 inch pots.

About five or six weeks after the preliminary pottings, careful-

ly knock the plants out of their pots. If no roots are visible around the soil, hastily return them and check again the following week.

If a reasonable number of roots are present, move them on. This helps to keep them in active growth for, if they are left to become pot-bound, they will probably be checked.

Begonias can be unforgiving, and it is important to water with care. Give too little and the tips of the leaves will soon turn brown. Give too much and the foliage will turn pale and start to rot.

After potting, water should be given sparingly until the roots are well developed; then it should be applied just as the soil shows signs of dryness, by filling the pot with water to the rim. If you have more than one, each will need to be treated individually. Once established in their final pots, the plants can be given liquid feed at seven to ten day intervals.

A begonia tuber is an investment which can pay dividends for many years if rested and stored through the winter. Don't be tempted to dry the plants off when flowering finishes, but keep them growing into autumn until the foliage shows signs of yellowing. At this point water can be reduced and the plants laid on their sides under the glasshouse staging.

When the foliage and stems have completely withered, knock the tubers out of their pots and carefully remove the old soil. Dust them over with flowers of sulphur to give some protection against storage rot, and store in boxes of dry peat or sand in a frost-free place until March. Then the cycle can start again!

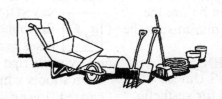

Your Gardening Week

FEEDING TIME This can be a busy time as crops grow to maturity. Many will benefit from liquid feeds at 10-14 day intervals. Tomatoes benefit from high potash concoctions, while general formulations will suit runners and French beans. Give bedding plants a boost as well.

EPIPHYLLUMS Epiphyllums enter their main growing period about now and can be encouraged with ample water and a programme of feeding through to the end of September.

PREPARE FOR LAWNS So that sowing or turfing can take place in September, August is a good month to prepare the ground for a new lawn.

HEDGE TRIM Give evergreen hedges a trim before the end of the month. This will allow new growth to harden before the advent of frost, minimising the risk of damage.

SHORTEN ARTICHOKES Unless required for aesthetic purposes, stems of Jerusalem artichoke can be shortened back to about 30cm (12in). This will not affect yield and will reduce the risk of their being blown over.

SOW STOCKS Beauty of Nice and Brompton stocks can be sown now for flowering under glass. The former will bloom from Christmas to late February or March to be followed by the Bromptons in late spring.

MAINCROP TURNIPS Maincrop turnips can be sown to the middle of the month for lifting in mid-October.

STOP TOMS Ordinary outdoor tomatoes can be stopped when they have set four trusses. Leave at least two leaves above the top truss to draw sap. Bush and other special outdoor varieties need little or no stopping.

NO SUCKERS Many floribunda and specie roses can be propagated by semi-ripe cuttings taken from shoots which have not carried flower.

A Clean Sweep With New Brooms

Anyone just the least bit interested in a garden should not be without a broom—a blooming one that is!

In the flower border, or just among other shrubs, they are a real bonus in that they provide superb splashes of delightful colours, from the creamiest of creams to the richest crimson, and, of course, mixtures of colour (see illustration A).

One thing I particularly value them for is for the fact that they provide blooms and colour at some height above other spring blooms.

One problem with the common broom (Cytisus scoparius) and its hybrids, and the Spanish brooms (Spartium junceum), is that they tend to get leggy and throw out long, spindly shoots.

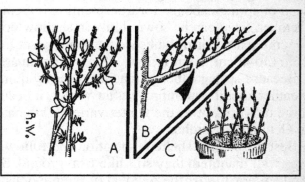

To counter this and to ensure that fullness of bloom which makes its so invaluable, those that bloom in the spring need to be cut back to encourage new wood for next year's flowers. This year's will have been produced on last year's new wood and that greener wood should, after flowering, be cut back by about one third, using a sharp knife (see illustration B).

Summer flowering Spanish brooms can also be pruned after flowering, but it is often better, particularly in colder climes, to leave cutting back until the following spring.

You can propagate new brooms from seeds but the job is somewhat tedious in that they take months, in some cases, to germinate.

Best, to be sure of success and true colours, to make cuttings—say 2-3 inches of this year's growth, to be struck with hormone rooting powder, six or seven in a pot (inset C). July and August is a good time to take cuttings.

187

Food And Flowers

Making mental notes is all very well, but sometimes they do seem to get lost. More certain is the diary; and this is a good time to take it out and make notes of how things are going in the garden. Over the years such notes can be a handy source of reference, although the vagaries of our climate can mean that what did well in one year will not necessarily do so the next.

The beginning of August in warmer areas is the time to sow seed of spring cabbage for transplanting in September or October. Seed can be sown thinly in shallow drills about 6in (15cm) apart. For the subsequent planting set the seedlings 12-16in (30-40cm) apart in rows 18in (45cm) apart.

Because spring cabbage reaches maturity quite quickly as weather conditions improve after winter, it becomes neither so large or so coarse as the winter varieties which come into season in October/November.

Best grown in a sheltered position and following a crop that was well manured, they still like firm ground. So it should be trodden down after the removal of the previous crop and prior to preparing a planting tilth. Very important is pH, and a dressing of lime to bring it slightly to the alkaline side will encourage growth and discourage club root. During early spring when growth begins, hoe nitro-chalk or at 2oz/square yard (60g/sq metre).

Having got some vegetables on the go, how about some flowers for early spring? This is the time when delightfully scented freesias can be potted and which should come into season during December and January. They may last into February and March.

John Innes No 1 compost will give acceptable results. Anything more rich may produce growth which is leggy and with a shortage of bloom. If you want to try a little muck and magic, then make your own from 4 parts of good loam with 1 part each of well-rotted manure and coarse sand.

Use 6in pots and set the bulbs 1 inch apart before covering with soil so that the crowns appear just above the surface. Stand in a sunny frame and cover with a layer of moist peat, which will keep the bulbs cool while roots form. Do not water until active growth has started. In the event of rain, set the framelights in place.

Towards the end of October, house the pots in a temperature of 18C (55F) and water regularly.

Window boxes and troughs planted with annuals can be a riot of colour at this time of year. But what about in winter, when the frost has blackened stems and seen off these tender splendours?

One way of enlivening their appearance through the darker days of winter, is to keep a supply of shrubs and dwarf conifers plunged in pots in a nursery plot. Many of the hebes have attractive foliage and are quite slow growing, though they can be cut back by frost.

The ivies offer an abundance of choice in variegation and leaf shape, and are hardy. Euonymous fortunei radicans 'Silver Queen' is well suited, with new leaves in spring unfolding to show a rich creamy yellow and gradually turning to green with a creamy-white margin. There are many more to choose from.

These shrubs can be lifted and plunged in the boxes, perhaps augmented with early-flowering bulbs. When it is time for annuals to take their place they can be plunged back in the nursery rows.

Over time they might become pot-bound or too large, in which case they can be planted out in borders.

It is time to be thinking about onions. Japanese varieties need to be sown in the first half of August in Scotland and the North, mid-month in the Midlands and towards the end of the month in the South. The resultant seedlings should be sufficiently robust to stand the winter, but not so far advanced that they bolt next spring. They can be thinned to a couple of inches next March, but the thinnings are not suitable for transplanting.

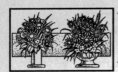
Friends And Foes

Most popular species of that delightful genus 'fritillaria' are F. meleagris, the snake's head fritillary, and F. imperialis, the crown imperial.

Other species are no less attractive to grow but can be a little difficult, requiring special attention to ensure that they perform well. There are, however, several that will respond to fairly ordinary circumstances and whose attractions warrant a trial. You may have to hunt around among specialist growers to track these down, but the hunt is well worthwhile.

First among these species is F. pallidiflora. This strong-growing and hardy species hails from the heights of Siberia. Growing to around 60cm (2ft), its sturdy stems are wreathed with large green leaves. From the axils of the topmost leaves appear clusters of flower. Numbering a dozen or so, the large flower bells range in colour from cream to greenish white and pale-yellow, their insides flecked with numerous tiny rose or plum-coloured dots.

Choose a warmish position to protect young growth from spring frosts.

Fritillaria persica may burst into flower as early as March, but again needs a sheltered position if frost damage is to be avoided. Its strong stems exhibit a bluish-grey bloom and can reach to 75cm (2ft 6in). The flowers of deep purple with a misty sheen are held in loose racemes.

Coming to flower about a month later is F. pyrenaica which is natively found in the Pyrenees. While smaller in stature, reaching 20-37cm (8-15in), it is very accommodating and will establish and spread in a situation to its liking. The chequered bells range in colour from mahogany-purple and crimson-purple to strong yellow. Look out for the species 'pontica', 'camschatcensis', 'michailovsky', 'pudica' and 'acmopetala'.

Where do all the slugs come from? I don't know the answer to

that, but I have a feeling I know where they all are!

Of the 25 species found in these isles, around seven can be regarded as garden pests; ranging from three species of keeled slugs which spend most of their lives underground through the field slug and garden slugs that grow to some 4cm (1.5in), to those near leviathans, the black and Bourguinat's slugs, which can reach 20cm (8in) long.

In the moist conditions they emerge at dusk and tear around the paths in search of food. If the dog has left a biscuit in the open, they seem to appear from all points of the compass and devour it by dawn.

Their prevalence is my own fault: a combination of masterly inaction in taking any control measures, combined with the cultural practice of using organic mulches, which seem to provide them with shelter and good cover for their eggs.

What still surprises me are the distances they can travel, the relative speed at which they move, the heights that they are prepared to climb and the rapidity with which they can devour succulent young growth.

Given that in the average garden slugs can be found at a rate of about 50 to the square metre, there are a fair number to handle. Total control is almost an impossibility and I'm quite happy to co-exist - well at least up to a point. It is a long time since slug pellets found their way out into the borders, and while concoctions containing aluminium sulphate are regarded as less harmful, I still opt for cultural methods of control where possible.

Where particular plants are known to be vulnerable they can be protected by rings cut from plastic bottles and pushed into the ground around them while young.

I still find that traps baited with milk or beer can result in quite a successful cull. I recall that some people who have conducted trials are less than enthusiastic about the numbers caught, and express concern that beneficial creatures are also prone to be lost. I suppose the numbers trapped depend to some extent on the numbers you start out with.

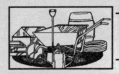

Your Gardening Week

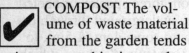

✓ COMPOST The volume of waste material from the garden tends to increase at this time and unless diseased is useful for composting. Dry material should be moistened to speed decay, and a dressing of sulphate of ammonia or a proprietary accelerator helps the process.

✓ STOP WEEDS Keep the hoe going on a frequent basis to prevent weeds becoming established and seeding.

✓ PLANT SEEDLINGS Seedlings of wallflower, myosotis, digitalis and the like should be ready for transplanting. Dress the nursery bed with general fertiliser, which can be raked in. Then plant the seedlings 225mm (9in) apart in shallow drills 300mm (12in) apart. The drill will make watering easier until the plants establish.

✓ REMOVE HEADS Removing the seed heads from bedding dahlias will encourage them to continue producing flowers.

✓ BLACKBERRIES AND LOGANBERRIES New canes which will carry next year's crop of blackberries and loganberries should be tied in as they grow. New plants can be had by tip layering the older shoots.

✓ WINTER SPINACH Sow winter varieties of spinach in succession through August and September, to provide crops from October through to April.

✓ PRUNE BLACKCURRANTS As blackcurrants pass out of bearing, a proportion of the oldest stems can be removed by cutting back to the base. This will encourage younger shoots to develop and help keep the bush vigorous.

✓ MORE BEANS? As early broad beans are harvested and if the ground is not needed for anything else, stems can be cut hard back to where small shoots are breading at the bottom. With luck these will grow more strongly and give a small second crop.

An Invitation To Butterflies

One particularly rewarding aspect of gardening is the fact that, given just a little thought, you can use even the smallest of areas to attract wildlife to enhance the garden.

A tree, for instance, a mountain ash, or a berry carrying shrub, will attract any number of birds, whilst a pond may attract either frogs and toads or dragonflies.

Most rewarding as introductions are those plants which, through colour or more particularly through scent, attract bees and butterflies.

There are a number of wild flower collections of seeds which provide the wherewithal to do the trick, but I find it more rewarding to select and introduce plants or bushes, so as to allow one to plan for colour.

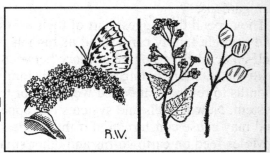

The most successful shrub in attracting butterflies is probably the Buddleia (see picture left). Generally speaking one sees the more common lavender variety, but there are others to fit into colour schemes too. I particularly like the Buddleia colvilei, which produces rose-pink flowers from June to July, and Buddleia globosa, producing orange-yellow flowers from May to June. These two varieties are half-hardy, whereas the more common, and earlier mentioned, lavender flowered variety, Buddleia alternifolia, is hardy. For further colour and varied flowering times Cytisus, or broom, is excellent. Most can be planted now, for they can be obtained container-grown.

Among the smaller border plants, some of the best for attracting butterflies are scabious, phlox and the vibrant violet-coloured Lunaria, beloved too of flower arrangers for the silky, silver, disc-like seed pods (pictured right).

All of these all so much colour to the garden — and attract even more.

Relocating Moles

M oles have never been a problem in any of my gardens, but the appearance of an abundance of fresh mining spoil in many of the places where I walk with the dog, shows that they are very active.

In the garden they can appear in a variety of situations and are very obvious in places like lawns, though less so in rougher areas or borders. While they prefer a light, well-drained soil they occur from uninhabited high moorland to well manicured suburban gardens.

They spend the biggest part of their existence underground, and a single family can extend its tunnels and chambers over half an acre! Breeding takes place between February and June, with the resultant young leaving their family tunnels after a few months to re-use abandoned workings or to set up their own new system. New tunnels and systems can appear at any time of year and may cause consternation if they appear overnight.

Moles feed on earthworms and other small invertebrates that are taken in and so do not cause a direct threat to plants. However, their extensive excavations can undermine roots and affect the growth of young plants, particularly in the vegetable plot. The aforementioned molehills can also look unsightly.

The main methods of control are by trapping, poisoning and the use of deterrents. In my time I've seen a number of contraptions for killing these furry beasts, and their appearance has suggested that their use is not for the faint-hearted.

Two types of trap are in general use: the half barrel and the caliper. They can be set in permanent tunnel runs, and half the game is tracking these down. The traps are then set in the tunnels and instantly dispatch any mole that ventures into them. The traps should be examined daily, and any that have failed to make a kill in a day or so should be repositioned.

For preference I think I'd rather work on the basis of discouragement, but the results may be less impressive or not work for long.

There are a number of repellents available which can be set in the tunnels. The moles, however, can take evasive action by quickly blocking the tunnel around the substance and making a diversion. Even where these are effective, regular topping up will be required.

Moles are sensitive to noise, and so noise generation can be tried. Rather than dash to the bottle bank following that romantic dinner, save the wine bottles and set them in the ground among the mole hills with the open neck exposed. Wind passing over the aperture will set up a singing sound sufficient to cause the moles to move away.

Euphorbia lathyrus, the Caper Spurge, which grows to around 90cm (3ft) and has large green bracts is generally recognised as discouraging moles for they hate the smell. You may need to set them densely though for burrows may still run fairly close.

The last method requires a box, a bike, a spade and a deal of patience! Choose a quiet spot with a good view of existing molehills. Settle down to enjoy the atmosphere but keep a sharp eye open. Sooner or later fresh earth will start to grow into a mound. This is the moment to approach with care. Push the spade into the soil behind the mound, lever down on the handle and turn out the soil with a startled mole in the middle. Place in the box and cycle to a pleasant piece of countryside before returning the captive to the ground.

Spring Green And Freesias

A t the moment, hydrangeas are clothed with their distinctive flower heads, confirming that consistent and rewarding displays can be had in successive years from these undemanding shrubs. If you look more closely in among the flowering heads you will find some non-flowering shoots. These can be used to make cuttings, either to increase stock for planting outdoors or to raise as pot plants.

Prune out some of the shoots, and make a clean cut just below a leaf joint to leave some 10-12.5cm (4-5in) of stem with three pairs of leaves. Remove the bottom pair.

If a lot of cuttings are made, they can be set in boxes of peat and sand or put directly into a propagating frame. For just a few, inserting three or four around the rim of a pot and placing in a polythene bag should do the trick.

Keep shaded in humid conditions and with a temperature around 16C (60F).

Small roots should appear within ten days or so. After four or five weeks, the cuttings will be well rooted and can be removed from the propagating frame or bag.

While plants destined for outdoors could be planted in autumn, they are susceptible to frost damage and would be better over-wintered with protection and planted out next spring.

Young plants destined for pot work could be potted singly but a single cutting will carry but a single bloom next year and look a little lost. Better to set three or four of them around the rim of a 12.5cm (5in) pot and grow them on in a glasshouse or on a window sill.

Having sown spring cabbage a couple of weeks ago, I'll be looking to clear the rest of the early potatoes so the seedling greens can be planted out in mid-September.

While my ground is on the heavy side, the plot vacated by potatoes is always a pleasure to work. Plentiful residues of

organic matter help make it friable, and the regular cultivation of earthing-up coupled with a canopy of dense foliage ensure that it is weed-free.

Cabbages enjoy a slightly alkaline soil and if needed, a dressing of lime can be worked in during cultivation. They also need a firm foothold, so the ground should be well trodden before the last raking leaves the planting tilth.

This is a good time to pot freesias, which may flower from December lasting into February or even March. The compost used should have a high humus content, and may be made from four parts of good loam mixed with two parts of peat and one part of coarse sand.

If available, well-rotted manure or compost can be substituted for the peat.

While mixing your own compost can be part of the pleasure, if you do not fancy the task John Innes No 1 will be fine. Don't use compost which is too rich or growth will tend to be leggy with little bloom.

Use large pots and place the bulbs 25mm (1in) apart, covering with compost until the crowns are left just proud. Place the pots in a sunny cold frame and cover with a layer of moist peat or ashes which will keep the bulbs cool while roots form. Do not water until active growth commences and in the event of rain, cover the frame with lights.

Toward the end of October, house the pots under glass in a temperature of 18C (55F) and water regularly.

Your Gardening Week

✔ **BOOST SPUDS** Potatoes may be small due to dryness in early summer. If rain has now fallen, encourage them by dusting fertiliser between the rows and hoeing in.

✔ **ENCOURAGE CUTTING** If you are intent to take cuttings of violas and pansies next month, select suitable parent plants and cut them back to encourage the production of basal growths which will provide cutting material.

✔ **PAPER AND PEN** It is a good idea to always carry paper and pen to make a note of attractive plants seen in other places. At this time of year, with plants in flower and the likelihood of some travel, it is all the more important.

✔ **ENCOURAGE EPIPHYLLUMS** The main growing season for epiphyllums starts about now and will continue through to the end of September. So encourage them with ample water and a programme of feeding.

✔ **DAHLIAS** Pick over bedding dahlias to remove any seed heads. This helps to keep the plants in flower.

✔ **GIVE SUPPORT** As fruit ripens on trees, their weight increases. Check over the branches to see if any need support, in which case they can be propped from below or supported by ties suspended from a tall pole set in the ground.

✔ **PAINT AND PRESERVE** Check over fences and structures and apply paint or preservative as required.

✔ **FEED BEANS** Earth up French beans to the bottom leaves and feed weekly with quarter strength liquid manure until the crop is finished.

✔ **TIDY BORDER** As early flowering herbaceous plants finish blooming, remove the old flower heads and trim back as needed to tidy. Remove any weeds establishing among the plants.

A Glut of Gladdies

Gladdies, or Gladioli to give them their proper name are not only Dame Edna's favourites but tops, too, with the average Brit. Among cut flowers they are, apparently, second only for choice to roses.

They are a joy in the border, giving height and and superb colour splashes. We all know and love the varieties boasting solid colours, but the range is also so wide, from the miniatures with flowers only 1 1/2 to 2 inches, to giants with flower spikes up to two feet long and in a staggering range of multi-colours.

To make your choice you really should obtain catalogues from suppliers, or select from the colour-illustrated selection of corns available from your local garden centre.

There are some superb newcomers; among them Pop Art, with showy arty shades of duo pink and yellow, or Royal Dutch, purple and white mix which has an orchid-like quality in its form.

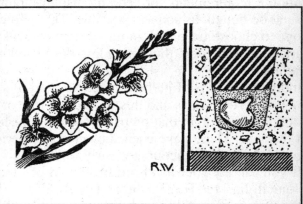

Gladioli like well-drained soil and a position which is sheltered from winds. Generally they tolerate most positions and, being tall, look well among low-growing plants. They are best grown in groups and planted where they fall from a scattered handful.

Before planting, place a stake to which the growing plant can be tied later. It is best to stake prior to planting, so as not to damage the corm.

Summer types can be planted from mid-March to April, but right now your could be planting some of the autumn flowering types.

A few days before planting mix in some peat or well-rotted garden compost and plant each bulb, point up to twice its depth. It's as simple as that.

Singing The Blues

Here we are in the middle of August, but already it is possible to sense that change in the growth cycle indicating that autumn is approaching. At this time, with many plants still blooming at their best, it is easy to forget the shortage of colour that could happen in winter and early spring. So this is a time to plan ahead for flower at Christmas.

During August, the first of the bulbs for spring-flowering appear in shops and garden centres. While there is still time to work out requirements for bedding displays, bulbs for indoor use should be bought as soon as possible. This will ensure a wider range to choose from and, in turn, allow batches of bulbs to be started in succession, thus extending the period when flowers are available.

Individual bowls of bulbs can be expected to stay in their best bloom for 10-20 days and this provides a rule of thumb to plan around. Don't forget that prepared bulbs are needed for the earliest displays. These have been subjected to a period of temperature control which encourages early flowering.

If you can lay your hands on fresh seed of Mecanopsis baileyi betonicifolia - the Himalayan or Tibetan Poppy - then now is a good time to sow. It is an advantage to use fresh seed from the current season for it germinates more readily. If such is not available, settle for the sealed commercial packet.

Sowings can be started any time through to early autumn, or be delayed until next spring. Use well-drained pots, pans or boxes with a compost consisting of equal parts of fine leaf mould, fibrous loam and coarse silversand. Peat can be used instead of leaf mound.

Sprinkle the seed very thinly and cover with a very light dressing of fine compost. Press down carefully with a piece of wood to firm in and then give water. Cover with glass and paper and keep in a warm frame or glasshouse until the seedlings show.

When late summer sown seedlings are up, do not delay in pricking off under framelights, cloches or into boxes for over-wintering in the glasshouse.

You should end up with one of the most impressive blue flowers to be found in the garden. It is a true perennial but needs encouragement to establish the perennial habit. Often it rushes into flower the first year then succumbs to exhaustion and dies out. The need is to discourage early flowering, and this can be achieved by removing stems as they are thrown in the first year.

The plant grows as a circular rosette of leaves close to the ground which should be around 20cm (8in) across. In May or June, loose heads of large poppy-like blooms are borne on stems up to 120cm (4ft) tall. While there may be some variation in colour, the true blues are astounding. Others can vary to pale lavender and for preference should not be used for seed.

A group well placed among shrubs or with a green background can be a splendid sight and the partial shade provided by shrubs and trees is just the right condition. Soil should be light and loamy, enriched with a little manure or leaf mould with ample moisture, but good drainage.

Set the young plants informally at 54-60cm (18in - 2ft) spacings. While this may look thin on the ground, they will grow to fill the space.

I suppose short-lived perennial is the description I should have used for these plants that will live for four or five years, flowering each season. This means there is a need to raise new stock on a regular basis, a task which is well rewarded.

There are many other species of mecanopsis, all of which are delightful; M. Cambrica, our native Welsh Poppy has bright yellow and orange flowers, the white-flowered M. superba has a boss of attractive anthers, M. napaulensis grows to 150cm (5ft) with flowers of mauve and pink while M. delavayi from China reaches only 15cm (6in) and has violet flowers. Certainly it is a group worth getting to know.

Prepare For Christmas Cheer

Have you noticed that bulb time is with us again? During the month, bulbs for spring flowering start to appear in the shops and garden centres. There is hardly a newspaper or colour supplement that does not seem to have a special offer on the go.

Nevertheless, it is handy to have one or two catalogues to hand, for specialist growers tend to offer a greater range of varieties, and their descriptions help in choosing varieties that you may not have tried before.

Whatever the method of purchase, it is a good idea to order early while the widest choice is still available. This is particularly important for bulbs which are to be forced, where a selection of early, mid-and late-flowering varieties will help spread blooming over a longer period.

Even if you only wish to have the odd bowl, it is fun to do it yourself. If you can stretch to a few, they also make good presents with a personal touch.

For Christmas flowering hyacinths it is necessary to invest in prepared bulbs. These have been subjected to temperature regimes which simulate an early winter and bring spring forward for them. Naturally they cost a little more.

Bulbs which have not been prepared can still be brought to flower early by giving them a period of coolness in which to establish followed by increasing warmth. Early varieties of tulip, together with many varieties of daffodil and narcissus which naturally flower earlier than hyacinths will be ready in thime for Christmas.

Individual forced bulbs can be expected to stay in bloom for from 10 to 20 days. Succession can be maintained by starting a fresh batch every two or three weeks.

As a rough guide, those started in early September should be ready at Christmas, those from mid-September to mid-October should flower in the second half of January and a batch put in at the end of October or early November should flower in February.

Choice of container is a matter of personal preference. Pots are adequate so far as growth is concerned, but bulb bowls look more attractive in the home. Pot-holders can bridge the gap. If you are aiming for succession and ornamental containers are in short supply, then the bulbs can be started in small pots or close-packed in boxes and then carefully potted into bulb bowls just prior to flowering.

Containers used from forcing to flowering should as a general rule have only one variety so that all are likely to flower together to make the best impact. Where grown in boxes, a selection of different types can be more readily made on the basis of their actual development. This also makes it easier to incorporate the likes of asparagus, which can improve the overall effect, particularly with hyacinths.

Both John Innes No 1 compost and specially prepared bulb fibre are suitable growing mediums, but make sure the bulb fibre is given a thorough soaking before use.

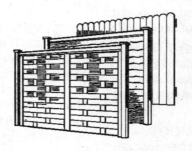

Your Gardening Week

CHERRY PIE Heliotrope or Cherry Pie is normally grown as a half-hardy annual. Cuttings can be taken in autumn and over-wintered under glass.

CLEAN GLASSHOUES Take the opportunity afforded by fine weather to move plants out of the glasshouse and give it a thorough cleaning.

GERANIUM CUTINGS A start can be made to making cuttings of zonal and ivy-leaved forms of geranium. Select shoots 125mm (5in) long without flower and take care to select them evenly from amongst the display.

PENSTEMONS Penstemons make fine border and bedding plants that flower through summer and autumn. Cuttings can be taken now from unflowered shoots and inserted in a frame of sandy soil.

START CYCLAMEN Rested corms of Cyclamen persicum can be restarted to growth after cleaning up and repotting.

LIFT BEETROOT When globe beetroot are about the size of tennis balls, lift them and twist off the leaves prior to cleaning and storing in moist sand.

ARTICHOKE SUCKERS Clean around globe artichokes, lightly fork the ground and topdress with well-rotted manure or compost prior to soaking with water. This will encourage suckers to grow, which can then be detached and potted in autumn.

FEED CARDOONS Continue to feed cardoons with liquid manure once a week until mid-September when blanching can commence.

RED CABBAGE Sow seed of red cabbage in a sheltered seed bed so that seedlings can overwinter to be planted out in spring. Sow thinly in shallow drills 15cm (6in) apart, and thin the seedlings to 10cm (4in).

VIRUS WATCH Inspect the foliage of dahlias for signs of mottling or discolouration which may indicate the presence of virus infection. Mark the plants for destruction in autumn. Dahlia mosaic virus is the most common but cucumber mosaic and tomato spotted wilt virus may also be found.

Hydrangeas

With many shrubs making new growth, now is a good time to make a start on increasing your plants by taking semi-hard cuttings.

Shrubs such as lavatera, escallonia and viburnum do particularly well if half-ripe cuttings (that is to say new shoots which are just beginning to turn a brawny colour at the base) are taken with a heel - and that means you leave a little of the old wood at the end of the new shoot.

They should 'take' quite easily if inserted about 2.5cm (1in) deep into a good seed compost. Four or five such cuttings can be put in a 12.5cm (5in) pot. Water well and cover with a polythene bag supported by stakes.

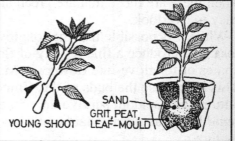

YOUNG SHOOT   SAND, GRIT, PEAT, LEAF-MOULD

After about three weeks you should be able to pot them up separately and, after a few more weeks harden them off before planting them outside.

Hydrangeas are very easy to propagate just now. Take cuttings, each about 7.5cm (3in) long, of ripe, greeny-brown shoots, which haven't borne flowers cutting them from the parent plant immediately below a leaf joint. Then remove the bottom pair of leaves (picture left).

Insert the cuttings separately in three inch pots (picture right) filled with a mixture of well moistened sand and peat, or a mix including sand, peat and leaf-mould.

Again cover with a supported polythene bag to help to retain moisture.

The ease with which hydrangea cuttings can be struck can easily be seen by another method of rooting. In this case you may just insert the cuttings in a glass jar filled with sand and water.

Good In Green

Many of the plants we choose to grow are selected on the basis of their flower display but often this is brief. Much more of the seasons can be covered by foliage and although it is easy to take this for granted, a little positive selection can produce an interesting range of foliar effects.

The greys, golds and variegated leaves have always caught our eye. It's useful to have those which change colour through the seasons, perhaps appearing a bright light-green in spring and deepening with time or more likely having good autumn colour. Then there are those that are green and stay green, which are easy to overlook.

While it is possible that the foxglove tree, Paulownia tomentosa, can produce a fine display of flower and be covered with spikes of foxglove-like flowers in May, it is unlikely to happen. This is because the buds of this Chinese tree are initiated in autumn and seldom survive the winter. So its flowers may be regarded as an occasional bonus, but the foliage remains as a feature.

Left to its own devices in a position sheltered from winds, open to the sun and possessed of a well-drained soil, the tree may grow to 9-12m (30ft). Alternatively it may be pruned on an annual basis to stimulate new growth and the production of large leaves.

Such pruning can be carried out in early spring when all previous year's growths are cut back nearly to the old wood. This encourages new shoots to appear that in turn are reduced to one or two of the strongest which may reach 3m (10ft) in a single season.

Normally the leaves will attain a length of 25cm (10in) and as much across but pruning, which sacrifices any hope of flower, may at least double this size.

The leaves of the Catalpa bignoides, the Indian Bean Tree, can have a similar effect. Though even encouraged by pruning they are unable to achieve the same size, they nevertheless are quite striking being large, soft and heart-shaped. There is also the bonus of flower spikes in August once the tree establishes.

Members of Juglandaceae, the Walnut family, the Pterocaryas or Wing-nuts have good growth to 30m (100ft) with a wide-spreading habit. It may however choose to throw suckers and become established as a thicket of short trunks.

The pinnate leaves made of numerous toothed leaflets may extend to 45cm (18in) or more and greenish flowers in pendu-lous catkins appear in summer.

This tree will do best in a strong, deep loam with plenty of moisture and is ideal for positions by lakes and rivers. Enjoying a sunny situation they become quite hardy but may be cut back in very severe winters while still young.

No room for more trees? In that case, come well down the scale and look at one or two herbaceous specimens.

The genus acanthus gives us a number to choose from. A. spin-osus reaches 120cm (4ft) with large, deeply divided and prickly leaves topped by purple, green and white flowers in July and August. A. mollis, with leaves to 60cm (2ft) long and its variety latifolius with even wider leaves are recognised as the best.

They make good specimen plants in a position where their characteristics can be appreciated. Their root system is strong, so they are resistant to both wind and drought. The top growth can stand erect without support. While propagation can be effected through root cuttings taken in autumn, such cuttings are best taken from established plants or the quality of leaf shape may be reduced. Division of the root may be practised in autumn or spring, otherwise seed can be sown in gentle heat during spring. Another mollis comes in the form of Alchemilla mollis or Lady's Mantle. Growing to 30cm (1ft), its rounded, wavy-edged leaves are a pleasant shade of light green. Although inclined to be invasive when established, it makes good ground cover and is useful in shady places. Propagation is easy by division.

Moving The Earth

Even if the weather can make it feel like the monsoon season it can be good fun in the garden. In fact rain can often spur me to fresh activity.

A good third of the garden is 'jungle' where I venture forth with care lest I disturb the tigers - and tigers there are aplenty, as several of the neighbourhood cats seem to find this natural area to their liking. The ground falls away into an enormous valley (hollow), the bottom of which is swamp (a little on the wet side) and reputed to be the haunt of crocodiles, though we have not managed to see one yet.

In fact, the bottom of this hollow lies a little above the natural water-table and at times of heavy or persistent rain is subject to flash-flooding. The temporary ponds that appear disappear in the space of an hour or so, but the ground rarely approaches dryness. It is a pleasant, cool green area shaped by the branches and leaves of beech, sycamore, ash and willow and populated by the likes of ferns, grasses, the odd clump of rush and a fine crop of brambles.

For good or ill, it provides a home to a family of grey squirrels, forms part of the network of land supporting owls, has slugs, spiders, wasp nests and burrows of solitary bees. Perhaps I should leave it alone!

Things have already gone a little too far for that. Because one of the sides is quite steep and subject to erosion, I have gradually been bulking it up with excavated spoil from other parts of the garden to produce a more gentle and accessible slope. In part this has been helped by the creation of a dry-stone buttress to retain some of the soil and this opened up the possibility of interesting paths and steps.

In the bottom of the hollow I've taken the plunge and started to excavate a pond, the success of which at this time will depend on the water table because I have not used a liner. Part of the

area around the pond remains at its old level and so provides a fairly boggy area. Around that I am raising the level a little with the excavated material to provide the opportunity of a dry pathway.

The area has always been a bountiful source of tree seedlings, producing for example enough young hawthorns for several yards of hedge.

In the past, young sycamores were allowed to grow quite large and several produced long, straight stems because they were growing close to one another in a group. A couple of years ago I felled several of these to let in a little light. Now the trunks are being put to use to retain some parts of the pond edge and some of the raised areas.

As to whether or not I should have left the area alone, the truth is that I could not. There is that part of me that sees things and wants to change them, hopefully for the better. I can also claim that making these changes creates new habitats and certainly has opened opportunities for a wider range of planting.

One of the things I was anxious to see was the effect of some extra colour and to know whether or not I would be disappointed at this intrusion into the gentle scene.

A visit to one of the smaller local garden centres produced Astilbe 'sprite', a dwarf form with interesting foliage and pale pink flowers. It fits in very well.

I also found Mentha aquatica, the water mint, which has the advantage of being native and can also be used at the table. It carries lilac flowers at this time and has a good mint scent. Another native is Filipendula ulmaria, the meadowsweet, and this came in variegated form. Reaching 60-90cm (2-3ft) this "queen of the meadows" carries creamy-white plumes of flower through summer.

As ever, there is still a long way to go, but with the direction of the team-leader (I can't call her foreman these days) and the help of our two garden assistants it is good fun.

Your Gardening Week

✔ HERBES Over recent years I've found a number of herbes which have rooted well from cuttings. I've then gone on to plant them out and they have grown away like mad. They look so well and carry so much flower that it is hard to contemplate cutting them out, but they do swamp other plants. They tend not to look so well when pruned so I'm trying to set up a four or five year cycle of propagation, growth and disposal to keep them in bounds.

✔ IN THE GLASSHOUSE There is now more of a nip in the air at night and more care is needed with glasshouse ventilation. In general the aim should be a day temperature in the region of 16C (60F) and a night minimum of 10C (50F). Unless we have an Indian summer, shading can be removed in a couple of weeks.

✔ OUTDOOR TOMS Outdoor tomatoes can be encouraged to ripen by giving them a light dressing of sulphate of potash.

✔ HEDGE TRIM Hedges of beech, chamaecyparis, thorn, thuja and yew which only need clipping once a year can be dealt with now.

✔ FOXGLOVES I am often blessed with fine display of self-set foxgloves, and abundant young plants making growth for flowering next year. In this case I leave the stems, which have carried flower a little longer to allow seed to fall. This should germinate next spring to flower in the following year.

✔ POINSETTIAS Rooted cuttings of poinsettia can be potted on. Once established, pinch out the tip to encourage sideshoots.

✔ BORDER CARNATIONS Border carnations and pinks layered during July should be rooted and can be severed from the parent plant, left carefully and planted into a prepared bed except in colder districts, where they are best overwintered in a frame.

Winter Colour

It may be difficult in weather such as that experienced during a hot summer to try and think about the winter ahead, but you really should if you want to make the best of bad weather times.

During the grey days of winter there is no more pleasant a sight than a sudden splash of colour. This is best achieved by introducing shrubs which not only bring a vast variety of leaf shades, but also colourful flowers and, or berries.

Preparations for the planting of such shrubs is fairly straight-forward and you can prepare and mark the sites now. Each hole should be dug to about 61cm (2ft) deep and the same across. Break up the sub soil so as to allow for better

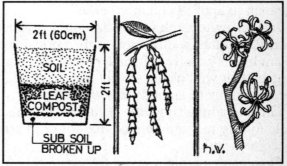

drainage, cover with a fairly deep dressing, perhaps up to half the depth of the hole, with leaf compost (leaf mould, rotted manure) and then top up with soil.

Allow to settle and make sure that the level is brought up with soil. Remember the importance of laying up that store of leafy compost, for that will be the basis of nourishment for the new plant for a long time to come.

As a few suggestions of plants to put in, try Garrya elliptica the Tassel bush (central picture) - with its eye catching grey-ish-green silk-like catkins which hang from the plants January/February; whilst the Chinese Witch-Hazel (Hamamelis mollis, see picture far right), which produces delicate blooms of twisted petal strips of yellow from a red base. These are most striking, bursting from bare branches and having a delightful scent.

Some Pruning Principles

Pruning is one of those jobs that requires degree of confidence, because once a cut has been made the result may be irreversible - or at least take some time to put right by fresh growth. That doesn't mean it is a job to feel daunted by, for in the most part nature is very forgiving.

The other thing to say is that it is not a precise art. There are often a variety of different approaches towards a common end. In the main however, the principles of pruning are simple and amount to applied common sense.

Just trying to think of a definition, I suppose pruning could be considered the modification of the normal habit of growth of a plant by the removal of some part of that plant. I have seen it argued that wild plants are not pruned at all, but consider that to be something of an understatement.

Grazing animals modify plant growth, and the wind can have a role to play in removing the likes of dead branches which have become brittle.

On a garden scale, I guess the two most important forms of pruning are to keep plants to within a certain size; or to achieve a particular aesthetic or design effect. Thus if a tree becomes too big or excludes too much light, we may reduce the number of branches or shorten them back.

If mowing is included in my definition, then lawns are regularly cut to achieve an effect - while in similar vein, hedges are trimmed on regular basis.

These are fairly blunt instruments, though, requiring a degree of skill and appreciation to achieve the best effects. However, it is when we seek to create the best possible growth or the best output of flower or fruit, that the art of pruning comes into its own.

To achieve the desired effect, there is a need to have some understanding of the habit of growth of the plant to be treated.

There is little point in cutting the likes of forsythia or ribes hard back in spring to encourage new shoots, when the main flower display is carried on older wood - the job must be left until flower has faded.

Equally, it needs to be understood that most woody plants are affected by apical dominance. At the end of each stem will be found a terminal or apical bud; below it, on the stem, will be found lateral or axillary buds.

They are set out in a variety of ways which vary in the different plant species. Some may be set in pairs opposite one another; others may alternate with buds spaced one on one side of the stem and the next on the other; while still others may form a spiral.

The terminal bud produces a chemical which circulates back to the subsidiary buds and has the effect of inhibiting their growth. Thus if the terminal bud is removed the inhibition is lost and the lateral buds grow more rapidly.

The degree of apical dominance varies with the species, Also during the growth cycle and sometimes in response to the seasons.

So, with a subject like Cornus alba sibirica we cut the top growth right back in spring, to encourage the production of many fresh young stems which are blessed with vivid red bark. With syringa vulgaris - the common lilac - buds are found in opposite pairs and the dominance is split between the topmost pair. This results in a regular forked pattern of growth.

One of the important decisions in pruning, is which bud to prune back to. One has to be selected so that the resulting shoot grows in the desired direction.

Thus, in roses we normally choose an outward-facing bud, to ensure that the middle of the bush remains open and uncluttered and that flower is carried on the outside of the bush where it it can be appreciated.

 *Your Gardening Week*

Post Haste

Working in the garden last week brought me close to a section of fence I had not inspected for some time. A pause for respite and gentle lean upon the fence, showed it to be a little shaky.

A visit to the local sawmill soon produced some replacement posts, but then the fun started. These days it seems to be a minor minefield to pick out the best sort of preservative which will do the job and have the a real chance of being "environmentally friendly" at the same time. I wonder if that should read "less environmentally harmful?"

Anyway, choice made, I set off with a can of liquid at a price which made a bottle of whisky seem fairly cheap. Mind you, the effect has to last for much longer.

I've reached the stage in life where it would be much better if the brand name and logos were printed on the side of the tin, and the instructions and safety advice elevated from small print to something a little bigger on the largest surface available. Now that could be a real contribution to safety!

Contained among the advice was the suggestion that: "where the wood comes into contact with the ground, it should be soaked for at least 24 hours." This seemed a fairly innocuous request, but what could I use as a container?

A search of the garage, garden and cellar produced a bucket that was not tall enough. The same problem applied with an old Wellington boot, the other one of the pair having been rendered less than waterproof at some time with a hole in the sole. I toyed with the idea of trying to smuggle the posts into the bathroom, but decided it was likely to be socially unacceptable, could lead to divorce, and in any case I did not want to run the risk of being left with a chestnut brown bath.

Eventually I stumbled across a spare piece of guttering. Yes it was long enough, and if I bought a couple of ends it would pro-

vide a long, shallow bath. Rather than just dipping the pointed end I have been doing the full length of the posts, though the job has been a little long-winded as they have to be turned to soak all sides and so are taking a couple of days each.

A leaflet giving information on the preservative mentioned that in tests two posts had been buried in the ground, one treated and one not. I'm not sure of the precise wording, but it indicated that when dug up after the best part of twenty years, the untreated piece was in the poor way while the other was just waiting to be put to good use.

While I am happy to be persuaded by the claim, all the posts I can recall that have succumbed to rot have done so at around or just below the soil surface, where the mixture of air and water produce a more volatile situation.

Thinking about this I noticed the remnants of a roll of repair tape. The fabric-based one, smothered in some sort of greasy compound, which can be run along glazing bars in glasshouses to prevent leaks. You know, the sort of stuff put on to make a temporary repair until the job can be done properly, and which is still there several years later. If it has a fault, it's because it can be a little messy to deal with.

What I am going to try is to excavate a reasonable amount around the posts once they have been driven in, and then bind them with some of the tape before replacing the soil. Whether it will have any effect I don't know, but if I'm still writing I'll give a progress report in a decade or so.

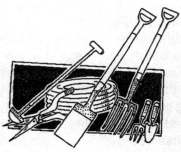

Your Gardening Week

✔ SOW LAWNS This is a good time to make lawns using seed. The days are shortening, and by the time the seed has germinated and the grass begins to grow we shall be well into autumn. There will be ample time for good root development before winter sets in, and little risk from sun scorch.

✔ APPLES AND PEARS Early varieties of apple and pear can be picked when slightly underripe. Take care not to leave pears for too long, or they will got soft from the middle.

✔ POT ALPINES Young alpine plants raised from cuttings in spring can be potted using a gritty compost. Overwinter in a cold frame prior to planting out next year.

✔ LIFT LILIUMS Lilium regale is early-flowering and often builds up into large clumps. These may be lifted and re-set. Plant about 15cm (16in) deep in well-drained soil improved with compost. Drainage can be improved by scattering a little sand in the planting hole.

✔ SOW POPPIES Poppies do not transplant well, so make a sowing outdoors where they can flower next year. The seedlings are hardy and will only require thinning.

✔ STRAWBERRIES Strawberry runners for forcing can be moved on into 15cm (16in) pots using JI No3 compost or equivalent. Pot reasonably firmly.

✔ SAVE SEED As the seed heads of annuals and perennials ripen, collect seed, remembering to label with care.

✔ BOOST CROPS Autumn green crops will benefit form a light dressing of general fertiliser hoed into the soil around them.

✔ SPRING CABBAGE There is still just time to plant spring cabbage, but do the job without delay. Water in well even if the weather is wet.

The Waiting Game With Geraniums

Geraniums always look magnificent in public garden settings. Just single specimens in pots are a joy to behold, but get them en masse and there you have a marvellous sight indeed.

The only trouble is their expense. But for that we could all boast a crowded bed of them. It is not much good, either, to run to seed, so to speak, for you don't get many per rather expensive packet.

The answer is undoubtedly to take cuttings from those you already have — a job which you can set about now. Select non-flowering, sturdy shoots about 7.5 cm (3in) long and cut them away from the plant cleanly. Then, remove the lower leaves so there is just a pair on top. Finally, cut again at a point just beneath the point where the lower leaves were removed.

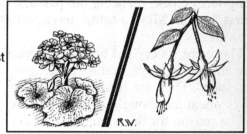

It is at this juncture that you should take a rest. Far too many go straight on to planting the cuttings. Be wise.... stop. Prepare the pots or boxes of either compost, or a mix of peat and grit, and water it and leave it to drain.

During this waiting time, leave the cuttings in the open, for, say, an hour or so — in the sun, if possible, to allow the wounds to harden off. This is the key to success, for the hardening-off will assist them in withstanding stem rot, which is the usual cause of failure.

When the cuttings have been set in the compost, cover them with a polythene bag (if in pots) or pop them into a propagator.

Do not overwater; they will do better if left on the dry side. When the cuttings show sign of growth you can pot them up separately.

Another favourite plant from which you can now take cuttings is the fuchsia. This is particularly easy to root. Just take some shoots which have not borne flowers, cutting just below a leaf joint and take off some of the lower leaves. Dip the end of the cuttings into hormone rooting powder and push into moist No. 1 potting compost — or ordinary garden soil. Again, pot up separately when growth starts.

A Sorry Loss

Last week I gave some views on the principles of pruning. As I sit at the keyboard tonight, I'm a little sad at the prospect of some pruning to be done. Well, pruning is an understatement - it's felling I really mean!

Each morning as I open the curtains on the landing window, I look out on the tops of two good specimens of Prunus serrulata Kanzan. With maturity the primary ascending branches have spread to make two well-rounded trees. They have acted as a long-term clock, marking the passage of years as buds in spring burst forth in May to bring masses of showy, double, bright pink flowers.

These are succeeded by coppery young foliage greening with the advancing days, and then changing once more as autumn advances. They are like two good friends, and my conscience nags me at the thought of their demise.

The reason for this state of affairs is my small contribution to stimulating the economy. My house has been blessed with what could be described as a large porch or small lean-to glasshouse. This has been useful to house a number of plants and to provide a sheltered sitting place to relax in the evening. Unfortunately, successive timber splicing and repeated applications of paint have failed to stem the spread of soft rot, and I decided that it had to be demolished before it fell on its own.

Recent weeks have seen negotiations with a number of small companies to work up a design and cost a replacement. Naturally, it seemed reasonable to choose something just a little bit large that could more readily be described as a conservatory, and that is what has affected the trees.

At first I tried thinning the crowns and shortening back a few branches, but having marked out the site it is apparent that they are too close - so tomorrow they go.

Having looked at one or two nationally advertised structures I did the rounds of local firms. It's amazing how many firms now do this sort of work. I looked at photographs, visited the odd job that they had already done, obtained a budget price and then chose one to work with. Given that much of the house is natural stone, and because I prefer it anyway, a wooden construction was chosen. Choosing the type of wood proved a little more difficult, leaving aside any environmental considerations. I spoke to several people knowledgeable in the use and longevity of wood. Brazilian mahogany emerged as favourite, and notwithstanding the impact on rainforests, it seems to weigh in at about 40 per cent more expensive than the next range of hardwood.

African mahogany, Phillipine Ihuan, hemasew, utile, 'clear' cedar, patch pine all appeared at the top of one list or another. Western red cedar - "but make sure to use brass screws and fittings because it corrodes steel." Even iroko, "because it weathers to look like oak but is cheaper." I make no recommendation - you pays your money and takes your choice.

In both the original and new structure, the timber sits atop a low wall. As the ground falls away quite steeply on two sides, it was obvious that more stone would be needed, for the wall is both longer and needs to be deeper to make up for the ground. Making what seemed a generous calculation, I cast around and eventually found a demolition in progress, arranging for six square metres (7 square yards) of demolished wall to be delivered.

Over the weekend I moved a number of shrubs away from the site, and yesterday work started on excavating for the footings. Two hefty lads set to with a will and shifted a mountain of earth. So far their digging has revealed two extras.

The surface water drain round the house has to be moved, and because of a quirk in the original construction and the sloping ground, footings that started out to be around two feet deep on one side became three, then four, and finally 2m (6ft) deep!

I'm told it's likely to be the biggest foundation ever seen under a conservatory, and tomorrow start to look for more stone!

Pruning For Vigour

Mowing the lawn is one of those jobs which we all recognise has to be carried out on a regular basis throughout the spring, summer, autumn - and even occasionally during winter in mild years.

I have come to the conclusion that a similar approach can be adopted to pruning; unless there are valid cultural reasons for treating a particular tree or shrub at a particular time.

Overall, the amount of growth made by our woody friends is significant. I'm sometimes surprised to find myself pushing branches aside, in order to walk along paths that seemingly a short time ago had been wide enough to accommodate a double-decker bus.

So now I'm as likely to be abroad with secateurs and small saw as mower and hoe. Thankfully, my acquisition of a chipper a couple of years ago means that the build-up of prunings can be dealt with on a regular basis.

With soft fruits, the timing of any treatment with knife or secateurs is important if done properly, but can be detrimental where this is not so.

In general the purpose of pruning is to ensure fresh supplies of young and vigorous growth to carry better crops. It also allows the removal of diseased or damaged wood.

Raspberries are a good example. The fruit is carried on this season's crop of suckers, which turn into canes. The older stems, having fruited this season, are no longer necessary and can be removed as soon as the fruit has been picked.

All the energies of the plant then go into building up the young canes, which ripen in the sun and are tied into their supports in late autumn.

With autumn-fruiting varieties which do not crop until August the treatment is different, and fruited canes are left until February when they are cut down to the ground. New canes

appear, fruiting later in the same year.

With blackcurrants, fruit is borne mainly on young shoots produced during the previous growing season, with older wood giving lighter crops and fruit of poorer quality. Thus a proportion of the older wood should be removed each year, cutting the stems hard back.

It is necessary to make some judgment as to the overall vigour of the bush, to be satisfied that sufficient replacement wood will be produced. Vigorous varieties will produce adequate new growth without hard pruning, while weaker varieties may need to be treated more harshly. The job should be done soon after fruiting.

Loganberries and berries of similar type carry fruit on new, young canes. They are treated like raspberries, with the old canes being removed after fruiting.

If they have been allowed to grow wild, this can be a difficult job with other than thornless varieties. This is a good argument for fan-training on a fence or wires, where the job is much simplified.

Blackberries are different, in that the canes will carry fruit for several years. With these it is reasonable to remove any over two years old, together with diseased or damaged stems.

Red currants are treated differently to their black counterparts. The fruit is borne in clusters on the old stems around the bases of the sideshoots, and so they are spur-pruned like apples. The side growths are cut back to four or five leaves in July, and then in winter are further cut to 12mm (.5in) from the base.

If the buds are prone to attack by the likes of bullfinches, this winter pruning can be left until spring. This is not necessary where they are netted over or growth in a fruit cage.

White currants are treated in the same way. Spur-pruning can also be adopted for gooseberries, where they are grown as a cordon on wall or fence. If grown as a freestanding bush, they can be left untouched except for the removal of old wood from time to time.

Your Gardening Week

WORK FOR THE WEEK

 SWEAT PEAS Early blooms of sweet pea can be had from sowings made at the begining of October, so it's time to order seed.

 DISBUD CYCLAMEN The appearance of cyclamen flowers is eagerly awaited. A better effect is achieved if the first to form are removed, allowing the strength of the plant to build.

 GREASEBAND Fix greasebands round the stems of apple are pear trees, to prevent crawling insects reaching fruit-bearing branches. To be doubly sure, place a second band higher up the trunk.

 PETUNIAS While bedding petunias are generally raised from seed, there is no reason why new stock cannot be raised from cuttings provided they can be housed for the winter.

HOUSE HOUSE-PLANTS Any houseplants which have been set outdoors for the summer should be brought in before frost arrives.

 REMOVE RUNNERS Check over strawberries, and remove any new runners that may be forming.

 LONG TOMS To extend the season of outdoor tomatoes, they can be detached from any support, laid down on straw and covered with cloches.

 LESS HUMID As temperatures decline, reduce the amount of damping down in the glasshouse or frame. High humidity and lower temperatures can encourage fungal infection.

PLANT EVER-GREENS Evergreen shrubs and conifers can be planted earlier than deciduous kinds. The soil is still warm, and they should establish well if planted firmly and watered in. Further watering and protection from drying winds may be necessary.

Just Geraniums

Given the mild weather there should still be time to take cuttings from your favourite geraniums.

This is a fairly simple and worthwhile job, for these are plants which, whilst giving a good display of themselves, really need to be seen en masse, which can be quite expensive if you buy-in.

Take short, sturdy shoots which have not flowered and cut cleanly below a joint (see left). Take off the lower leaves so as to retain only the top two or three.

Then, lay them aside for a couple of hours before progressing further, so that the cut ends will dry, or "heal". This will help to prevent rotting.

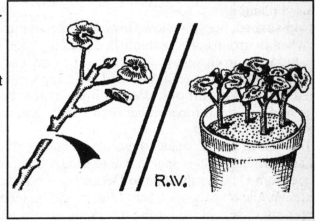

R.W.

Four or five inch pots with drain holes, should be filled with John Innes No 2 or a finely sieved mixture of loam, sand and peat.

Dip the ends of the cuttings in hormone rotting powder before planting to about half their length in the pots. You should get five or six cuttings around the edge of such a pot (see right).

Ideally they will need to be kept in fairly warm conditions, preferably a greenhouse, so as to make roots in a few weeks. They can be kept like this until around March, when they can be put into their own separate 10cm (4in) pots, to bring them on for bedding out in May.

The Excellent Eranthis

O ne of those plants which is aptly titled is Eranthis: its name being derived from the Greek er, 'spring' and anthos, 'flower'. This, the winter aconite, is the earliest bulbous plant to come to bloom in the year. The time of its opening will depend on both weather and position, but it may be as early as January or as late as March in cooler climates.

Eranthis belong to Ranunculaceae, the Buttercup family. They are hardy, low-growing perennials which are ideal for naturalised planting.

Cup-shaped, bright yellow flowers make an impact, particularly when in groups. Well established plantings can carpet the ground with green foliage and yellow flower. They are held on stems around 75mm (3in) tall, and their appearance is heightened by a frill or ruff of leaves set immediately below the petals. The root is a small tuber rather than a bulb, and can be bought now.

Tolerant of partial shade, these plants are ideal for the edge of an area where grass is sparse due to shade. Planting can take place from October through to December – but the sooner the better. While a spacing of 5cm (2in) might be recommended, a better effect is achieved if the tubers are gently scattered on the ground and planted where they fall.

Having said that, try to ensure a reasonable concentration. Don't spread them over too large an area or their impact will diminish.

If you would like to enjoy some a little earlier, keep a few of the tubers back. During October or November, set them close together in pots or pans and cover with 12mm (.5in) of compost.

Grow in a cool glasshouse or on a window ledge that does not catch too much sun. After flowering, the plants can be set out in the garden to join their companions.

There are several types to try. Eranthis cilicica is bright yellow and E. hyemalis a nice lemon yellow. Eranthis tubergenii produces larger flowers of golden yellow, and 'Guinea Gold' is fragrant in deep yellow flushed with bronze.

If you find yourself with space to spare in a cold frame or the borders of an unheated glasshouse, how about raising another crop of potatoes?

Soil beds can be forked over and at the same time enlivened with a dressing of general fertiliser. Egg-sized potatoes from an early crop make ideal seed, but whatever is to hand is worth a try rather than letting the space go unused.

Before planting, ensure the bed is moist; if needed, applying water the night before. Set the tubers 15cm (6in) deep, 30 cm (1ft) apart in rows 37 cm (15in) apart. Earth up as normal.

If your glasshouse or frame does not contain border soil, there is no need to be left out. Potatoes can be planted in pots and should do just as well.

Usually tubers can be set one to a large pot around 25cm (10in) in diameter. If these are not to hand, you might improvise with boxes or patio planters, but they should be light enough to move.

Use a proprietary compost, or prepare your own using loam and leafmould in a ratio of 2:1, to which general fertiliser can be added.

Fill the container to about two-thirds its depth and plant the tuber(s). This level of compost is not dictated from frugality, but allows further compost to be added as growth is made, simulating earthing up! The containers can be stood outdoors while weather permits, and then placed in shelter.

If you don't have a cold glass house or frame, there is no need to be left out. Place the containers in a sheltered position and when the weather deteriorates, cover with a large, preferably thick, plastic bag.

Although the risk is greater, we have been blessed with a succession of mildish winters, and you might manage to raise a crop of new potatoes for Christmas or soon after.

A Lucky Escape

I had a bit of a shock the other day. In the roadway outside our boundary runs a sewer - quite a large one I think, and deep. Over the last couple of weeks a large wagon with hoses and water jets has appeared on three or four occasions, in an endeavour to remove a blockage; without success it seems.

A telephone call from the head gardener at home advised me that some laddie from the council's engineers was there wanting to gain access to our land and "could I come at once?"

I arrived to be met by a plan which showed the outline of our garden - and much to my surprise, a thick red line showing where a branch of the sewer ran beneath it.

The drainage engineer explained that there was a blockage which they had been unable to move, and so they had sent a camera along the pipe to ascertain where it was. He needed to check the measurements, and they would probably need to come in with a digger and break into the pipe.

As he spoke his finger hovered over the plan and my heart skipped a beat, and then another. He was pointing to the 'jungle' with my newly excavated pond, stone walls, interesting paths and new planting.

I wondered whether to try to scare him away with tales of tigers and crocodiles, but knew there would be little point. A month ago this would not have mattered, but now!

On we ventured, and he measured the line, checking for the position of the cast-iron pipe with some electronic sensor. Fortunately for me we ran out of ground and hit the fence before he reached the required distance, and he left to see if my unlucky neighbour was in. A big thankful sigh from me, and I could almost swear that I heard a crocodile shedding tears of relief.

Although the sun is still finding its way through, that smell of autumn is starting to scent the air. Salads fill the table once

again, and remind me that it is time to make further sowings of lettuce to stand the winter.

We tend to think of lettuce as a summer crop, but some of the varieties are quite hardy and can see the winter through with only minimum protection. These hardy varieties can be sown now to mature in May, or a forcing variety can be sown at the beginning of October which, with cloche protection, should be ready for use in April. The hardy varieties will also benefit from cloche cover, reducing the risk of loss and bringing them on a little more quickly.

Choose a position sheltered from the North and the East to avoid the coldest of winter's winds. The land should be well-drained and preferably a lighter loam. Where water does not get away easily it may be worth making a raised bed.

Of course, at this time of year the ground will already have carried its share of the summer crops. To prevent growth being too lush and soft, avoid fresh manure.

Equally the application of fertiliser should be treated with caution. The chances are that residues from the previous crop will suffice, and certainly nitrogen should be avoided, at least until spring when growth can be given a boost.

As my ground is on the heavy side, I tend to use the plot that has carried potatoes. It still has goodness in it, and potatoes always seem to improve the structure of the soil.

Of the varieties, Valdor, Arctic King and the smaller Winter Density can all be tried without cloche protection. Under cloches or perhaps in a frame, try Kweik or May Queen.

Sow thinly in shallow drills 30cm (1 ft) apart. As the seedlings grow, thin initially to 50-75mm (2-3in) and later to 125-150mm (5-6in). A final thinning to 225-300mm (9-12in) is best left to spring when any casualties can be taken into account. Winter Density is a more compact variety, and its final thinning can be kept to 150mm (6in).

Keep a wary eye open for slugs!

Your Gardening Week

STORE SUPPORTS As stakes and canes come free from cleared crops, remove them from the soil and clean and dry them before storing.

SPACE CABBAGE If you have cabbage to plant, space some at 30 x 22cm (12 x 9 ins). After Christmas alternate plants can be used as early greens, leaving the reminder to grow to maturity.

PLANT EVERGREENS Provided we do not experience a prolonged dry spell, from now through to mid-October is a good time to plant evergreens.

MORE FRUIT Take cuttings or currants and gooseberries, selecting healthy wood from productive bushes.

CAMELLIA CUTTINGS Camellia cuttings can be taken now from vigorous, mature bushes. Detach terminal buds with a leaf and a heel of ripe wood, and dip in rooting powder before inserting in lime-free compost.

SLOW MOW As the rate of grass growth diminishes, ease up on mowing the lawn. There is still time to seed bare patches.

MANURE As the digging season threatens, marrows are best harvested and stored in a cool, airy room where they will keep for some time.

APPLES GALORE A lack of frost in winter will ensure a good set of blossoms in spring, and result in a good crop of apples. The earliest varieties are ready in July and August, and now we are into the mid-season types. These ripen fully on the tree and will keep for some weeks if handled with care. The late, long-keeping kinds are usually picked in October and finish their ripening in store.

Picking And Storing

Late summer and early autumn are lovely times for the gardener. Not only are the trees at their best as their leaves change colour, but in many instances there is the pleasure of picking and enjoying their crops.

The time for picking apples and pears will, of course, vary the length of the country. Whilst you cannot therefore rely on a calendar to let you know when picking should start, there are some invaluable pointers.

First, there is the appearance of windfalls on the ground. Then the colour of the fruit will give a hint that the time is ripe.

Not all the crop will be ready at the same time. The ripening process begins at the top of the tree, continuing on the

sides and finally reaches the middle. Thus it will be necessary to pick on two or three occasions.

The final test that shows fruit is ripe for picking must be made by hand. Gently lift the fruit in the palm of the hand and give it a slight twist. It is ready for picking if it comes away easily from the branch.

As for storing, the late maturing varieties are obviously the best. Apples and pears will need slightly different conditions, except in so far as the fruit should be well separated, both as far as physical contact and varieties are concerned.

Pears like a cool, dry atmosphere and should be arranged in boxes with thin slats to hold them upright and apart in rows (see illustration left).

Apples keep better in a slightly warmer, moist atmosphere so as to prevent their skins shrivelling and splitting. Again, wooden boxes are best for storage, but each fruit should be wrapped in a square of newspaper (illustration right) to prolong their storage life.

Your Gardening Week

Damsons, Wasps And Roses

If the lack of a late frost in spring allows a high level of fertilization, then top fruit usually does well. The Victoria plum is particularly rewarding, with drooping branches laden with fruit. Another thing affected by the weather is the amount of damage caused by wasps. Generally, if wet and blustery weather coincides with ripening, then wasps are discouraged from taking to the wing.

By the way, my normal practice is to leave wasp nests alone. It is interesting to see how they establish in different parts of the garden in succesive years, and provided I find out where they are (so that I don't inadvertently disturb the nest) I find them an acceptable part of the scene.

The only exception to this was a couple of years ago, when they found their way into the house wall through an area of perished pointing near the back door.

Some obviously like the idea of being indoors. Recently we had some rewiring done in mother's bungalow. One startled electrician made a rapid exit from the extremes of the roof space when he spotted a nest. This was disposed of with the help of the pest control officer from the council. He had hardly left the premises when a piece of old wiring being pulled from its run in a wall demolished another nest. This time the wasps were angry and, despite beating a hasty retreat, one of the team was stung several times.

That's a bit of a diversion from plums. What I wanted to mention was the advantage of growing damsons. Many of the varieties available have arisen from chance seedlings derived from prunus institia, which occurs in its wild form as the bullace here and in other parts of Europe. It is thought that the name derives from Damascus, where the fruit was in cultivation B.C.

The fruits have good flavour and are suited to pies, puddings and jam. Beside that, the trees are reliable and their self-fertility means that only one needs be planted if space is at a premium. Not choosy as to site, their main requirement is that the ground should not dry out in summer, and they are tolerant of rain, wind and a shortage of sunshine.

Of the varieties to look for, Bradley King has large sweet fruit which ripens in mid-September. It is thought to have been raised in Nottinghamshire, and is first recorded in 1880.

The Merryweather Damson, which comes in late September or early October, has fruit like a small plum - and is likely to be a cross between a damson and a plum - was introduced in 1907.

The Shropshire Damson is likely to have been a selection from the wild, chosen because its fruit was larger than the common type. It produces a crop of juicy, sweet, medium-sized fruit in season in September and has been grown since the eighteenth century.

While abroad with the knife, why not make a few rose cuttings? The plants you raise might not be as long-lived as those budded onto rootstocks, but they come cheap and will fill a space, although they will need three years to make a reasonable size.

Old-fashioned and rambler roses are the easiest to root, followed by floribundas and miniatures. Hybrid teas and climbers are more difficult.

Cuttings are made from this year's wood which has ripened. A rule of thumb is that it is ready when thorns come away cleanly and easily when pressed on the side.

Make them about 20cm (8in) long, though miniatures should be a little shorter. Remove all but the top or three leaves and press off any thorns.

Set the cutting outdoors in an adequately drained nursery plot. Take out a slit trench, run a layer of sand in the bottom and dip the cuttings in rooting powder before placing them two-thirds into the ground and firming in.

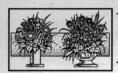

Lovely Lavateras

Lavatera arborea, the tree mallow, makes a strong impact with its size and flowers. While it is not entirely hardy and may be cut back by frost, the relatively mild winters of the last few years mean that many have escaped this fate, and so attained significant size.

Even when frost damage occurs, it may be expected that they bounce back in spring unless the conditions have been quite severe. The new shoots can quickly reach anything from 2-3 m (6-10 ft), depending on conditions, forming a large, open shrub. The flowers are pale purple and extend from summer into autumn.

Lavatera olbia has reddish purple flowers and grows to around 2m (6ft). Its variety rosea is rose-pink. Flowering occurs from June to October, and the overall appearance is heightened by a soft, grey down.

All like hot, dry conditions although even in coolish and wet summers, mine have performed well. While their size suits them to a position at the back of a border, they reward a greater prominence and make an effective specimen.

Other than the variegated form of L. arborea which has white variegated leaves, new stock may be raised from seed sown under glass in February or March in a temperature of 16C (60F), or set outdoors in late spring. Cuttings can be made in mid-summer, but are best kept in a close propagating case until well rooted.

I also continue to be impressed by the annual form, Lavatera trimestris, and its varieties Mont Blanc and Silver Cup. Seed may be sown in the final flowering position during September or April. Alternatively it may be sown in heat under glass from January onwards. Both varieties have a strong, self-supporting branch framework and attain a height and spread of around 60-75cm (24-30in). As you might expect the flowers of Mont Blanc

are white, though with a hint of pink in the bud. They open to around 7cm (3in). Silver Cup belies its name a little in that its basic colour is glowing pink, though enhanced with silver streaking. Its flowers are a little larger and completely smother the plants when fully open. A further variety is Ruby Regis, with rose-red flowers and mid-green foliage.

Planting continues in the reclaimed part of the 'jungle.' At what seemed fairly large expense I invested in a fairly large plant of Gunner's manicata, although through time I expect to see a lot of plant for my money.

This is often described as a plant for setting by large stretches of water, be they river or lake, because of the possible ultimate size. In fact, in all but the most favoured districts it will not achieve world records and can be constrained by going easy on the manure.

Some call it the 'prickly rhubarb,' and while this is not a name that appeals to me, its foliage is not dissimilar. It does, however, achieve greater size, and leaves to 2.75m (9ft) in diameter have been recorded on stems nearly as high. Unless it becomes really well established and spreads as a clump, this makes it no bigger than many a shrub.

During winter the crown needs protection. This can be provided by using the leaves when they are cut down by frost and augmenting them with bracken or litter. The largest plants need a good feed and will respond to a generous dressing of manure in spring.

A large planting hole should be prepared and enlivened with loam, manure and compost. The site need not have direct access to a pond or lake, but in this case ample water will need to be applied in summer. Avoid windy sites or the leaves may become tattered.

The flowers are greenish and carried on spikes to 180cm (6ft) tall. If desired they may be cut out in spring, the energy saving being diverted to growing larger leaves.

Your Gardening Week

WORK FOR THE WEEK

✔ WORM CASTS With dew and humidity, moist worm casts are more persistent. It is a good idea to scatter them before mowing, lest the flattened heap provides a toe-hold for weeds.

✔ FINAL TRIM The growth of hedges will be slowing down, and any that need tidying can be given a final trim.

✔ TAKE NOTE Make a note in your diary of new plantings and their rough position. It's amazing how labels can disappear over the year.

✔ JERUSALEM ARTI-CHOKES Jerusalem artichokes will have made all their growth. The stems can be cut back. While tubers may be left in the ground until needed, if the space is required they may be lifted and stored as potatoes.

✔ KEEP LEAVES OUT If you have a garden pond, it is a good idea to cover it with netting at this time to minimise the number of leaves entering the water.

✔ DRY SOIL Where materials such as manure or compost have to be borrowed from around the garden, try to move them into place while the ground is dry, even if not used immediately.

✔ MAKE SPACE Many summer plants in the glasshouse can be dispensed with or given a rest. Gloxinias have finished blooming and can be allowed to dry slowly. Large, tuberous begonias and achimenes can be treated in the same way. Use the space created for winter-flowering plants or to hold stock plants for next year.

✔ INSULATION It is time to think about insulation for the glasshouse. There are a number of systems using polythene or bubble polythene available. If this material is attached to the structure, make sure that ventilators are kept separate so that air can be switched on if needed.

Sweet Pea

Among the flower arrangers' favourites for summer displays, sweet peas must come pretty near the top. For nearly three hundred years the sweet pea has been grown in Britain and during that time there have been changes in its development.

Now we have a wide variety of choices from the "old fashioned" varieties to the newer highly scented and brilliantly coloured ones, to the even newer dwarf types, which are so easy to grow in the border of smaller gardens. They need little support - just a bunch of twiggy shoots will do to hold up their 45cm (18in) height - and they look good as an end feature.

To get early blooms next year you really need to start work now. First prepare a trench. This will need deep digging but should not require further manure, providing the plot is in a good fertile condition.

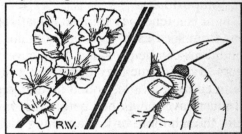

If you want to reach exhibition standards you will need to double dig and where the second spit was removed, dig in plenty of rotted manure. Then refill and allow to settle after applying a couple of handfuls of bonemeal to the top spit.

After settlement and hopefully a downpour - or a watering - you can prepare for sowing the seeds of your choice.

The next job is to prepare the seeds. They will need to soak in water for 24 hours to enable them to swell for the skins to break more easily. Black skinned varieties will need a little more care to ensure germination; being thick skinned they may need to be chipped by breaking the skin with a very sharp pocket knife (see right). Draw the drill 5-7cm (2-3in) deep and sow about 7.5cm (3in) apart.

Do not water for two or three days, but then give them a thorough soaking. From thereon, keep them moist throughout germination. No protection is needed during the winter.

Productive Canes

Autumn colour continues to improve on many deciduous trees, chrysanthemums and dahlias still show strongly, and a fine flush of flower has appeared on autumn-flowering heathers.

Stripping summer bedding to make way for spring flowering plants need not be a loss. There are always a few of the tender plants still at their best. These can be potted up and given an extended life with little protection. The remainder add weight to the compost heap.

There is a tendency to raise Impatiens and Begonia semperflorens from seed each year; but both are perennial, and if frost-free conditions can be provided, they may be kept through successive years. By this time they tend to be a little ragged and can be trimmed back a little, potted up and kept on a glasshouse bench.

I must have mentioned before that raspberries are my favourite fruit, though more or less anything picked fresh from a bush cannot be faulted. It's interesting to know that the wild raspberry can be found growing as a native plant in most parts of these isles, and that is a pointer to the fact that cultivated varieties are likely to do well. Needless to say, some soils do suit them better than others. The best crops can be expected from a well-drained loam capable of retaining moisture, and amply supplied with organic material. Any soils which lie wet in the winter should be improved.

Calcarious soils, however, are unsuitable. When the pH rises over 7, iron and manganese are locked up and the plants suffer chlorosis from the shortage. Something slightly on the acid side with a pH of 6 is ideal, though pH5 will be too acidic.

Though raspberry canes are available for planting from the end of October, November is generally regarded as the best month for planting.

This allows time for the roots to extend and establish before any top-growth is produced in spring. Nevertheless, if circumstances dictate, planting can continue through the winter, even to April.

So, there is time to select a site, order varieties and prepare the grounds.

Raspberries can be planted in single rows, set with 45 cm (18 in) between each cane. Ideally, rows should run north/south to allow even development on both sides, and with at least 1.8 m (6 ft) between rows this should allow reasonable space for inter-cropping.

Alternatively, they can be grown against a fence or wall, but development will tend to be one-sided and picking becomes a little more difficult.

Good support will be required and you should be prepared to set posts at least 1.5m (5ft) high at 4.5m (15ft) intervals, and suitable bracing at the end of each row. These can either have suitably spaced single strands of galvanised wire to which the canes can be tied, or crosspieces can be attached to the posts to allow a double run of wire within which the canes can be contained.

Remember that good drainage is required, and so on wet ground give consideration to either cultivating deeply to improve the situation or creating a raised area. The disadvantage with the latter course of action is that in dry periods, the surface will be more likely to dry out. So you would need to be prepared to apply water at such times, especially since raspberries are surface-rooting.

In contrast to the need for good drainage, there is also a requirement for ready access to soil water, and so the structure must ensure that it is retained in sufficient amounts to be accessible to the roots, but without waterlogging.

This is best achieved by ensuring there is plenty of organic material within the soil. Either well-rotted garden compost or stable manure can be dug in and, in addition, apply a dressing of superphosphate.

Branch Into Blackcurrants

A good fruit garden can provide healthy supplies of black-berries, rasberries, currants and gooseberries. Although my favourite is the raspberry, the currants come a close second. Gooseberries are good, but I tend to the view that black-berries and blackcurrants do best when mixed with apple. Of course that is when they are used in pudding or pie; but all of them bring heightened pleasure that the non-fruit grower would do well to experience.

I suppose from a cultural point of view blackcurrants are the easiest to grow. They need little care and attention other than the suppression of weeds, fairly straightforward pruning, and a dose of nitrogenous fertiliser from time to time to ensure high yields.

They will thrive in most districts, preferring a soil with good drainage though retentive of moisture - which they will absorb in large amounts. They flower early in the year, during March or April, and so some shelter from the coldest winds is desirable. This increases the likelihood of insect activity, essential to ensure good pollination. Planting can take place through to mid-March, though the earlier the better. Soil should be deeply dug and have a generous dressing of manure worked in.

If manure is not to hand, use compost enriched with bone meal and hoof and horn at 85g (3oz) of each per .8m^2 (1yd^2), together with 28g (1oz) of sulphate of potash. Planting will often have to be delayed until early November to give the ground a chance to firm down. This respite also provides the opportunity to send for catalogues, choose and order cultivars, and arrange the delivery of plants.

There are many cultivars old and new to choose from. By judicious selection of earlies, mid-seasons and lates, fruit can be had in succession from July through to early September. One caviat to this is that if your site is exposed to frost or cold winds, and you fear that flowers may be damaged, it may be better to settle

on cultivars that flower later in the spring.

It is worth mentioning that, while blackcurrants do need a rich soil to perform at their best, they do not like excessive acidity. Thus, if you suspect that your soil is on the acid side it is probably worth carrying out a pH test. The aim should be a pH of around 6. If it falls below 5.7 then liming will be beneficial. Use hydrated lime at 57-85g (2-3oz) per .8m^2 (1yd^2) or ground chalk at 85-113g (3-4oz) and scatter evenly over the surface.

When plants arrive, unpack them straight away and check their condition. If they appear at all dry, plunge them in water for 24 hours. This is probably a worthwhile exercise even when they seem all right.

Spacing might vary a little with the vigour of the cultivar, but a general guide would be to set plants at 150cm (5ft) in the row with 180cm 6(ft) between rows. Don't skimp on the planting hole; make plenty of room to accommodate the roots.

The bushes can be set 5cm (a few inches) below the original nursery mark. This means plenty of buds will be below soil level and should result in strong new growth from the base to form a 'stool'.

Don't expect any fruit next year. While it would be possible to take a crop from the branches already on the bush, the future will be better served if they are cut back to just above soil level after planting. This way the bush has a full season to make roots which will sustain the crop in the following years. During next year around half a dozen good shoots should be produced which will carry fruit in the following season, and these should be left alone. The only exception is if any are weak or badly placed. If so, they may be cut back during autumn.

Your Gardening Week

LETTUCE Plant winter lettuce in cold frames, keeping them well ventilated when conditions allow. Take precautions against slugs.

COMPOST Make a fresh compost heap, so that the one in current use will provide material for digging-in later on.

POT PLANTS Any long-term pot plants that will not be rested through the winter should be checked over. If the compost is exhausted or in poor condition, repot while there is time for the plants to re-establish before winter.

DON'T DELAY ON ROSES If you intend to plant roses, send your order in as soon as possible. Although planting can take place through the winter as conditions allow, I like to have the job finished by mid-November.

EARTH UP Celery and leeks should be ready for their final earthing. While you're at it, draw a little soil around the stems of winter greens to give them extra stability.

LIFT AND DIVIDE Either now or early spring is the time to get in among the herbaceous perennials, to lift and divide those plants which do not resent disturbance. Early-flowering types are best dealt with now, while the later flowerers can be left over.

BEANS Any French beans from a July sowing can have the cropping season extended if cloche protection can be given. At the same time, think about making a sowing of broad beans, but only in a sheltered spot on free-draining soils.

LAWN CARE Use a spring-tinned rake to comb lawns in at least two directions to remove thatch and accumulated debris. Mow with the cut set high, and then top-dress with sandy compost. Any areas of compaction can be relieved prior to this. A boost can be given by applying a dressing of autumn lawn food.

Flowering Hedges

Too often when we think of hedges, we tend to consider the leaf bearers such as privet, conifers or the tough but rather woody hawthorn Crataegus monogyna.

There are many other shrubs to try, however; roses, Hebe and the flowering Quince, flowering currants and the evergreen honeysuckles, such as Lonicera nitida.

The latter will quite readily reach a height of 1.5-2m (5-6ft), but if you want a screen of up to 2.5m (8ft) go for Lonicera syringantha, which gives lilac flowers and a delightful sweet scent.

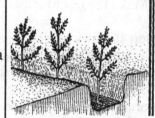

If you have any of these already in the garden, take cuttings. Each should be about a foot long and with the bottom leaves stripped off (illustration, right).

Of prime importance if you are starting a hedge is to bear in mind that it is likely to remain in position for some years. Prepare the site well to receive your cuttings to ensure that nourishment will be readily available over a long period.

First mark out the site of the hedge and dig a trench about 60cm (2ft) deep, putting of the soil to one side. The rest of the earth should then be dug over and mixed with well rotted material before turning back the rest of the soil.

Let the soil settle before opening a trench about six inches deep to receive your cuttings, which should be spaced at intervals of about 15cm (6in). This will allow enough plants, so that any that fail to root can be removed (illustration, left). It will certainly be as well to reduce the plants to a final position allowing 30cm (12in) between each.

Whether you intend to grow the hedge from your own cuttings or bought in plants, as soon as new growth starts, keep the plants restricted in height to encourage growth low down.

Dahlias And Cranberries

It won't be long now before frost blackens the green leaves of dahlias, a presage of the needs to cut back stems and prepare for winter storage. Dahlias were introduced from the warmer climate of Mexico in the 18th century, and generally have to be lifted and dried to survive the winter.

While you may wish to remove the foliage straight away because it becomes unsightly, the tubers can be left in the ground for up to a fortnight, so that a time can be chosen when the ground is dry. Make the cut to leave about 15cm (6in) of stem.

When lifting, insert the fork at a reasonable distance to minimise the chance of damage to the tubers. Remove the soil, and if the tubers are very wet leave them to dry in the open before bringing inside.

Labelling is important and is best done at lifting to lessen the chance of a mix-up. It is also a good idea to make notes on colour and height, so that the design of any display can be enhanced in future years.

Once inside, the tubers should be set upside-down and left for a period to allow all moisture to drain from the hollow stems. After this set the roots in boxes, covering with sand to keep them cool and slightly moist. This helps prevent them from shrivelling.

Set the boxes in a frost-free place, and make checks every three or four weeks to ensure that storage rots have not set in. Any affected tubers can be removed from their boxes and treated with fungicide before drying and returning to store.

If you have the benefit of a light and well-drained soil, it may be worth leaving the tubers in the ground. However, don't risk them all on a first trial occasion.

If you have an area where acid-loving plants such as rhododendrons and heathers thrive, them why not pop in the odd cranberry, so that your own jelly can accompany Christmas dinner? The best to choose is Vaccinium macrocarpon, the American cranberry, which grows more strongly and has larger berries than our native Vaccinium oxyccocus.

It makes a prostrate creeping shrub which flowers pink in summer. There follows a crop of large red berries in September and early October which may be picked for jelly.

Planting can take place from now through to spring, choosing a site with light shade. The soil should be well supplied with leaf-mould,which can be forked in; and after planting a good dressing of leaf-mould mixed with sand can be spread over the surface.

The aim is to simulate a moorland environment, and flooding with water once or twice during the summer will do no harm. As the leaf-mould become depleted, further dressing can be given in future years.

Once established, the wiry stems and box-like leaves make good ground cover. If tending to become straggly, they can be clipped over in April.

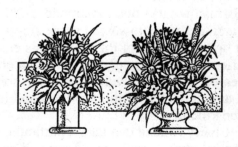

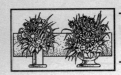
Care In Winter

It is noticable that the seasons are moving on and conditions becoming more cool and damp. The greatest disappointment for me has been the rapidity with which darkness has fallen, curtailing activities outside. Especially as I have a little catching up to do in terms of tidying the garden for winter, removing weeds, cutting back unwanted growth, collecting leaves to turn into leaf-mould and so on.

This is important and helps to minimise the amount of work we face in spring when there is a lot of work to be done. But we should bear in mind that some of the materials removed do afford protection to less hardy plants, and so should be replaced with other materials.

This is probably true of some of the less hardy herbaceous perennials, but both neatness and frost protection can be achieved if the crowns are covered with a mound of bark, leaf-mould or bracken. Some herbaceous perennials such as the kniphofias or 'Red Hot Pokers', have evergreen leaves and these can be pulled to a point and tied in at the top to give added protection to the crown.

Despite surviving in extremes of cold, some alpine specimens can succumb in British winters due to dampness. It is normal practice when planting alpines to spread stone chippings on the soil surface right up to the neck of the plant. This ensures good drainage and carries water away quickly. If by any chance the stone has disappeared or became well mixed with soil, drainage may be impeded and the collar of the plant - at and just below soil level - may be killed.

Those with grey, hairy foliage can take a particular dislike to the vagaries of the weather as moisture, deposited on the foliage during foggy, damp days, is frozen at night when the temperature plunges - only to be thawed again when the next day dawns, bright with winter sun. The physical effect of this successive pat-

tern of freezing and thawing can be sufficient to injure and sometimes kill the plant. With tender specimens the answer is to provide cover, either with cloches or by fixing a pane of glass or piece of stout plastic above the plant. Use bent wire as supporting legs.

Although the main tree and shrub planting season has not started into full swing, deciduous forms can happily bed down for the winter in their dormant state. Do, however, spare an extra thought for evergreens, which still carry the majority of their foliage. They are particularly vulnerable to the effects of dry, cold winds which remove water from the foliage at a faster rate than the newly planted and unestablished roots can make up.

The answer with these is to provide protection from the wind by erecting a wind-break or screen on the windward side. This is easily achieved with two or three stout stakes and a piece of plastic mesh or hessian. On smaller specimens, push three bamboo canes into the ground and tie these in at the top. Cover with a polythene bag which should be slit open at the top to prevent sweating. In very cold conditions, however, the slit can be closed with clips.

Plants such as roses, which are to be pruned in the spring, can have long shoots tipped back to reduce the amount of movement caused by wind.

Even after pruning this may still occur. Take the first opportunity to firm soil back to the stem or, if the ground has become hard, fill the gap with compost.

In the glasshouse, try to avoid sudden fluctuations in temperature by ventilating with care and keeping draughts to a minimum. Water should be given sparingly and splashes avoided so that humidity is kept low. Too much moisture in the air will encourage botrytis. Keep an eye on the glass itself, which soon becomes dirty. If the opportunity arises, given it a clean to let in as much light as possible.

❑ ❑ ❑

Your Gardening Week

✔ **START DIGGING** As land becomes vacant in the vegetable plot, a start can be made to digging when ground conditions are good. Remember to leave the ground rough to allow maximum penetration by frost.

✔ **PROTECT STRAW-BERRIES** Strawberries potted for forcing early next year should be given protection against frost. Plunge the pots in sand or leaf-mould or stand in a cold frame.

✔ **TOP-DRESS FRUIT** Where heavy crops of fruit have been carried on fruit trees, it is a good idea to apply a top-dressing of compost. Where there is a low-level graft union, carefully remove some of the existing soil first, so that the surface level is not built up to a point where the scion or variety could take root. Cover with a mulch of manure.

✔ **BORDER CARNA-TIONS** Young plants arising from the layering of border carnations during August can be detached and transplanted. In areas subject to cold or excessive damp, pot them singly and overwinter in a cold frame.

✔ **PLANT BIENNIALS** Biennials such as foxglove, Canterbury bells and honesty can be planted where they are to flower next year.

✔ **CATCH CATERPIL-LARS** Caterpillars of the cabbage white butterfly may still be in among brassicas, so check them over, including the growing points of Brussels sprouts.

✔ **ASPARAGUS BEDS** Cut back asparagus foliage and carefully clean the bed of weed and any self-set plants, before applying a layer of manure topping with soil or good garden compost.

✔ **PRUNE GOOSEBER-RIES** Once the leaves have fallen, gooseberries can be pruned. On young bushes, cut back the leading shoots by about half to encourage growth. On older bushes, the laterals can be cut back depending on their vigour.

Storing The Best Of Bloomers

To ensure the continued development of an eye-catching garden, there's much to be said in favour of keeping the best of the past year.

Plants are expensive especially if you are starting a new garden or if you are trying to fill in bare spots. If, therefore, you have favourite plants which have done particularly well or blooms which have proved particularly startling or long lasting, you'd be well advised to keep them for next year.

Careful storage is the answer. Dahlias should be left until the first frost. Then gently lift them with a fork, cut the foliage back to about 15cm (6in) of the soil mark; clear the tubers of soil and leave them on greenhouse staging or raised slats of wood upside down so that moisture can drain down the stems (see pic left).

After a few weeks they can be put right side up in boxes of dry soil or compost for the winter.

Gladioli need lifting when the leaves turn yellow. Clean off the corms and hang the plants in a dry airy space. After a few weeks, cut off the leaf stems to within 15cm (6in) of the soil level. Before cleaning all the soil off, remove bulbils from the corms and keep them in paper bags together with loose skin. Then hang in nets for the winter.

Begonias, some of the most beautiful and colourful bloomers, will need lifting as complete as possible until the corms have dried out. Once lifted, place them in boxes until the top growth has withered. Then remove the corms, clean them off and plant them in small hollows in a box filled with either leaf mould or dry sand, growth side up (pic right). A cool but slightly moist place will suit them well.

247

Autumn Lawns And Flowers

O n balance, it seems to have been a good year for lawns. Only latterly, on my heavy soil, have the moist conditions led to the creation of muddy patches. Of course it has to be recognised that this has coincided with conservatory construction and a fair amount of moving about with excavations and import of materials.

Earlier in the year we saw a prolonged dry spell, so that much ornamental and sports turf turned from green to brown. I know that in this area golfers and bowlers were starting to panic lest their sacred turf should fail to recover. Then came the rain - and almost overnight the green returned.

These significant variations in conditions do tend to exact some toll. In addition, the relatively moist summer has meant that mowing has been a regular occurrence which, taken with the leeching effect of rain, means that food reserves can become depleted.

With the mild conditions experienced over the last year or two, regular mowing has continued well into the autumn, with even the odd cut in winter or early spring. Again with heavy ground this is a job for late in the day, when there is the best chance that dew will have evaporated and the surface dried.

At this time there is more to do than just mow. Not least is the need to rake or brush away leaves and other debris on a regular basis. Ideally any scarification should be carried out in September; but here things have fallen a little behind, and so I await one of those clear autumnal days to catch up.

The removal of thatch opens up the surface allowing air to circulate more freely and stimulates the growth of runners and sideshoots.

I'll also continue to apply topdressing. While previously this would most likely have been a mixture of loam peat and sand, I have simplified my needs to well-riddled leafmould just mixed with sand, and spread after the surface has been spiked.

While I know that mist can be a hazard to the traveller, of late there have been some thoroughly attractive mornings. Mist and haze held in place by invert layers in the atmosphere have created beautiful effects in the morning sunlight, and in the garden this season of mist and mellow has its bright spots.

Sedum spectabile has come into its own, as slightly rounded broad-topped clusters of pink flower burst forth to grace the attractive foliage.

Asters serve us well with free-flowering displays, starting in the height of summer and persisting through into autumn. There are many cultivars to choose from, some growing to near six feet (180cm) are ideal for the back of the herbaceous border. One growing to half that size but worth looking out for is Aster frikartii. Orange-centered lavender-blue flowers appear in July/August, and its free-flowering nature gives good effect.

With more delicate appeal, one of the treasures of autumn is Schizostylis coccinea, the Kaffir Lily. As one might expect with a name like that, it hails from South Africa and is a little on the tender side. In colder areas it can be grown in the open until September and then potted and brought indoors to flower.

Flowering is completed by December, when the pot may be set in the shelter of a frame until April when the rhizome is returned to the ground.

In favoured areas it may be left outdoors, and even in cooler places it is worth trying in a sheltered sunny position such as a border at the bottom of a wall. However, the soil should be moist and rich.

Strap-like leaves reach to 60cm (2ft) and racemes of pretty star-shaped flowers appear in October and November. The rhizomes grow rapidly and can be divided in March/April.

Check Trees!

With buddleias, I always find myself facing a difficult decision in spring on whether or not to prune them. The tall, arching stems have their appeal, although they can become a little too large for some situations. Certainly cutting them hard back in early spring stimulates the ready production of new shoots, and encourages flowering, better than if they were left untouched.

The thing I don't like is the period, albeit brief, when a collection of short, ugly and knobbly stem bases pop up around borders. The answer is to plant them behind some other shrub which is a couple of feet high, and carries foliage at this critical time.

The other day, while on my travels, I popped over to look at a sycamore, still in full leaf and which had fallen over with no evidence of high winds at the time. As I neared it, the reason became clear.It was not a particularly vigorous tree, though it had made sixty or so feet in height. I guess that when it started to grow or was planted, the ground in which it stood was reasonable.

Then, for some reason, the water-table changed. Certainly the ground was wet and the turf was flecked with rushes. Through time the tree roots had rotted away until just a lump remained at the bottom of the trunk.

Looking at it I could imagine that something as simple as a magpie making a heavy landing on a high branch would be sufficient to send it over! It served as a reminder that trees need to be inspected on a regular basis.

I'm still surprised at the number of dead elms that remain standing, obviously several years after succumbing to elm disease. Their pale, brittle, bark-stripped branches are a stark reminder that action is needed before hefty branches start to tumble earthwards of their own volition.

There are still elms around so far unaffected, for whatever quirk of the disease-carrying beetle's flight-path. They stand as a reminder of how important and effective that beloved tree was in the landscape. Sadly, with each succeeding year, the remorseless infection goes on.

A few weeks ago I noticed a snippet in a newspaper, the gist of which was that a resistant stock of elm was being bred from previously infected trees. Unfortunately I did not follow it up, and while I hope it may be the case, my own experience gives no great cause for hope.

In and around my garden are a number of young elms. Not seedlings I suspect, but rather suckers that have arisen from the roots of affected and long since removed trees. In their first few years they are vibrant with health, strong in growth and with good leaf colour. Then, it seems, on attaining a certain size, they brown and die.

If you believe you have an affected tree, it is pleasing to note that most local authorities are still able to give impartial advice on the condition of trees, or to indicate contractors capable of undertaking any necessary works in a reasonable manner. Even so, it always makes sense to obtain more than one quotation.

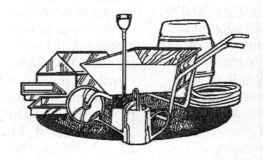

Your Gardening Week

 SPRING FLOWER When planting crocus, grape hyacinths, scillas and the like out in the garden, keep a few back for potting for an early indoor display.

 LIFT GLADIOLI Loosen the ground with a fork and then lift gladioli. Cut off the stem just above the corm and ensure that they are dry before placing in store.

CUT-BACK CHRYSANTHS As outdoor chrysanthemums finish flowering, cut them back and them lift the stools and store them in shallow boxes of compost kept in a frame.

 PROTECT ALPINES As the likelihood of cool, humid conditions increases, alpine plants with hairy or downy foliage will benefit from protection. This is normally achieved by covering with a sheet of glass or plastic supported on wire legs.

 LAY TURF There is still time to prepare lawn areas by laying turf. The ground is still sufficiently warm to encourage new root growth, allowing a reasonable amount of establishment before growth really slows down for the winter.

TREAT YOURSELF Splash out and treat yourself to an extra bag of tulips, which can be planted before mid-November.

SPROUT CARE Remove yellowing leaves from Brussels sprouts and firm the plants in well with your feet. If they are in an exposed position it may be worth staking them.

EARLY PEAS If you have the space and the time, why not try an early sowing of peas for an early crop next year? Take out a broad drill 15cm (6in) deep, rake in a little bonemeal and broadcast round-seeded varieties such as Feltham First.

 LIFT AND PICK Lift and pick all perishable crops for storage in the near future.

Soft Fruit Cuttings

One of the delights of gardening is gathering the goodies be they cut flowers for vases, vegetables for the dinner table or fruits for desserts.

But, come October, you can make efforts at increasing your stock of soft-fruiting plants such as gooseberries and black and red currants.

Blackcurrants are easy. Hardwood cuttings, each about 22cm (9in) long and taken from good healthy bushes, will root easily when planted in a trench to a depth so that only 3 or 4 buds are left above the ground.

Choose well-ripened wood and cut with sharp secateurs just above a bud (see pic left). Trim the tip off above a bud, so as to make a cutting just about 22cm (9in) long, and plant 15cm (6in) apart (see pic right).

R.W.

Press the soil firmly around cuttings with the foot and keep moist throughout the summer. It will take about a year before you can remove the new plants to their permanent growing positions.

For gooseberries, choose shoots of this year's growth, about 30cm (1ft) long, and pull them from the parent plant with a heel of old wood.

Remove the top 5cm (2in) of the cutting and all spines and buds, except about three or four at the top. Plant 15cm (6in) deep in a trench, and 15cm (6in) apart.

For red currants, again take hard wood cuttings about 22cm (9in) long, but rub off all except the top four or five buds. Again plant at a depth of about 15cm (6in) and 15cm (6in) apart.

Mount Stewart

Chance and mid-September found me in Northern Ireland for an all too brief spell. Names like Lurgan, Portadown and Dungannon, which previously I had only known through distressing news of the "troubles", transformed into attractive towns set in idyllic countryside. Here it seemed that all the world could be made up of a succession of small farms, each with its own white-painted bungalow. How nice it was that the scale of the holdings and the field patterns meant that hedgerows abounded, and all surrounding Lough Neagh - tantamount to an inland sea, with its 65 miles of shoreline.

A visit to the Mountains of Mourne wrought a remarkable change. On the lower slopes of these granite peaks the holdings were just as plentiful. While the ubiquitous white bungalows continued, hedgerows had given way to walls with their own distinctive character. The action of glaciers in the past has left a gritty soil littered with rounded boulders. These were and still are collected and built into thick, drystone walls, clearing land for agriculture at the same time.

A few miles brought me from the thin peaty soils of the exposed mountains to the richess of the Mount Stewart Garden. Situated at the head of Strangeford Lough, some five miles south-east of Newtownards on the A20, this 80-acre garden enjoys a sub-tropical climate, a lime-free soil and around 35 inches of rain a year. While much of the estate bears testament to the rough parkland planting of the 18th Century, it conceals and protects a jewel of a garden, largely created by the 7th Marquess of Londonderry and his wife Edith Lady Londonderry who took up residence in 1921.

Here is an assemblage of outdoor rooms, each with its own character, leading one on in anticipation of fresh discoveries, until a turn of a corner reveals a larger landscape. The wealth and variety of plants is such that I should think it worth a visit any day of the year.

I suppose what impressed me most was the rampant vigour of growth. Here were cannas which made me feel small, and actinidias which scrambled to the tops of 70-foot trees, cordylines of stalwart proportions, large Irish Yews and enormous Tasmanian Blue Gums reaching to the best part of a hundred feet. Around the Fountain Terrace and on a smaller scale, Ophiopogon planiscarpus nigrescens formed dense clumps of curving grass-like leaves, near-black in colour and topped with spikes carrying dark berries to match.

Rosa setipoda with stout, erect stems carrying few thorns had lost its beautiful clear pink flowers, but carried a fine crop of large flagon-shaped crimson fruits. The leaves are glandular underneath, and give off a sweet-briar fragrance when crushed. A small specimen of Ilex aquifolium 'Silver Milkboy' showed attractive dark green leaves with a central blotch of creamy-white and strong spines. This plant can be prone to reversion, and any green shoots appearing should be removed.

The Dodo Terrace was built in 1925 and contains amusing animal statues. Rosemaries, lavenders, camellias and rhododendrons set the scene, and lead through to the Italian Garden whose parterres were based on those of Dunrobin Castle in Sutherland. The Spanish Garden is flanked by tall, clipped hybrid cypresses which are being trained into splendid arches. Further clipping was evidenced in the Shamrock Garden, enclosed by a yew hedge in the shape of the shamrock and containing a topiary Irish harp.

Around the corner was a fine specimen of Myrtus appiculata. This import from Chile had made quite a large tree and was bedecked with solitary white flowers. While these pass, the cinnamon-coloured bark remains, peeling off in places to reveal a beautiful creamy, inner surface beneath.

Operated by the National Trust, its hours of opening vary through the year and further information can be had by telephoning (0124774) 88387.

Pour On Boron But Only If You Must!

Recently I was asked if borax could be made into a solution and poured onto the soil before setting seed. The simple answer is yes, but you do need to understand why.

Borax is used to correct a deficiency of the minor plant food boron; but an excess of the element can also have detrimental effects. If you suspect such a problem the best course of action is to arrange for a sample of soil to be tested for its chemical content.

In respect of the soil type, it might have been produced from parent rocks which naturally have a low boron content. The condition is also to be found in very sandy soils, where their free-draining nature and lack of retentiveness allows chemicals to be leached out relatively easily. In some circumstances there may be adaquate boron in the soil, but for one reason or another the plants are unable to take it in.

So, some knowledge of the soil in the area can be a help, but don't forget that where development has taken place, it is not unknown for builders to transport 'top-soil' over fairly long distances. In common with 'Rambling Sid Rumpold', I think the answer lies in the soil!

So far as symptoms are concerned, a good example of this can be found in cauliflowers, where the curds develop brown patches. When cut through, brownish patches and hollows are also to be found inside, and the curd has a bitter taste.

The effect of boron deficiency is closely related to the availability of calcium, and the symptoms of either deficiency are similar in many cases. Besides cauliflowers, other brassicas - beetroot, celery, lettuce and sweet corn - can all exhibit severe symptoms, as can apples.

The effect on other brassicas is similar to that in cauliflowers.

With cabbage and Brussels sprouts, the pith of the stems can be brown and hollowed. Celery exhibits browning of the leaves, with corky mottling and cracking of the leaf stems. Lettuce shows tip-burn and leaf scorching. In sweet corn the growing point dies out, light stripes appear on the leaves, and cobs fail to develop. If you happen to grow sweet corn and such stripes appear, don't charge in with a dose of borax straight away. Similar light markings on the young foliage can be caused by fruit flies.

With apples and pears, young shoots can be affected by die-back in spring, but this may be due to other causes. Similarly the foliage and fruit may be affected. The leaves become narrow and thickened, while the fruit may show cracking and corky tissue both on the surface and inside. Again the situation is complicated in that viruses such as apple green crinkle, apple rough skin and apple star crack can produce similar symptoms on the skin. All this serves to confirm that a soil analysis could be a good investment.

If the balance of probability is in favour of boron deficiency, then action can be taken. There are two options to consider.

Firstly, borax can be applied, either in solution or by raking it in at planting time, at a rate of 28 grammes per 17 square metres, or the Imperial rate of 1oz to 20 sq yards. While the treatment acts quickly, it is not persistent and repeat applications will be required in subsequent years.

Secondly, boron is found in reasonable amounts in some plants, and so a dressing of seaweed meal or manure will often correct the situation.

Where growing plants are affected and there is a chance of saving them, apply a foliar feed containing trace elements.

If all this sounds fairly complex, opt for the easy way out. In general, such nutritional deficiencies are rare, particularly in garden soils which contain an adequate supply of organic matter. Pest, disease or in years other than this, even drought, might be at the root of the problem.

Your Gardening Week

BROAD BEANS Given sheltered conditions and a free-draining soil, broad beans can be sown at the beginning of November. Try Aquadulce or Bunyard's Exhibition.

EARLY PEAS If you have the right conditions, a round-seeded variety of peas can be sown from now through to mid-November. The seedlings need cloche protection, and you may expect an early crop in late May or early June.

AVOID DRAUGHTS Your house plants may have stood well for the summer, but now the season has changed and cold air is about. Check their positions, try to ensure they are not exposed to cold draughts.

TAKE CARE Remember that this autumn sees you a year older, so take a cautious approach to jobs like digging. Doing a little and taking a rest until you are run in, is better than rushing at the job - and then finding yourself laid low with backache!

HARVEST LEAVES When harvesting leaves for leaf-mould, don't just clear paths and lawns. Keep an eye open for any build-up in other parts of the garden, remembering that some smaller plants can be smothered and caused to damp-off. Grid tops and gutters should be kept clear.

TIDY ASPARAGUS As the fronds of asparagus turn completely yellow, they can be cut back near to the ground. Remove any weed which has established in the bed, and then top-dress with a mixture of soil and well-rotted compost.

PLANT IRIS Bulbs of Spanish, Dutch and English iris can be planted now, either in rows to produce flower for cutting or informally in borders or rockeries. Set the Spanish and Dutch 20cm (8in) apart and 5-7cm (2-3in) deep, and the English iris a little deeper.

Planting For Drift Of Spring Colour

One of the joys of gardening is undoubtedly the sight of beds, or containers, massed with the later flowering bulbs from March to the end of May. Among those bulbs, tulips are, perhaps, the most useful, coming in probably one of the widest colour range of any of the flowers and a superb selection of form, from the traditional tulip shape to the more open ragged varieties.

Now is, of course, the time to be planting bulbs, especially now that wallflowers are ready to go in. If is a useful tip to mix wallflowers with bulbs, the former providing a nice background with plenty of colour whilst you are awaiting the flowering of the latter.

Whilst daffodils and narcissi are the first to go in, plant the wallflowers first. These will provide markers for the bulbs to go in between. Do it the other way round and you will find that in planting wallflowers you will almost certainly disturb, or damage, bulbs planted earlier.

Tulips can be left for quite a number of weeks after the daffodils for planting, but you will be wise to try and complete the job by the end of the month, if only to get it over with satisfactorily before bad weather sets in.

Try and prepare the bed at least a week before planting the bulbs, turning in a dressing of bonemeal at the rate of two ounces to the square yard, five or six inches deep. Let the ground settle for a week and then plant the bulbs just 10cm (4in) deep and with about 15cm (6in) between each.

Tulips tend to look their best in broad drifts of the same colour, or in smaller pockets set amongst other spring flowering plants, as illustrated left. They look good, too, interspersed with wallflowers (see picture right).

The first tulips are the species ones, followed by the brilliantly coloured Early Singles (which have the more traditional tulip shape) in April and, later, the Early Doubles with their large flowers and the exquisite exotically shaped Parrots.

Back To Nature

L ast week it was a pleasure to think about the delights of Mount Stewart; but my visit to Northern Ireland also afforded a complete contrast.

A trip to Peatlands Park afforded the opportunity to see a more natural environment, and to ponder afresh on the intricacies of 'the peat debate'.

Extending to some 250 hectares, the Park was acquired by the Verner family in the 17th century. Up until the beginning of this century it was little used but for hunting, shooting and turf cutting. This led to the planting of pine and rhododendron, the latter now perhaps being thought of as a spreading weed!

From 1901 the land was acquired by the Irish Peat Development Company which, despite its name, was I believe London-based.

They carried out a commercial peat extraction operation in the bog areas, installing some 16 kilometres of narrow gauge railway track in the process. This operation ceased in the late 1960s, and the site was taken over by the Department of the Environment, which maintains it through their Countryside and Wildlife Branch.

There is a small, attractive visitor centre, containing a small and amusingly interpreted display, examining peat extraction in its historical and environmental perspectives, allowing you to form a view on the pros and cons of peat extraction. A section of narrow gauge railway has been reconstructed, and a smoky diesel engine provides a rickety ride through the centre of the bog.

Most of all is the opportunity to walk around and enjoy the environment. About half of the park is designated as two National Nature Reserves, which support a wide range of flora and fauna.

The Mullenakill Reserve extends to 22 hectares and consists

mainly of uncut raised bog vegetation. Operations on adjoining land have led to a lowering of the water table, so that sphagnum mass has been reduced and replaced by heather, sedge and cotton grass.

Here in season are to be found butterflies such as the Large Heath, Green Hairstreak and Silver Washed Fritillary. Here also exist curlew, snipe, woodcock and long eared owl, together with mink and Irish hare.

The Annagarriff Reserve is large, extending to 77 hectares with mixed topography and habitats. In the 19th century deer and game birds were the prime product, and the reserve is a mixture of wooded hills with bog land between.

Although felled earlier this century, part of the wood can be classed as ancient woodland with a rich ground flora and understorey. In addition to rare insects and plants there are sparrowhawk, jay and blackcap together with badger, both colours of squirrel and long-eared bat.

Information about all these areas, together with opening times, can be had from the cheery warden on (01762) 851102 and the park is immediately north of Junction 13 off the M1 motorway.

Last week I mentioned the possibility of sowing broad beans for an early crop.

While there is the danger that in really hard conditions the plants will be wiped out, in a normal year they will not, and autumn-sown crops should be ready to harvest four or five weeks before anything raised in a New Year sowing.

Select a well-drained site, and aim to set the rows on a north-south axis to make the best of winter and early spring sunshine. Cultivate trenches by double-digging, incorporating manure and bonemeal as you go.

After well treading the ground to make it firm again, take out a 22cm (9in) wide and 7cm (2.5in) deep, flat-bottomed drill in which to sow. It may be necessary to protect against mice, and twiggy brushwood pushed in alongside the rows will reduce the effect of winds.

Rhubarb, Rhubarb...

I was talking about gunnera manicata and its large, rhubarb-like leaves a few weeks ago; but there should also be space for the real thing.

I suppose rhubarb is one of those crops you either enjoy or do not. While I may have a preference for other fruits and vegetables, I nevertheless like rhubarb pie with custard and always keep at least a few crowns on the go. It is easy to grow, requiring a minimum of attention. Producing useful amounts of sticks from a relatively small area, comes into use early in the season, before other fruits are on the go.

I say other fruits for comparison, because rhubarb is normally used as a desert, but it is in fact a vegetable native to China and Tibet.

Unless you plan to use crowns for forcing on a regular basis, there is no reason why a plantation cannot continue to crop for up to ten years. Just a few crowns will be sufficient to supply most families. Given this period of time, it is worth devoting a little effort to preparing the ground. Rhubarb thrives best on fairly heavy soil enriched with heavy dressings of manure or compost.

Good manure can be incorporated at a rate of one hundred-weight to ten square metres, while compost can be used at a barrow-load to the square metre. Ideally the pH should be slightly acidic at around 5.8.

At the moment the foliage of standing crops is still dying back, but by next month crowns will be available for planting. They are best put in early, although planting can be completed any time through to March while ground conditions allow. If the crowns available to you are large, they can be divided into sets by cutting them with a spade. Each set should have at least one healthy bud.

These are planted 90cm (3 feet) apart in either direction, at a

depth whereby the buds are not more than 5cm (2ins) below the soil surface. Use your boot to ensure that they are firmed in well.

During next year a strong root system will be formed. It is advisable not to pull sticks, so that all food produced by the foliage is devoted to building up the crown. In the following year a crop may be taken, but it is better to take only a few sticks so that the plant is not weakened. In successive years a full harvest may be enjoyed until the crowns reach the end of their useful life.

While maintenance is minimal, it is desirable to keep soil fertility high. This can be done by applying a dressing of manure or compost during February, and forking it into the soil surface with sufficient care to avoid damage to the crowns. Follow this with a handful of general fertiliser scattered around the crowns when pulling is over.

Provided perennial weeds were removed before planting, the dressing of compost should be sufficient to keep annual weeds at bay until such time as the dense cover of foliage supresses any further weed growth.

Other than that, all that is needed is to remove any flower heads which start to develop. Plants bent on flowering will be unproductive.

The main cropping season starts in mid-April. Sticks should be pulled once or twice from a number of crowns to meet immediate needs, rather than from separate crowns in succession. Over-pulling will result in poorer crops in the following year, and as a general rule pulling should cease in July. In any event, acidity will increase as the season progresses.

Availability of fresh sticks can be increased, and the season extended, by forcing. Crowns of at least three seasons' maturity should be used for this purpose. If it is intended to be a regular occurrence, it is a good idea to plan beds so that young crowns are maturing to replace those which have been forced, but more of that another time.

Your Gardening Week

✔ **EARLY SHRUBS** If you are in the market for shrubs such a forsythia, syringa, deutzia and azalea, not to mention roses, why not pot some for forcing under glass to give an early display of colour. They may be grown on and used in this way for a number of years, or planted out, where they will return to their normal cycle of growth.

✔ **FORCING LILIES** Lilies for forcing can be brought into heat around thirteen weeks before flower is required. Maintain a temperature around 10C (50F) until growth has started, and then increase to 18C (65F).

✔ **HERBACEOUS PLANTS** This is the time when existing herbaceous plants can be lifted and divided, or new plantings made. On cold and heavy soils it might be advisable to wait until spring; but elsewhere, the job done now will give the plants a head start. Take the opportunity to cultivate and enrich the ground.

✔ **DIVIDE CHIVES** Where chives have been growing for three years, it is advisable to lift, divide and reset as small groups 15cm (6in) apart.

✔ **PROTECT SPINACH** Perpetual spinach can take a bit of a bashing. If spare cloches are available, cover at least some of the plants to provide more tender and less weatherbeaten leaves.

✔ **TIP ROSES** Roses are slightly tender, and so cannot be fully pruned until winter has passed. It is nevertheless a good idea to tip back the stems to reduce wind-rock.

✔ **DRY ACHIMENES** Achimenes can be dried off and set under a bench until needed. In spring, the tubercles are knocked out and re-potted.

✔ **WINTER CHERRIES** Winter cherries are budding well, and will benefit from dilute feeds with liquid manure. If the berries are late to colour, a little sulphate of potash will assist.

The Time For Roses

A lot of people believe that, when the nights are drawing in, there's precious little to be done in the garden. Those folks that like to raise some produce of their own for the table-will be only too aware that October and November are indeed pretty busy months.

For instance, there are cuttings to be taken of currants and gooseberries; there's winter pruning of established bushes and fruit trees, and there's an awful lot of digging to be done, to ensure that the frost can get in and raise it to the condition required for planting in the spring.

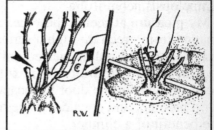

But for those who either have not the land or who prefer to concentrate on flowering plants, there could not be a better time to plant roses.

Set about selecting those that you would really like to have in the garden. If you increase the number of varieties, this should lead to a longer flowering season.

Other than doing some careful pruning and keeping a watch for bugs such as greenfly, roses really do a good job in the garden. Give them a good start, however, and they'll do you proud.

Having made your choice and obtained your plans, make sure that they have not dried out. If so, immerse the roots in water for a day or two. Then check them out. Using sharp secateurs, cut out all the dead wood, weak or damaged shoots, cutting back to an outward facing bud (see picture left).

Check the root system, too, cutting back any that are long and straggly, so as to leave nothing more than, say, 8 to 10 inches long. Any roots that are damaged should be cut back to just above the damage, and the thin, wispy, fibrous roots should be retained.

When it comes to planting, make sure that you do not do so too deeply. Take out a hole the shapes of the root system, and to a depth, so that the old soil level on the rootstock will be at the same height as a cane laid across the hole (see picture right). When you have turned the soil back in, tread firmly with the toe of the shoe, from the outside, working in towards the plant.

Colour Change

Why don't we have more climbers on our houses? I ask the question, but I don't have an answer. What prompts the thought, is the joy I experience at this time of year, when whole walls change colour due to the climbers which cover them. The main show comes from members of the family viticaea, with beautiful names that roll off the tongue, like Parthenocissus tricuspidata, Vitis cognetiae and Ampelopsis aconitifolia.

My pleasure at seeing these beauty-creating plants as they change from green through a series of oranges and yellows, to bright autumnal red, is marred only by the stark contrast and prevalence of bare walls. So next time you arrive home, don't head straight for the door to escape the cold and damp, but pause for a moment and consider if the house would look better with the benefit of a climber.

Other than planting trees, this is the simplest way to substantially increase the size of your garden and add to its three-dimensional effect. It is worth remembering that most true climbers can cover a large area of wall, and make a tremendous impact while requiring only a small amount of planting space.

Among the most commonly available is Parthenocissus tricuspidata, the Boston Ivy, producing large, deciduous leaves with three lobes which have good red and crimson colour in autumn. The cultivar 'Veitchii' is slightly smaller, with leaves which are purple when young and exhibit particularly strong autumn colour.

The Virginia Creeper, Parthenocissus quiquifolia, is tall growing and ideal for larger areas. There is often confusion in identity, but its leaves are five-lobed. Somewhere in the middle in terms of the number of lobes on its leaves sits P. henryana, which has three to five oval leaflets in each leaf. It is one of the most attractive, with green leaves enhanced by silvery-white veination, especially when grown in partial shade.

Of the ornamental vines, Vitis coignetiae is probably the most spectacular, producing well-coloured leaves up to 30cm (12in) across and having the vigour to climb walls or tall trees with ease. It colours over a long season, slowly suffusing from purple and red through orange to yellow.

You may like to try 'Brandt', a hybrid of the grape vine, Vitis vinifera. Besides producing leaves of dark red and purple with veins tinged green or yellow, it will produce numerous bunches of sweet, dark-coloured grapes. Given the support it can reach 9 metres (30ft). Vitis vinifera 'Purpurea', the Teinturier Grape, may also produce fruit after a hot summer. It has red-tinged foliage which, for something different, turns to deep purple in autumn. Ampelopsis brevipedunculata 'Elegans' is interesting, with foliage mottled white and tinged pink. Compared to the others it is both less vigorous and less hardy, but from a size and ornamentation point of view, is well suited to a patio.

While any reasonable garden soil will serve to nurture parthenocissus, the vitis will benefit from a rich soil and prefer milder areas. Once established, these species will cover a large area and eventually training and pruning will be required - if only to prevent doors and windows disappearing!

It is also advisable to restrict growth to below the house eaves for, if allowed higher, tendrils and stems can easily penetrate between tiles or slates and displace them, while deciduous stems can block gutters and down-spouts. It is also important to check the wall surface before planting. While sound brick or stone is unlikely to suffer, screed surfaces applied as a skin could succumb to the weight of a vigorous plant and be torn away.

Although these considerations must be weighed seriously and probably answer the question I posed - at least in part - don't allow yourself to be put off unnecessarily. When measured against the advantage of blending house and garden and the beauty displayed, the risks are small, the maintenance manageable, and the returns great.

Hardwood Cuttings

O ne way and another, there are methods of propagating plants at most times of the year. I still find it one of the most satisfying activities in the garden. True, nature's bounty tends to provide a wealth of useful seedlings, but there is a joy in sprouting seeds and putting roots on cuttings.

Just thinking about seedlings, I came across a nest of young plants the other day. From their leaves I take them to be buddleias. They had sprung up by the kerb at the side of a path, their roots running down into the pores of the tarmacadam. A gentle and steady pull slowly gave them to my care with roots in reasonable condition, and I have lined them in a nursery row to see what they grow into.

That is in some way irrelevant, for at this time a wide range of trees and shrubs can be increased by way of hardwood cuttings. Here, ripened wood of the current season's growth is prepared and inserted, either in open ground - where it may be given cloche protection - or within a frame.

Not all species will respond to this treatment. Many and various are the techniques that have been developed to extend the range of plants that can be increased from such cuttings. These may involve bottom heat, the use of chemicals, wounding tissue opposite buds and so on. But for most of us there are a number of rewarding plants which can be increased by the simplest application of this technique.

As a rule, a warm, sheltered site creates the best chance of success. Added to this, it is essential that drainage should be good. Where soil is on the heavy side it can be improved by adding sand or sand and organic matter. It is not uncommon to dribble sand along the bottom of the slit trenches into which cuttings are to be inserted.

In difficult cases - where land is low-lying for example - an option is to create raised beds about 120cm (4ft) across.

Generally the season for taking these cuttings starts towards the end of October, extending to December; but best results seem to come from cuttings made immediately after leaf fall.

The quality of the parent plant will affect the chances of rooting and the vigour and quality of new stock. The stems chosen should be healthy and vigorous, and can be made into cuttings 15-22.5cm (6-9in) long. Cuttings made from the base of the stems are best, although with long stems there is no reason why several cuttings cannot be made. Of course it's the exception that proves the rule, and cuttings from Sambucus and Laburnum for instance, should be taken with a heel; so it's only one per stem in such cases.

A cutting is taken with a heel by pulling it away from the older stem, so that a sliver of wood and bark comes with it. This has the effect of protecting the base of the stem from rotting. If this heel is large or ragged it can be trimmed up with a knife.

Where no heel is taken, the bottom cut can be made at an angle, just below a bud, while the top cut is made horizontal - an invaluable guide to ensuring the cutting is inserted the right way up.

We all know that with softwood cuttings, taken in the summer, and which have plenty of leaves, one of the biggest problems is to keep them from drying out until the roots can take in sufficient water to keep them turgid.

With hardwood cuttings taken in the dormant season, the cooler temperatures, absence of foliage and setting them well into the ground, means that they lose moisture only very slowly.

Cuttings are inserted by taking out a V-trench with one side vertical and sufficiently deep to accommodate the cuttings to two thirds of their height. Dribble in sharp sand, stand the cuttings against the vertical face, push back the soil and firm in well - and stand back to await results.

The cuttings will start to root in spring as the soil warms up, and are best left undisturbed until the following autumn, when they can be lifted and lined out.

Your Gardening Week

✔ **ROTATE** On the vegetable plot, don't forget to rotate your cropping plan both to reduce any build-up of pest or disease, and to create the right levels of food in the ground for various crops. In general, lime for brassicas, incorporate manure for legumes, and apply general fertiliser for root crops.

✔ **ROOT PRUNING** Any root pruning due to be carried out to reduce vigour and induce fruiting, should be carried out before conditions deteriorate.

✔ **CUT MINT** Use shears to cut back clumps of mint to near ground level. Take the opportunity to remove any weeds which may have become established, and then apply a top-dressing of compost or leaf-mould. The old growth is not suitable for drying, but an extra supply can be had by lifting a clump of roots, potting or boxing them and placing them in a glasshouse or by a window, where the temperature will not fall below 13C (53F).

✔ **ENGINE CARE** Four-stroke engines on garden machinery that is not to be used for some time, will benefit if a little protective oil is squirted into cylinder and then the engine rotated until both valves are closed.

✔ **LIFT OR LEAVE?** Although parsnips and horseradish are hardy, and the flavour of parsnips is improved by frost, it still makes sense to lift and store a proportion of the crop to allow for days when the ground is too frozen for lifting.

✔ **PINCH SPROUTS** Encourage the topmost Brussels sprouts to swell by pinching out the stem tip.

✔ **STORE CHECK** As the air becomes cold and humid, check all crops in store on a regular basis.

✔ **MORE STOCK** Continue to propagate trees and shrubs by taking hardwood cuttings. Lift, box, and keep in a dryish frost-free place until spring.

Sow Now For A Dish Of Early Beans

One of the joys of gardening is the ability to have fresh produce for the table — and even more of a joy is to be able to get that produce earlier than most. Early beans and peas have a special appeal, but to enjoy them you will have to start sowing pretty soon. There are two things to be wary of: firstly, they will need well drained soil; secondly, beware of predators. Mice really enjoy these winter titbits.

For those growing beans there is the reliable Aquadulce — early to mature and which will provide one of the earliest dishes of beans.

Another that can be grown in succession from November to February is The Sutton, which is ideally suited to those who want to try their hand in a small garden.

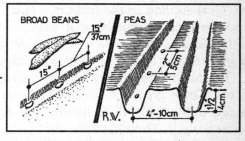

For peas chose Feltham First, which is a dwarf one and which therefore needs no support. It does well with or without cloche protection. Meteor is another hardy one for November planting, doing well in cold and exposed areas and still providing one of the first dishes of peas. Before sowing either of these vegetables, dig the ground over well to ensure that it has not become compacted. Just to help further winter hardiness, you can give a dressing of sulphate of potash at the rate of about half an ounce to the square metre. The addition of other fertilisers is certainly not necessary pre-sowing, but is best left to give a boost in the spring when growth is beginning to make headway. Then, dress with Growmore at three ounces to the square metre.

For broad beans set them at about 15 inches apart (see left). Whilst The Sutton is usually grown in single rows, Aquadulce is usually grown in double rows 9 inches apart with the beans sown at 6 inch intervals. For the peas take out parallel drills about one and half inches deep and 3 to 4 inches apart, sowing the peas some 2 inches apart (see right). It is, perhaps, safer with peas to sow more than one at each station, because they do tend to be a little more susceptible to winter conditions.

 **Your Gardening Week**

Not-So-Rampant

If, despite last week's reassurances you bridle at the thought of rampant climbers on your house walls, all is not lost. This week I wish to consider what may be described as wall shrubs or creepers that can imbue bricks and pebbledash with colour and life, but on a smaller scale.

There is a difference, for while ampelopsis and vitis climb by means of coiling tendrils, and parthenocissus produces clinging flattened discs, today's selection will require some additional physical support in the form of trellis or wires. Trellis has a presence becoming something of an architectural feature in its own right - and so should be well designed and constructed of pleasing materials. This will incur some significant cost.

The cheap, simple and adequate alternative is to use straining wires. These are run horizontaly through strong screw eyes plugged into the wall so that the wires are held 5cm (2in) or so away from it. They have the further long-term advantage that if replacement is required it can often be achieved by plugging fresh eyes and running new wires without removal of the plant. Replacing trellis might involve cutting the plants right back or struggling to disentangle growth and give it temporary support while new trellis is manoeuvred into position.

Traditionally a north wall provides a home for the morello cherry, allowing a fruit crop to be taken as well. From an ornamental point of view the graceful Garrya elliptica takes precedence, though it needs protection from the direct assaults of icy winds. Its shiny, dark green, wavy-edged ellipse-shaped leaves provide a foil for graceful clusters of long and slender silvery-grey catkins held on male forms in February. It can be used on any aspect, is evergreen, and can grow to around 3.5m (12ft).

Pyracanthas may also face in any direction. They will tolerate sunless conditions and their evergreen foliage, clothed with hawthorn-like flowers in early summer and followed by masses of scarlet, orange or yellow berries, makes them a good choice. P. coccinea 'Lalandii' is orange fruited, and the larger leaved P. atlantoides has good red fruit. They may easily exceed 4m in height and spread, and will require cutting back after flowering to keep within bounds.

Also suited to any aspect is Jasminum nudiflorum, the winter jasmin. This semi-deciduous climber can grow to as much as 6m (18ft) and flower from November through to February. Early on its wiry green stems are covered in small, bright yellow flowers, which are followed by trifoliate leaves.

Although it will grow in any aspect, best results are obtained in a sheltered, sunny position, facing south or south-east. If grown on its own, as the blooms fade tie in the strongest of the shoots which have flowered, cutting the remainder back to within 5cm (2in) of the old wood. I say 'if grown on its own' because I like to grow this jasmin through another shrub such as pyracantha, where together they provide an enhanced feature.

For early colour in spring, the deciduous chaenomeles or Japonicas take some beating. While more normally grown as a free-standing shrub, they adapt to wall training and seem to succeed well in both sun and shade, but prefer the former. Provided lateral shoots growing away from the wall are kept in check by spurring back in summer, they fit well on shorter heights of wall, beneath windows for example.

There are many to choose from, but C. superba 'Knap Hill Scarlet' is noted for the volume of its orange-scarlet blooms which persist from spring into early summer.

C. speciosa 'Simonii' has darker blood-red semi-double flowers and a dwarf habit, while C. speciosa 'Moerloosii', also known as 'Apple Blossom', has thick clusters of delicate pink and white flowers.

A camellia such as C. williamsii 'Donation' is also worth a try facing north. A rapid grower, easily raised from cuttings, it pleases well with a generous display of large, semi-double peach pink blooms.

Tool Care

There is never a shortage of jobs in the garden; but at this time of year a little bad weather can be a boon, creating the opportunity to catch up on those jobs which otherwise may be forgotten. One such important task is the cleaning and servicing of tools so that they are sharp, oiled and ready for whatever work is to come.

Perhaps the most important tool is the knife which is in regular service for making cuttings. The quality of cut depends upon keeping a well-honed edge. Here an oilstone should be used to provide a keen edge.

Like most things, its use requires some practice so that the blade is held at the correct angle to the stone. If the angle is too shallow, the edge of the blade will become thin and will not withstand regular use.

In particularly bad cases it will burr over and become useless. Conversely, if the angle is too steep, the edge will become bevelled and lose its sharpness.

Keeping the oilstone in good order is also important for, if it is used for a variety of different width blades, its surface may become uneven so that it is difficult to obtain a level finish on the blade. This can be corrected by dressing the stone, but I like to avoid the problem by keeping different stones for different blades.

Scythes and sickles are not so common these days having, to a large extent, been replaced by rotary mowers, strimmers and weedkillers. Nevertheless, they are still handy tools but must be treated with respect.

While the blades are kept touched-up during use, the end of the season provides an opportunity to attack them with a file and then to put back a good regular edge.

Great care is needed, for when weilding the whetstone it is easy to stray too close to the blade and end up with badly cut

fingers.

With rotary mowing machines, because the blade is hidden there is a tendency to assume that it will be all right. During the course of a season the blades can take a real battering, especially if your ground is on the rough side.

With petrol driven engines, disconnect the plug lead so that there is no danger of the engine firing. Ideally, remove the plug so that there is no compression, before removing the blade. This can then be touched-up using a file. If the blade is badly worn or distorted it should be replaced.

With cylinder mowers the task of keeping the blades in good order in not quite so straightforward. A good quality machine that has been kept at a good setting so that the blades and sole-plate provide a good cut may not need attention for several years, especially if it has been used on fine turf.

Where things have gone wrong and poor setting has resulted in uneven wear, or hard objects caught in the blades have caused distortion, both cylinder and plate may need to be re-ground. This task requires specialist equipment and should be carried out by a service engineer.

The chipper/shredder is another tool for which the state of the blades has a significant effect on performance. The rough, blunt blades which smash soft, green material are less important; but the chipper blades are critical.

When removing them for sharpening great care is needed for, when properly sharp, they have a razor-edge and it is easy to cut fingers.

With the model I have, these blades are double-sided so while the edge that has been in use may be dulled, the other still poses a threat.

I have found it useful to keep a spare set of blades. This means that one set is in use, while the others are kept sharp and ready for changing when the need arises - which is fairly often. The highest level of productivity with the minimum strain on the motor is achieved by these means.

Your Gardening Week

 PLANT PAEONIES Paeonies can be planted now. They need deep, rich soil and prefer a little shade to full sun.

 SPARE BULBS Any unused bulbs can still be potted for a display in late winter.

 CORDON RULES When planting grafted fruit trees to grow as cordons, the golden rules are to make sure the graft union is well above the soil surface; and that the scion or variety is on the topside when the stems goes in at an angle.

 SOW CARROTS Forcing carrots can be sown now, though they will have to be grown under glass.

 MORE ARTICHOKES Check around globe artichokes for signs of suckers. Any found can be detached and potted up to increase stocks.

 PINCH FUCHSIAS Young fuchsias, grown from cuttings taken in late summer, can have the growing tips pinched out if bushy plants are wanted.

 HEDGE COVER When planting hedges, it's a good idea to obtain one or two extra plants. Grown in a border or nursery plot, these will serve to fill any gaps created by losses.

 EXTRA NOTE When new stock is to be planted remember that labels can disappear, so make a note of what goes where in your gardening diary.

 DIG BROAD AND DEEP When taking out planting holes make them broad and deep, sufficient to accommodate roots with a bit left over. Any skimping at planting time is only rewarded with poor growth.

 SAVE PEA STAKES Clean and store those of this year's pea stakes which are still servicable. Take advantage of pruning to collect additional material.

Ponds In Winter

While some years it may seem a somewhat superflous addition to the gardening scene, a pool, in general, does provide a restful feature in the garden.

To ensure that you can enjoy it every year, it is necessary to give it as much care as the rest of the garden, particularly in preparing it to withstand the ravages of the winter ahead.

Of prime importance is net protection, not only to thwart marauders who might be tempted by the golden coloured stock, but also to keep the whole thing sweet and fresh, by acting as a trap for leaves and other debris which might otherwise foul the water.

Chicken wire will do the job for you. Just stretch it across the pool and anchor it at the sides with pegs hammered in at an angle (see picture left) or hold it down by large pieces of stone.

Where there are plants at the margin, cut a hole in the netting and turn back neatly (as shown).

Before putting on the net cover, give a thought to the oxygen requirements of the pool, particularly for fish, should the thing be turned into a mini-rink. Trying to break the ice can well have dire effect on the stock, shocking the poor fish to death.

Make provision for easy openings to be made in the ice by floating some pieces of polystyrene block, or a number of large rubber balls on the surface. Anchor them with galvanised or plastic coated wires to the edge, so that you can get at them when necessary.

Polystyrene blocks are particularly good for the job, because they always remain slightly warmer than their surroundings; further, they are easily gouged out to provide an airhole if there are any difficulties.

Up The Wall

L ast week I was looking at a number of shrubs suited to enhancing walls which face north. This week I want to move round one hundred and eighty degrees. This brings us to south facing walls, where the main problem is in narrowing down the choices. With shelter, there is a chance to choose something a little exotic.

Who can fail to show pleasure at a flower-laden wistaria in May? Happy in any normal well-drained garden soil, they need support to allow their long racemes of flowers to be displayed to best advantage. Some two or three years establishment may be needed before blooming commences, but the wait is well worth-while.

Most popular is Wistaria sinensis from China, either in its blue, white or dark purple form. It may grow to near 20m (60ft), but can be kept to a third of that by regular pruning. It is recognised by its leaves made up of 11 leaflets, and by its branches which always wind in an anti-clockwise direction. If something smaller is needed then W. floribunda, the Japanese wistaria, should be ideal. With a similar range of scented flowers, it can grow to around 10m (30ft) or be kept small in similar proportion. Its leaves hold 12-19 leaflets.

If you can engineer sufficient clearance for the racemes, try Wistaria floribunda 'Macrobotrys' which sports fragrant lilac flowers tinged with purple on racemes up to 1m (3ft) long. While a nice thought, it is probably more suited to growing on a larger pergola.

Outside the most favoured areas some shelter is needed, for the flower buds are susceptible to damage from both north and east winds as well as late frosts.

Once established a regular pruning regime must be followed, both to keep growth tidy and in bounds and to help promote flowering. In late July or early August, when flowering is over, the current season's stems are cut back to around five buds or 15cm (6in) from their base. In late winter - February - all sideshoots should be cut back to two buds. This is also the time to cut back strongly growing plants which might have become too large for their position.

Something a little more subtle and grown primarily for its foliage is Actinidia kolomikta. A hardy deciduous species it may attain as much as 6m (20ft), its slender stems bearing leaves up to 15cm (6in) long, rounded at the base and pointed at the tip. While gently attractive in their green guise, during May and June they assume a new importance as they become partly or even on occasion wholly suffused with white and pink. White, slightly fragrant fruits appear in June to be followed by yellow-ish egg-shaped fruits about 25mm (1in) long.

Also requiring shelter, Cytisus battandieri - the Moroccan Broom - is a fine choice. An excellent wall shrub, its strong growth can easily be kept in check by pinching back lateral growths.

The leaves are similar to those of laburnum, but of grey cast with a silky sheen caused by fine hairs. In June and July cone-shaped clusters of golden-yellow flowers appear, possessed of a pinapple scent.

If you can find a well sheltered position it would provide a place for Carpentaria californica. This is the only species of its genus and is related to philadelphus. It will grow to just over 2m (7ft) with long, narrow leaves which are green above and softly woolly beneath. The fragrant white flowers, 50-75mm (2-3in) across and enhanced with golden anthers, appear in clusters dur-ing July.

While I have seen a variety of names used for some of the Olearias, it may be that O. gunniana, O. phlogopappa and O. stellulata are just about the same thing. In any event I'll settle for Tasmanian Daisy Bush as quite descriptive. With shelter, this medium-sized shrub with narrow-toothed leaves which are also aromatic, produces masses of panicles of white flowers in May.

Choice Fruit

Peach is a word that has entered our vocabulary not only to describe a particular form of fruit, but also as an indication of something of exceptional quality, something that is 'choice'.

In itself that seems to amount to a fairly healthy recommendation, and a pointer that we should consider growing our own. You might wonder if there is any point with good reason, since peaches and nectarines are common in grocers' shops and supermarkets in their season.

As ever, the answer is that you cannot beat growing your own for pleasure, and that no fruit tastes better than when fresh-picked and eaten there and then.

The site and method of cultivation is guided by the climate, although it is fair to say that peaches are more hardy than is generally realised. The more inhospitable the climate, the more they are likely to benefit from being trained and grown against a south or south-west facing wall.

Extremes of cold are unlikely to cause the premature demise of the trees as they will stand temperatures as low as -9C (-15F). But problems may arise in spring when early blossom, appearing in February and March, is susceptible to frost damage.

In marginal positions the effect of frost can be reduced by giving protection at night. Sacking or plastic sheeting can be pressed into service for this, but must be removed in the mornings to allow access to pollinating insects.

One big advantage of peaches and nectarines is that they are self-fertile, removing the need to identify a suitable companion for pollination. Nevertheless, during the flowering period pollinating insects are likely to be at a premium, so hand pollination is a practice worth following.

If you have glasshouse space available, an alternative would be to grow the bush in a large pot or container. At the end of

January, as flowering approaches, the plant can be housed until the fruit is set, and then moved outdoors again.

When planting direct into the ground, site selection is important. The position should be sheltered but sunny. Although the peach will perform in a wide range of soils it is essential that they are well-drained. Where necessary, the drainage can be improved by excavating a planting pit and placing rubble in the bottom, topped by chopped turves.

You might wish to try more than one variety: but have you the room? Peaches are grafted onto rootstocks, the two main ones being St. Julian A, which is semi-vigorous, and Brompton, which is vigorous. On the former, bush trees can be spaced at 15-18 feet while wall-trained fans need 12-15 feet. On Brompton these distances increase to 18-24ft in both cases. For most gardeners the St. Julian is adequate.

If you are tempted to try, the first task is to approach your nursery or specialist grower to see what varieties are available and to find out which will perform best in your area. There are several to choose from. Some I mention are suited to growing under glass, and that is a topic I will return to.

'Amsden June' has medium-sized fruits with white flesh and good flavour. It produces a moderate crop in mid-July and is suited to outdoors or under glass. 'Duke of York' has very good flavour with tender, pale-yellow flesh. Ripening in mid-July, it crops well and is suited to growing against a wall or under glass. 'Peregrine' comes in a little later, during August, with good crops of large fruit. It can be grown in all three situations and is ideal grown as a bush in warmer areas. 'Redhaven' follows a similar pattern, though with smaller fruits.

Although its flavour is not the best, 'Rochester' is a good hardy variety, suited to all three situations and ripening in August. Look out also for 'Royal George', ripening in late August/early September, and 'Bellegarde', ripening in September, both of which are suited to growing under glass or on a wall.

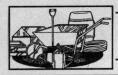

Your Gardening Week

 KEEP PRUNING Complete the pruning of bush fruits as soon as practicable, remembering to leave late fruiting raspberries until February.

 LATE TURFING If any late turfing is to be carried out, protect both the ground to be worked on and any stacked turf, or frost may cause the job to stop. Check recently laid turf for lifting caused by frost, and firm back when the frost has gone out of it.

 SAVE LEEKS If you intend to save leek bulbils, cut the heads before there are hard frosts. If they are not fully plumped, cut the stems long and stand in water. Once large enough they can be removed from the water and allowed to ripen until after Christmas, with a view to planting at the end of January.

 WINDWARD STAKES When staking trees, remember to place the stake on the side which receives the prevailing wind. This way the stem is blown away from the stake and bark is less likely to be chafed.

 DIVIDE POLYANTHUS Polyanthus which have made good crowns can be lifted and divided if you wish to spread their benefits around the garden. Otherwise leave them as big attractive clumps.

 MORE JASMIN! Increase stocks of the 'Winter Jasmin', Jasminum nudiflorum, by taking cuttings now and inserting in a cold frame.

 ORDER DAHLIAS While putting this year's stock of dahlias away for the winter, check next year's requirements and send your order for fresh stock as soon as possible to avoid substitutions.

LETTUCE CARE Regularly examine lettuce in frames or under cloches. Ventilate thoroughly on mild days and water carefully. Put bait out for slugs if there are any signs of their presence.

Go On, Force Yourself For A Rhubarb Treat

It's nice around Christmas time for the gardener to be able to come up with some produce, out of season, for the delight of family and friends.

It's the time for eating, of course, so the idea is to come up with something special for the table...and what better after all the Christmas puddings, mince pies and cream than a home made rhubarb crumble and custard!

So start now by gently lifting a crown of rhubarb ready for forcing. Leave it on top of the ground (see left) for about a week in the hope that it will catch a touch of frost. This, it is said, increases the sugar available in the plant and helps to produce tastier sticks.

The next stage is to put the crown in a box of really rich soil. Then add a layer of straw to help conserve warmth. Water it well and cover completely with a black plastic bag so as to cut out light.

Placed in a nice warm garage, or somewhere similar, the stems should be ready for pulling in 4 to 8 weeks.

You can, of course, force rhubarb in its garden position by covering the crown with a tea-chest or a plastic bin (see picture right) upturned and roped so that it is not blown away. Pack around the cover with straw, leaves or even manure if you have it — anything which will generate heat.

This method is however rather slower, for it will be something like 2 months before there is need to check for growth. Pull them when they are about a foot long.

Winter Colour

It was dark when I went out of the back door. The previous evening it had not seemed anywhere near as bad, for the reflected rays of a nearby street lamp were enough to lighten the gloom. The only difference was that successive hours of wind and rain had removed the remaining light, golden leaves from the likes of birch and maple which, when covered with moisture, had sufficient presence to give depth and dimension to that part of the garden.

Now the conifer hedge and dull rhododendron leaves seemed only to absorb the light. It was a moment for inward reflection. One which served to show how important it is to maintain some colour and interest in the garden through the winter months - and perhaps to think about installing some garden lights.

There are many plants which flower through the winter, but which tend to be overlooked, probably because less time is spent in the garden during the cooler, short-day seasons. Nevertheless, their comparative scarcity makes them more attractive; and while their displays may be less spectacular than summer flowering specimens, they reward closer inspection with colour, form and often scent.

Of course viburnums are well known for their flower and scent at this time of year. In fact there are many species of this genus which can overlap to supply interest throughout the year; but sticking to autumn, winter and early spring, there are several to consider.

The deciduous viburnum bodnantense makes a medium to large sized shrub, of upright habit, with densely-packed clusters of sweetly-scented white flowers with a rosy tint, appearing from October onwards. These are considerably resistant to frost and look well on cold winter days.

Two clones are available, the best of which, 'Dawn', produces clusters of richly scented flowers in late autumn and winter, while the other, 'Deben', opens pink buds to reveal white scented flowers from October to April.

Viburnum farreri (or fragrans), also deciduous, forms a rounded bush to around 4m (12ft) in height, and carries pink buds which open to white, sweetly scented flowers from November through to spring.

Related and similar, v. grandiflorum has larger flowers which appear as a carmine bud, opening to deep pink flowers which fade to blush white. They appear in dense clusters during February and March.

Of the evergreen types, v. tinus, the laurustinus, is one of the most popular. While not native, it has been grown here for over 400 years. Making a medium to large shrub, it is dense and bushy in habit with masses of glossy, dark-green, oval leaves. Although tolerant of shade, sunshine is necessary to ensure good flower production. The resultant flowers, pink in bud and opening to white, are carried on flattened cymes from late autumn to early spring.

Another evergreen is v. burkwoodii, which produces fragrant white flowers from January to May. There are a number of clones, including 'Anne Russell', 'Chenaultii', 'Fulbrook' and 'Park Farm Hybrid'.

In general the viburnums are hardy shrubs thriving in most soils, provided they are moist. While frost or snow may cause damage to some blooms, more will appear to take their place. Species can be raised from seed, although all types root easily as cuttings or layers.

Sarcococca confusa, the Christmas Box, makes a small shrub to near 1.5m (5ft). Densely branched, but of spreading habit it bears small tidy elliptic leaves which are suitable for cutting. The small, white, richly fragrant male flowers are held in short-stemmed clusters, with tiny insignificant female flowers between. They appear from December through to February, and are followed by black berries. Slow in growth, they succeed well in fertile soils and are suitable for chalk soils.

Fan For Fruit

L ast week I launched into peaches; and I hope I might have
persuaded you to give one a try. If so, and you have chosen to opt for a fan, the easiest way forward is to select
one that has already been part-formed by the grower and is well
supplied with shoots.

Of course a wall or fence is needed to train it against, and to
provide that useful extra amount of shelter. The young fan
should be planted 15-22.5cm (6-9in) away from the base of the
structure to allow room for growth, and should lean slightly
towards it.

After planting, apply a mulch of well-rotted manure.

Before planting, it is good idea to set wires in place which will
carry canes to which the shoots will be tied. The lowest one can
be set about a foot (30cm) above ground, with successive ones
spaced 6in (15cm) apart. If attached to a brick wall the easiest
spacing is two courses. The canes can be tied in place using thin
wire or rot-proof twine.

Setting forth with the secateurs can sometimes cause the
adrenelin to flow while pondering where to make the cuts. In
fact producing a fan is an interesting task, but takes about three
years to achieve.

The first pruning can start in the Februrary after planting, by
cutting back to a lateral about two feet (60cm) above ground.
This should have at least two laterals or buds beneath it, one on
either side. All other laterals can be cut back to one bud.

By early summer, fresh shoots will have appeared. Select three
in good strong condition. Ideally they should rise from just
below the bottom straining wire. The topmost is trained vertical-
ly and the others to either side. All other buds and shoots can be
cut or rubbed out.

The two sideshoots will continue to grow and can be gradually
trained at an angles of 45 degrees. By mid-summer they should

reach to some 18in (45cm), at which time the vertical shoot can be cut out entirely.

Throughout the remainder of the season, all that is needed is to tie in further extension growth as it is made.

In the following February, the secateurs come out again. Look for a slender, pointed wood bud, or a triple and which consists of one wood bud and two rounded flower buds, placed about 18in (45cm) from the main stem.

Cutting back to these will again encourage the production of new shoots.

In mid-summer it is shoot selection time again, and four need to be chosen on each lateral. Of these, one is to extend the existing branch.

Two more should be chosen, reasonably spaced, on the upper side of the branch, and one on the lower side. Fix canes in place against which to train them.

Any remaining shoots are nipped back to one leaf, as are other shoots which may subsequently appear.

In the third February the leaders are shortened back by about a third, making the cut just above a downward-facing wood bud. Guess what happens in summer!

At this point there are eight main branches in the fan. The leading shoot is left to continue making extension growth. A further three shoots are chosen on each branch and tied in to achieve an even spread. Any buds facing the support structure which, if allowed to grow, would be difficult to deal with, are rubbed out.

Now we are almost reaching the exciting part. The remaining shoots provide the basis of those which will carry fruit in the following year.

To maintain order, nip excessive ones back to the first leaf, aiming to allow the development of shoots about 4in (10cm) apart on both top and bottom of the fan branches. Allow them to grow to 18in (45cm) and then pinch out the growing point, tying them in to canes in late summer.

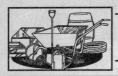

Your Gardening Week

GLADIOLI Gladioli, lifted and tied in bundles or placed in boxes to dry, may be ready for cleaning. If the foliage has withered completely, force the old corm from beneath the new with your thumb nail. Pull off the dried leaves and store in a dry, frost-free place.

WHAT - NO CATALOGUES? If you find yourself without catalogues, send off straight away. The season for planning next year's displays and produce is upon us.

CAMMELIA CARE Pot-grown cammelias, under glass, should be well budded. While benefiting from protection, they should be kept in a cool side. Make sure there is adequate ventilation on days when the sun appears, or fluctuating temperatures may cause buds to drop. Feeding can continue at fourteen-day intervals until the buds show signs of opening.

FORCE RHUBARB If you intend to force rhubarb, crowns may be lifted now and should be left exposed to frost for a couple of weeks before being brought into the glasshouse or shed. There they should be packed in boxes using soil or rotted leaves, watered, and then completely blacked out.

STEADY BEGONIAS Spring-flowering begonias should be grown steadily through the winter at 13 C (55 F). Stop giving feeds, to prevent the formation of soft growth.

POT CYCLAMEN While this year's cyclamen will soon be at their best, seedlings for next year, sown in late summer, should be ready for potting up using J.I. No1 compost.

CHRISTMAS HYACINTHS If you boxed or potted hyacinths for Christmas, now is the time to bring them into the glasshouse. Cover with paper to draw the stems and do not give too much heat to begin with.

Winter Protection

Of one thing most gardeners can be almost certain - a cold snap is likely to catch them out. No matter how much you get into winter, really cold weather always seems to be still a bit away. Then suddenly you - and worse still your plants -- are caught. The scene is one of devastation as stalks are broken and leaves shrivel.

The ideal, of course, is not to be caught. Quite a lot can be done, as you tidy up the beds ready for winter. When delphiniums have been cut back, draw the soil up round the clumps to protect the root system and cover them with ashes. Cut back peonies and cover their root systems with some strawy manure.

The foliage of red-hot pokers and that front garden favourite, the pampas grass, can be twisted and tied (as shown in illustration right).

Remember that shrubs - and particularly those in pots - should be prepared ready for quick covering. Give each a central stake and then place a number of outward pointing stakes around the plant, so that sacking, paper or a polythene cover can be laid over them. The surrounding stakes will hold the cover away from the plant and in the border can be held down with stones, or more easily tied around pots and tubs (as shown in the illustration on right).

One thing to remember with plants which are covered in this way, however, is that an opening should be available to allow air in during frost-free periods.

With plants such as camellias, take extra precautions, whether they are in tubs or in the border, by pegging down a good layer of straw over the area of the root system. A period of frost, particularly following a wet period, will penetrate deep down and kill off the root system.

Hairy-leafed rockery plants can be protected by placing pieces of glass, tent-style over them.

Whatever you do — don't be caught out. Make the basic preparations now.

Your Gardening Week

More Winter Colour

In last week's article I started to look at winter-flowering plants, and barely managed to run through suitable viburnums. While flowering shrubs have that extra appeal, any variation in colour and form is to be welcomed; and there are one or two conifers that come into their own at this time.

Cryptomeria japonica, the Japanese Cedar, is the only species of its genus. While the type grows to make a large tree useful for timber, it has given rise to a large number of clones of widely differing habit, colour and size. Of these, 'Elegans' has a lot to offer. Of shapeless, bushy habit, it may ultimately form a small tree, reaching to near 10m (30 ft) after many years. Soft foliage is formed, which is retained during growth and clothes the bush well. During summer it appears blue-green, but during autumn and winter becomes a warm bronze-purple.

I believe sometimes it may set seed; but more readily is propagated by taking 5-7cm (2-3in) cuttings during autumn and setting them in a cold frame. It will not do well on alkaline soils, requiring a moist, acid soil, preferably in a sunny position. Keep an eye open for heavy falls of snow, which can break branches.

A sport of 'Elegans' also worth looking for is 'Elegans nana' (or 'elegans compacta'). Significantly slower in growth and smaller in stature, its foliage is more feathery and turns to rich purple in winter.

I know at this time of year, when we think of piceas, it's the green needles of picea abies - the Norway Spruce or Christmas Tree - that spring to mind. However, out in the garden it is picea pungens glauca, the 'Blue Spruce', that comes into its own.

While there are several attractive forms available, it is p. p. glauca 'Koster' which is probably the most popular. It grows slowly to make a small to medium-sized tree, perhaps attaining 7-8m (25ft). Although it is broadly conical in form, there is an irregularity in growth which creates a different shape in every aspect. The branches are covered with densely packed needles of an intense silver-blue. Look out also for 'Hoopsii' and 'Moerheimii'. Although they will succeed in wet and cold soils, these spruces will not perform well on dry, chalky or shallow soils.

I always have a soft spot for yews with their form, their longevity, and the impression that they rightly belong in our landscape. I do feel, however, that they are not as widely planted as they deserve.

Taxus baccata - the Common Yew or English Yew - is one of three native conifers and is usually to be found on chalk where it occurs naturally. However, given good drainage it will grow in soils towards either end of the pH scale.

The type has again given rise to many interesting variations. Of these, Taxus baccata 'Elegantissima' is the most widely used of the golden forms. Dense in habit, it grows to make a large bush with ascending branches. When young the leaves are yellow, changing to green in the centre and straw yellow around the margins with maturity.

Of upright habit and slow growth, T. b. 'Fastigiate Standishii' is dense and columnar, with tightly packed erect branches and golden-yellow leaves. Also worth considering is T. b. 'Semperaurea'. Slow-growing with widespread ascending branches, its crowded branchlets are clothed with bright old-gold yellow leaves in spring. These age to rusty yellow, a hue which persists for the rest of the year.

Finally a couple of thujas. Thuja orientalis 'Rosedalis' maintains interest throughout the year. Slowly growing to form a dense, ovoid bush with attractive soft young foliage, it appears bright canary yellow in spring, changing to pale green in summer and finally to a glaucous purple in winter.

On a larger scale T. plicata 'Zebrina' is similar to T. plicata, but grows more slowly at around 30cm (12ins) or so a year. The flattened foliage is light green, banded across in stripes of creamy yellow which, in late spring, causes the whole bush to take on a golden hue.

A Garden 'Must'

As the weather closes in and Christmas draws near, I find it a pleasing distraction to think about spring. Besides picturing the first snowdrop, and anticipating the strong colours of daffodils and tulips, I look forward to the splendours of the flowering cherries.

It is nice to daydream from time to time; but the presence of Cherry blossom trees reinforces the mental picture with each passing year.

While the tiniest of gardens or a fairly hard heart may militate against such a tree, I think it is an easy matter to decide there should be room for a cherry in the scheme of things. The hard work is in deciding which is best, for there are many to choose from.

There are a variety of forms of growth, from upright to round and spreading, and the planting situation has an influence on that choice. They may be grown as single specimens in a lawn, set as part of a mixed border or, if your garden is large enough, concentrated in a strong group.

In this latter case the options are to mix varieties to give a selection of shapes, colours and flowering times, or to plant several of the same type and make a bold statement. While single varieties are attractive, especially when massed together, probably semi-double or double-flowered types can be planted to best effect in the majority of gardens.

All the normal rules of planting apply, and any garden soil that does not become either too dry or waterlogged will suffice. Best results are achieved, however, on a slightly heavy and slightly alkaline soil.

Although it would be good to get on with planting straight away, the luxury of choosing any suitable day up until March means that there is time available to make a selection. Of course, any trees delivered should be given water and, if planting is

delayed, be heeled-in until they can be attended to.

At this time of year, if you have identified a planting site, but await delivery, it is a good idea to cover the ground with litter such as leaves to prevent frost entering the soil.

As already indicated, the choice is wide. I'll start with some of slender, upright kind. While having their place in larger gardens, they can be accommodated in quite small plots.

The first to spring to mind is Prunus 'Amanogawa'. This is generally likened to a Lombardy Popular in its habit of growth, though of more manageable proportions. It grows to around 20ft (6m) in height with a spread of 3ft 6in or just over a metre. The vertical branches carry in abundance upright clusters of single and semi-double flowers, coloured pink and with a pleasing fragrance. These appear in April to mid-May and are followed by green leaves which turn yellow with splashes of red in autumn.

If there is a fault with this tree - and it should not discourage you - the slender, upright branches become quite long and can outstrip their strength. They then tend to bend outwards towards the tips under the weight of flower, foliage, or even snow. If necessary, this can be dealt with by tying in the branches or by shortening back the current season's growth.

Growing a little larger, Prunus hillieri 'Spire' is another attractive choice. Of conical shape, it extends to around 26ft (8m) with a spread to 10ft (3m). Single pink flowers are produced plentifully during April and it produces good tints in autumn.

In the future I'll look at some more of these beautiful trees, and attempt to persuade you to plant at least one!

Your Gardening Week

 PRUNING CARE
When pruning out larger branches with a saw, first make a cut on the underside, to prevent bark tearing back as the branch comes away. With some branches it is a good idea to cut through initially some way from the final position, leaving a smaller and more manageable piece to be removed with less chance of damage.

 CLOCHE CELERY
The tops of celery can be protected, either using straw or by placing cloches along the ridge.

 PINCH CHERRIES If a new flush of growth starts to appear on Christmas cherries - Solanum capsicastrum - and threatens to hide the colourful fruits, it should be pinched out.

 CHECK BEDDING
Look over spring bedding. Remove any debris which may have lodged between the plants, remove weeds if these are starting to establish, and look out for signs of slug activity. Bulbs may still be planted, but complete the job without delay.

 EARLY LETTUCE
Order lettuce seed so that early sowings can be made, in frames, during January.

EASY LIFT Where vegetables such as parsnip and Jerusalem artichoke have been left in the ground - and they do taste better when freshly lifted - cover a part of the plot with leaves or straw, to stop frost hardening the ground and making lifting difficult.

PROTECT LEGUMES
Early peas and beans from an autumn sowing will benefit from the protection of a little soil drawn up around them to make a windbreak - unless they have the benefit of wind protection.

EARLY BULBS If bulbs planted outdoors have been encouraged into early growth by mild conditions, protect shoots from what is to come by dressing with sand or fine, dry compost.

Perk Up Those Poinsettias!

Pot plants always make popular presents, with a great variety to choose from. But often the recipients are concerned about their care.

Firstly, ensure that the plant is positioned so that it is away from draughts but in good light. Try, also, to ensure a fairly even temperature. It is unwise to put pot plants on window sills, for though the light is good, there are invariably draughts, and there is the temptation to leave them there at night - on the cold side of the drawn curtains. Next, do not be tempted to over-water - one of the main reasons, undoubtedly, for the early demise of plants in the home.

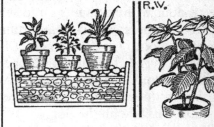

Better to let them go on the dry side, and then to water thoroughly with tepid water To maintain the best conditions then, follow those basic rules. Some plants will, however, require some special care. Azaleas and solanums (the Winter Cherry) need extra humidity and will, therefore, benefit from regular spraying with tepid water.

A great gift favourite at this time is a potted cyclamem; another plant liking a moist atmosphere but one which because the corm should not be wet directly, will require watering from underneath.

In all these cases it is a good idea to try and stand the pots on a dish or tray of pebbles filled with water to just below the tops of the pebbles this will ensure that the moist conditions necessary are provided constantly.

Yet another favourite is the poinsettia. This plant really does need special care. The latter will certainly lead to it not being around much into the New Year.

As for watering this plant, wait until the leaves begin to droop, then give the plant a good soaking and leave it until it dries out again. Under no circumstances be tempted to give it a daily topping up with water. Finally, to retain its colourful bracts, ensure it has plenty of light.

Your Gardening Week

No Pre-Christmas Dig?

W hat a depressing month November can be. It's fine if the days are clear, crisp and bright, but more often than not it seems to be rain, rain and still more rain. Even when there is a respite, it often does not occur at times to allow much to be done outside. The general prevalence of dark clouds and absence of sunsets make the days seem very short indeed.

The result of that is that I keep off the ground as much as possible. My soil is on the heavy side, and I only have to stand at the back door with my boots on to see it turn to mud. So, even though there are leaves to clear, pruning and general tidying to be finished, not to mention digging, I just let it go for a while.

Of course every cloud has a silver lining. It's nice not to have to be a slave to the garden for a few weeks, and I enjoy the opportunities to wrap up in waterproofs and set off for long, wet walks in the hills with the dog.

It also gives me time for that crucial big decision – whether to house the Christmas tree in the conservatory, or bring it to its traditional place in the parlour.

Mention of Christmas reminds me that it is time to think of decorations. One of the most popular items in a display, even if there is only a little of it, is Viscum album – better known as mistletoe.

There are, in fact, some 60-70 species of this parasitic shrub to be found throughout the temperate and warmer regions of the world; but the only one likely to be found in cultivation is Viscum album.

This is a British native found in the southern counties and extending into South Wales and the Midlands. A hardy evergreen, it can be found growing on a wide range of trees – principally apple, poplar, lime, hawthorn, maple, pear and oak. If any of these are to hand, then it should be interesting to try and grow your own supply for the future.

Probably the only chance that many of us have to get stocks is at this festive season and, as sowing should not be carried out until spring, the seed must be preserved. All that is needed is to keep the sprays in water until late March, April or May.

The translucent white berries each contain one seed in a sticky, viscous fluid. There is no ground preparation to undertake, for all that is needed is to smear the berries on the underside of a decent-sized branch.

On the assumption that you intend to make use of any resultant crop, choose one which is accessible!

Birds may pose a problem, being appreciative of this new source of food, so give protection with a little netting until the pulp hardens and fixes the seed to the branch.

The chances of germination may be increased if a small notch is cut into the bark and the seed set in it. Even when this occurs, growth will be slow over the first two or three years.

While that sowing is some time away, there is work to be done now. If you have a glasshouse and some heat available, it is time to start sifting through the seed packets to find the likes of tomatoes.

So long as you can provide a minimum night temperature of 10-12C (50-55F), tomatoes can be started, though you will need a temperature of 16-18C (60-65F) to ensure germination. When the seedlings have formed their first pair of true leaves, prick them off into 3-inch pots of No1 compost. Place near the glass to ensure that they receive the maximum of light and do not become drawn. They will be ready for planting out in the glasshouse during March.

Pick A Cherry

Last week I praised the virtues of ornamental cherries and got so far as to mention a couple of varieties with slender, upright habit. There are many more forms to choose from so that, whatever the situation, there is likely to be one to fit.

One of the best ways to choose is to plan well ahead and give yourself the opportunity to see the trees in a nursery or, better still, in an arboretum, botanical garden or park. This way you have a real chance to see how they will grow, and if you can manage to achieve such visits in spring, an opportunity to appreciate their flowering capacity. One that displays its flower within easy reach is Prunus 'Kiku-shidare Sakurs'. You may also find it listed as 'Cheal's Weeping Cherry'.

Growing to make a small tree, it has arching, pendulous branches which spread to around 10ft (3m). It flowers during April and is most attractive when decked with deep rose-pink double blooms carried in dense bunches. These are followed by leaves which are tinged bronze when young, and turn to a shiny deep green with maturity.

I still enjoy Prunus 'Kanzan', even though it has been widely planted. As its branches reach upwards they spread, rather as the hairs on a flattened shaving brush, to form an inverted cone or

In early April the flower buds take on a dark, purplish-red colour until, towards the end of the month, they open to reveal fully double flowers in beautiful deep pink, whose effect is heightened by being carried in clusters on long stalks.

Once established in good condition it is a vigorous grower, generally reaching about 26ft (8m) in height and with similar spread. Although perfectly acceptable when planted in a lawn, I prefer to see it among lower-growing shrubs. Its habit is sufficiently erect to allow planting by the side of paths.

'Kanzan' has sometimes been confused with 'Hisakura', which does not achieve the same size and whose single flowers gener-

ally open a little earlier.

If you can accommodate something larger still, then 'Tai-Haku' is worth a thought. This, the Great White Cherry, may reach to 30ft (9m) or more, again with similar spread. It is among the finest of the cherries and probably the best of the whites, with large, single flowers two and a half inches (6cm) across appearing in April.

Their effect is enhanced by the appearance of young foliage in rich coppery-red. Later the leaves turn to green and in autumn they turn through red and yellow before falling.

Another good white is Prunus 'Shirotae'. It makes a smaller, but still vigorous tree growing to around 20ft (6m) with wide-spreading branches which are horizontal or slightly drooping. Again the flowers are large but may be single or semi-double, and with the benefit of fragrance. They appear in April and are held in long drooping clusters.

Of course choice is not restricted to these Japanese flowering cherries. Prunus serrula is worth growing for its bark, which glistens and shines in a deep reddish-brown. Both leaves and flowers appear in late April. The leaves are narrow like those of willow, and the flowers small and white.

If you have a leaning to plant native species, and the space and willingness to provide food for birds, then the likes of Prunus avium can be considered. Also known as the Gean, Mazzard or Wild Cherry, this is one of the most attractive of our native trees. Generally it grows to 50-60ft (15-17m), although specimens to near 90ft have been recorded.

The flowers appearing in April or May form small, drooping clusters. The leaves of light green turn to rich red and yellow in autumn, and the bark is glossy brown, often peeling into thin, papery strips.

Look also for the cultivars 'Decumana' which has large leaves and flowers, and for 'Plena' which with its masses of double, white flowers is among the loveliest of flowering trees.

Your Gardening Week

WORK FOR THE WEEK

HEELING IN Though my normal practice is to heel in new trees or shrubs if they can't be planted straight away, if the ground is especially wet then I resort to straw and sacking, rather than disturb the soil.

CHOOSE WITH CARE When buying poinsettias, choose plants with healthy bracts and good colour. Also check the small flowers in the centre of the head. Ideally these should just be showing colour. If they have already opened fully or gone over, then the display will be that little bit shorter.

KEEP CACTI DRY During the winter period, cacti should be kept in a cool, light position and only given a minimum of water. Too much may lead to fungal attacks. If this occurs, improve the environment with dry, buoyant air, cut out the affected parts and treat with fungicidal dust. If the plant's appearance is badly affected, plan to replace by taking cuttings.

SOW CELERY If heated glass can be made available, then celery can be sown now to give crops from mid-May onwards. Successional sowing at 14-day intervals will provide crops until this time next year. Remember that heat will also be needed to grow on after sowing, and if this is not available delay until the end of January.

DIVIDE FERNS Well established clumps of fern can be propagated by division, though the job should be completed before growth recommences in spring.

LOOK CLOSELY While spring and summer's flamboyant displays of flower may take our breath away, many plants have attractions at this time of year if only you will take a closer look. Watch out for viburnums (some well scented), hamamelis, the "Witch Hazel", mahonia and, of course, winter flowering heathers.

Pot A Present

Buying presents for plant lovers and gardeners does make life easier in the run-up to Christmas. Another plant or a new tool is always acceptable. When it comes to tools the range is wide, both as gardening aids, be it for outside or inside use, and therefore for price.

Miniature sets of tools - dibbers, forks and spades - are excellent for those who do their gardening in pots or glass bottles. For those who have an outside patch there are a hundred and one aids - from comparatively cheap hand tools, to powered diggers, a bit on the pricey side as gifts, but a boon to anyone who finds fork and spade-work too difficult. Seeds and bulbs of favourite or unusual plants make splendid gifts.

Others of a more lasting nature, include roses and other shrubs, which may be planted now or later. Pot culture makes it possible to buy most of the favourite flowering shrubs and roses at this time and, even if the weather is not kind enough to allow for them to be transferred 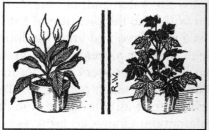 to permanent beds, they can happily be left to grow on in their containers, until the weather is more clement.

So at this time of the year, pot plants come high on the list of favourite gifts. Choose them with care and they will give pleasure for many weeks to come.

Select plants that look healthy, rejecting any that have broken or discoloured leaves, or that have roots out of the bottom of the pot.

If you are purchasing flowering plants, then choose those that are in bud, rather than those in full bloom. Check, too, that there are no infestations of pests, such as bugs or whiteflies on or under leaves. And do not be tempted to take a pot that is bone dry. Prefer, too, to take plants from inside shops, rather than those standing outside in the cold, and cover them with paper to protect them in transit.

If you know where the plant is to be sited, seek advice on the best plants for the spot. Spathiphyllum (left), for instance, is a regal plant with lily-like flowers, prefers the shade, warmth and humidity, but will survive well down to 50 deg F. The Fatshedera (right), is an easy grower, provided one is sparing with water in the winter.

Oranges and Lemons

I f you live in a favoured area, or at least are able to provide protection under glass in winter, or better still are able to maintain a minimum temperature around 7C (45F), then there is some chance that you will be able to raise citrus fruits with some success.

Given the range of fruits which are readily available in the shops for many months of the year, it might be thought a waste of time. But many of the plants are ornamental, there is a degree of novelty value and, of course, if you do manage to ripen fruit, you will have the pleasure of savouring your own produce.

In a well favoured area, outdoor planting against a wall is ideal. In other places the options are to grow the plants in a glasshouse or conservatory border, or to set them in containers which can be taken outside for the summer and brought inside for winter. If all this sounds too much, you might choose a Calamondin Orange to grow as a small pot plant.

The Calamondin Orange - Citrus mitis - hails from the Philippines. It will grow quite happily in a 12.5cm (5in) pot and make a bush 30-45cm (12-18in) high. It will produce flower and fruit while still small, the white fragrant flowers appearing mainly in spring, to be followed by fruits developing over several months. They grow to around 4cm (1.5in) across, and tend to be bitter, but are ornamental.

Of the larger fruits the mandarin is the toughest, followed by Seville oranges, grapefruit, lemon and lime. Being semi-evergreen they are more prone to frost damage than our deciduous fruit trees. Nevertheless if temperatures cool gradually in late autumn and early winter, growth will slow down in tandem and damage is less likely. A sudden frost, however, is likely to damage young shoots.

So container-grown plants should be brought inside when temperatures drop. A shed with plenty of light will do, or a glasshouse, both with just enough heat to keep out frost. On mild days in autumn and spring they should be placed outside, being brought in as the temperature drops. Then from early summer until autumn they can be kept outside in a sunny, sheltered position.

As you might gather from the need to take plants out on mild days, any grown under glass need well-ventilated conditions. Good light in winter and a minimum temperature of 7C, or slightly higher for limes, are also needed. Avoid stagnant, humid conditions and give light shading from May to September.

Propagation is an open question. New plants may be raised from pips sown in spring. However, not only will the seedlings vary, but it may take several years before the plants start to flower. It is better to invest in two- or three-year-old bushes which should have been grafted on appropriate rootstocks.

Of course there are pitfalls. Aphids, mealybug, scale and whitefly may need to be controlled. More critical, though, is the need to maintain consistant temperatures if satisfying, ripe fruit is to be produced. Ideally, for some six months after flowering, night temperatures should not fall below 13C (55F). With oranges and mandarins temperatures over 18C (65F) are needed if full flavour is to develop.

Less demanding is Meyer's Lemon, which can grow to make a medium-sized or large shrub with short-stalked, large, dark green leaves. It responds well to being grown in a pot where, even with its size restricted, it is capable of producing fruit to match any found in shops.

A closely related monotypic species which is hardy appears in the form of Poncirus trifoliata. This, the hardy orange or Japanese bitter orange, makes a shrub which can reach 3m (10ft). It has interesting form, with flattening branches carrying strong green spines up to 6.5cm (2.5in) long, but relatively few trifoliate leaves. Large, fragrant flowers are carried on leafless stems in April and May to be followed by small, yellow, bitter oranges some 5cm (2in) across.

Your Gardening Week

A Plant With A Future

Not long now before the festive season has us in its warm embrace - VAT on fuel permitting! Whether for the decoration of our own homes, as pre-planned gifts or a last-minute purchase, pot plants add to the joy. Few have the potential of the Christmas cactus.

They may easily be overshadowed by the large and colourful bracts of poinsettias, or the massed blooms of chrysanthemums and Indian azaleas. Yet they can become large and impressive and last for many tens of years with only a modicum of attention and care. Equally, they will tolerate some degree of neglect, although their appearance may suffer.

To me the Christmas cactus is forever Zygocactus truncatus: but to the botanist it has been re-classified as Schlumbergera truncata. You may also find it called Crab Plant or Lobster Plant because of its shape and habit. Originating in the forests of Brazil and Mexico, there are a number of species in cultivation which have been useful in providing hybrids and cultivars. These can extend the flowering season from September through to April, and offer a range of flower colours from pinks, oranges and purples to white and even yellow.

Their main requirements are for light, warmth and humidity and these, aided by repotting and feeding as required, will produce large plants with many tens of attractive flowers, and which may last for 50 years or more. Needless to say, most of them do not survive for this length of time, succumbing to starvation or over or under-watering.

For flowering at this time of year, all the usual pitfalls relating to house plants in winter are to be avoided. A minimum temperature around 15C (60F) is desirable when they are in bud. This may be reduced to 10C (50F) after flowering. Draughts and sudden fluctuations in temperature should be avoided or bud drop may follow, and if their normal position is on a window-sill,

bring them away from the glass when frost threatens.

In nature they grow as epiphytes, and this is reflected in their compost, which should be free-draining, with plenty of organic material. They also prefer this to be a little on the acid side with a pH of 5.5 to 6.5. John Innes No. 2 without the lime added – but with extra leaf-mould and sharp sand – will do, as will an ericaceous soilless compost, although I always lean to the former with longer-lived species.

If you want to start from scratch, make your own compost with good loam, leaf-mould and sharp sand in equal parts.

Watering should be exercised with the usual care, the compost never being allowed to dry out completely and also not becoming waterlogged. Having said that, I know of many such plants which stagger through periods of drought, alternating with excessive soakings, and which have survived for several years. Because the plants prefer an acidic environment, lime-free water should be used if reasonably possible.

The summer provides an interesting time, with the plants needing to be shaded from full sun. Common practice has been to set them in the branches of a tree where the dappled shade suits them, though an alternative is to plunge the pots in a cold frame.

At this time a regular programme of feeding can be carried out using a high potash formulation, such as tomato fertiliser in weak solution. This programme can continue through August, and will ripen new growth and encourage flowering.

New plants can be had by taking cuttings in spring or early summer. Select cuttings of a couple of days for the surface to heal, then insert in a mixture of peat and sand, keeping them in a moist atmosphere and with a minimum temperature of 15C (60F).

After about four weeks gently tug some of the cuttings and, if good root growth is being made, pot them into 5cm (2inch) pots until established. When moving on into a larger container, it is normal to set three plants around the rim to achieve an even spread.

WORK FOR THE WEEK

✔ **CHRYSANTHS** As chrysanthemums finish flowering, cut stems back to 20cm (8ins), knock them out of their pots, shake soil from the roots and set them in boxes. These stools will produce shoots which can be taken as cuttings in January/February.

✔ **KEEP PLANTS WARM** If you are likely to be away from home for a few days, don't leave houseplants in the window. Move them to the centre of the house, which should stay warmer.

✔ **PINCH PEAS** Sweet peas can have their growing tips pinched out when the stems reach 7.5cm (3in). This will encourage bushy growth.

✔ **EARLY STRAWBERRIES** The first batch of strawberries for forcing can be brought in now. Take care to check that they are clean and do not harbour any pest of disease which might affect other plants inside.

✔ **KEEP BERRIES** If holly used in decorations has not been soaked in a glycerine solution, then the berries can be given a coating of hair spray to help stop them shriveling.

✔ **ORDER EARLY** If you haven't done so yet, get on with preparing your seed order.

✔ **CLEAN HOUSEPLANTS** Light is already at a premium, so houseplants should be cleaned to ensure that as much as possible reaches the leaves. Shiny-leaved types can be gently sponged, while those with hairy leaves can be dusted with a fine paintbrush.

✔ **CHECK STORES** Check over all crops in store and rogue out any which show signs of storage rots.

Houseplants

Now, when flowers and colour are scarce in the borders outside the house, it is particularly pleasing to be able to bring some colour inside, in the form of pot plants. Single plants — be they foliage or flowering — in pottery or china containers, provide a spot of colour and interest in any room. Much more interesting, however, is the introduction of large containers which may provide grouping of both flowering, berried and foliage plants.

Of the plants available at this time of the year, solanums and peppers provide brilliantly coloured berries, whilst cyclamen and the Christmas cactus, will give an excellent and long-lived range of colour.

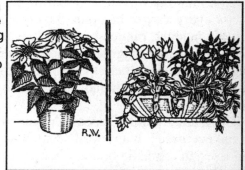

When it comes to finding a plant, there is much to be said for going for something which has size. Chrysanths fit the bill, of course, and so do some cyclamen, though a mature flower-packed plant will probably be quite expensive. Of the larger plants boasting colour, choose perhaps the ever-popular poinsettia (illustration left), its dark green leaves set off a foil for either red or white bracts surrounding what are otherwise insignificant flowers.

Bear in mind they do not like to be moved about. Place them in a south facing window, but well away from draughts. Ensure that they do not dry out and they will display over a long period.

When the bracts begin to fall stop watering and, when the stems are bare, cut them back (sealing the wounds with charcoal) to come up again next year.

Large pots and troughs make excellent containers for mixed arrangements (illustration right). I prefer to fill the container with peat and then to set the chosen plants, still in their containers, into the main container. This allow you to give individual attention to watering needs to a certain extents, and certainly makes it easy to replace plants within the general arrangement when they have given of their best.

Your Gardening Week

Magnificent Magnolias

All of a sudden I was taken back to the early part of the year, and my mind remembered a short drive along an urban estate road in the Midlands. Here the houses had adequate – but not excessive – front gardens, all with space to allow cars to manoeuvre and park, and all with mature collections of shrubs and trees.

While some shapes and forms were common to many, and the pavements held an avenue of regular lime trees, what caught my eye on that day was the number of magnolias.

Not every garden had one, but enough so that several were always in sight, ranged beside a long and gentle bend. I always tend to consider magnolias as specimens, best set in a contrasting environment where they stand out from the crowd and do not compete one with another. But here the effect was most pleasing.

There are around 80 species of magnolia, some deciduous, some evergreen, many well scented and most with bark which releases an aromatic odour when crushed. However, essentially they are grown for their magnificent flowers.

I believe they have traced back for over five million years, which amounts to a recommendation in it own right!

In general they need a reasonable depth of soil, preferably enriched with organic material. While waterlogging should be avoided, a plentiful supply of moisture is needed. Some need shelter, particularly the early-flowering kinds, whose buds may be damaged by spring frosts and cold winds. Some benefit from woodland shade, and the large-leaved kinds are best protected from strong winds. They are tolerant of clay soils, able to withstand atmospheric pollution, and a few will tolerate lime.

So for the best results there is a need to give some thought to choice and situations. However, Magnolia soulangiana is perhaps the easiest to grow and, therefore, in its various forms, the most widely planted. It will only tolerate a moderate amount of lime, and is no use for shallow, chalk soils.

Its hardiness is well established and it has the additional advantage of growing at reasonable rate and coming to flower when young. The roots are thick and fleshy and resentful of disturbance. Care should be taken when handling and planting, to avoid damage which can result in the affected parts rotting. For this reason there is merit in using container-grown specimens. It is also a good idea to undertake planting in late April or early May, when growth is most active.

This magnolia grows to form a large shrub with wide-spreading stems and may reach 4.6m (15ft). The scented flowers are large and tulip-shaped, and have petals of white stained with pink or purple. These appear initially in April on bare stems, and continue into June.

Of the clones, 'Lennei' is excellent. Of vigorous spreading habit, it produces many stems with large leaves up to 25cm (10in) long. The flowers, like large goblets, have thick, flashy petals which are rose-purple on the outside and creamy-white stained with light purple on the inside. Sometimes repeat flowering occurs in autumn.

Others to look for include 'Alexandrina', which is vigorous and erect in growth with large flowers of white flushed purple at the base. I also like 'Brozzonii', which has among the largest and latest flowers, again in white and purple.

Propagation by seed takes a long time, with no certainty as to the form of the offspring given the hybrid ancestry of the parent. Layers can be set in spring, or cuttings struck in June in a propagating case with bottom heat if available.

From a cultural point of view there is little to do, other than enjoy the flowers. A top-dressing of organic material is beneficial each year in spring, particularly during the early years. Pruning is not desirable, but if it becomes necessary it should should be done when flowering is over. Evergreen species, however, are best pruned in spring.

Heaps Of Goodness

How can I write about something to do in the week of Christmas? Despite the commercial pressures to book next season's 'holiday in the sun', or to scramble at some 'not-to-be-missed' super sale, it is, after all, the season of peace and goodwill. Where can you find these scarce ideals?

To my mind, there is no better place than the garden or glasshouse. Both can provide a welcome respite from the cacophony of crackers, the tabernacle of television, the farrago of food, the daze of drink, or even just the washing-up!

Of course care is needed, for festive excesses dictate that only gentle exercise should be considered. The essential tasks of watering and ventilation should not be missed, but other than that, time can be well spent on contemplation and planning for the year ahead. To this end a range of catalogues can be very useful.

One of the things to think about is composting. Not only does this provide supplies of humus which is most beneficial in creating a well-conditioned soil, but it also contributes to a reduction in the amount of refuse which has to be processed by your local authority. It also has the distinct benefit of reducing demand for the likes of peat, and is cheaper than buying other forms of organic material.

All that seems reasonably positive, so what about the negative aspects? These are very few, in that all you need is a space for the heap, a preparedness to collect suitable material, a sprinkling of fertiliser to encourage decomposition and a willingness to turn the heap once in a while, so that it rots down evenly.

There are several types of compost-making containers on the market, but these are not essential. Equally, if you have a streak of do-it-yourself zeal, you could construct a wooden bin with a detachable side, remembering to leave gaps between the timbers to allow for aeration.

At the other extreme, a free-standing heap works well, but I opt for a length of galvanised pig fencing. This has horizontal and vertical wires and is reasonably robust.

A panel about 4m (12ft) long can be bent round into a circle to hold material and is both self-supporting and portable. Just bend back the ends of the horizontal wires, and they can be hooked on to the verticals when the circle is made.

Virtually all waste vegetable matter which is soft enough to rot down in a reasonable time can be used. Things to be avoided include hard, woody substances; material which is infected with virulent diseases; and the roots of persistant perennials weeds such a couch grass, convolvulus and ground elder.

In general grass mowings are good, but if you treat lawn areas with weedkillers or fungicides, do check the instructions for advice on how long it should be before subsequent mowings are used for compost or mulches.

While the finer leaves such as beech should be reserved for leaf-mould, coarse leaves are ideal. Peelings from the kitchen, tops and stems cleared from the vegetable plot and soft hedge trimmings can all go in. The stems of brassicas should not be discarded unless infected with club root disease, but they should be chopped or crushed to render them more digestible to the heap.

There are one or two general rules to follow when making a heap: Within reason it should be as large as can be accommodated. This means that more heat will be generated in decomposition and the proportion of uncomposted material is less.

Water is important and the heap should not be allowed to dry out.

Conversely it should not become waterlogged, and so a covering may be needed in very wet periods.

One important ingredient is patience. Even a heap started in summer might take three months to mature, while one started in autumn could take six to eight months before usable compost is ready.

Your Gardening Week

✔ **AIR LETTUCE** Lettuce under cloches or in frames should be checked over regularly and ventilated in suitable conditions. Only occasional watering will be needed, and is best done on an individual basis. Avoid splashing the foliage by pouring gently onto the soil.

✔ **FIRM STRAWBERRIES** If strawberries, planted in autumn, have become loose, work a little fine compost around the collar and firm back in. Similarly, check hardwood cuttings and firm if needed.

✔ **CLEAN CLOCHES** The glass of frames and cloches soon becomes dirty, so take advantage of good days to clean them. Remove to a suitable spot before washing, so that the ground is not waterlogged.

✔ **MAKE A DATE** If you have any dates left, save the stones and sow in a temperature of 55F (28C). The airing cupboard might be handy for this, but bring the seedlings into light as soon as they germinate. Pot up into No. 2 compost

✔ **REPAIR TIME** Take opportunities afforded by poor conditions to repair pots and boxes. Boxes can be kept going for another season or so, with the odd additional nail. Cracked plastic pots and trays can be glued to stop them becoming unusable.

✔ **PRUNE FRUIT** Any fruit-tree pruning that is needed can be carried out now.

✔ **TOOL CARE** When using secateurs, take care not to use them on branches bigger than they were intended for. There is a good chance of straining the blades, rendering them useless. Invest in a pair of heavy loppers, or use a small pruning saw for bigger branches.

✔ **LILLIES** Propagate lillies by planting scales to half their depth in boxes or pots of No. 1 compost. Set in a cold frame

Cover-ups And Fat Balls For A Happy Christmas

Winter is the time of year when those who have started early planting to get early crops, need to take especial care of seedlings and the like.

It is the time when winds can play havoc; when snow can severely damage young plants and when tender seedlings provide tasty morsels for hungry birds.

Protection is the obvious answer. Wind can, of course, be thwarted by covering the plants completely with sacking or polythene - always remembering that, on good days the covers should be opened enough for the plants to get the benefit of fresh air.

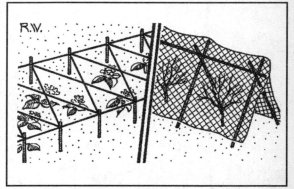

This cover-up will, of course, provide protection against snowfalls. At special risk here are the seedlings and young plants which are best protected by either of the two methods shown in the accompanying illustrations.

The solution on the left is best for seedlings. All that is necessary is for two lines of pegs to be driven in along each side of the bed and then to stretch cord or wire between them, as shown. In really bad, cold weather this can act as a support for polythene sheeting.

For taller plants try the solution on the right. A series of crossed poles with a top support, over which bean netting or chicken wire can be stretched. Again, in severe weather, you have the support for further cover.

As for the birds, these two methods should cope with them, too. But don't forget the birds. Do make sure there is bird feed for them, hung well out of the reach of cats. Don't forget that they'll need water, too.